RELIGION, EMOTION, SENSATION

TRANSDISCIPLINARY THEOLOGICAL COLLOQUIA

Theology has hovered for two millennia between scriptural metaphor and philosophical thinking; it takes flesh in its symbolic, communal, and ethical practices. With the gift of this history and in the spirit of its unrealized potential, the Transdisciplinary Theological Colloquia intensify movement between and beyond the fields of religion. A multivocal discourse of theology takes place in the interstices, at once self-deconstructive in its pluralism and constructive in its affirmations.

Hosted annually by Drew University's Theological School, the colloquia provide a matrix for such conversations, while Fordham University Press serves as the midwife for their publication. Committed to the slow transformation of religio-cultural symbolism, the colloquia continue Drew's long history of engaging historical, biblical, and philosophical hermeneutics, practices of social justice, and experiments in theopoetics.

Catherine Keller, *Director*

RELIGION, EMOTION, SENSATION

Affect Theories and Theologies

KAREN BRAY

AND STEPHEN D. MOORE,

EDITORS

FORDHAM UNIVERSITY PRESS ❖ NEW YORK ❖ 2020

Library of Congress Cataloging-in-Publication Data
Names: Bray, Karen, editor. | Moore, Stephen D., (date) editor.
Title: Religion, emotion, sensation : affect theories and theologies /
    Karen Bray, Stephen D Moore, editors.
Description: First edition. | New York : Fordham University Press, 2020. |
    Series: Transdisciplinary theological colloquia | Includes
    bibliographical references and index. | Summary: "Religion, Emotion,
    Sensation asks what affect theory has to say about God or gods, religion
    or religions, scriptures, theologies, and liturgies. Contributors
    explore the crossings and crisscrossings between affect theory and
    theology and the study of religion more broadly, as well as the
    political and social import of such work"— Provided by publisher.
Identifiers: LCCN 2019028490 | ISBN 9780823285679 (hardback) | ISBN
    9780823285662 (paperback) | ISBN 9780823285686 (epub)
Subjects: LCSH: Psychology, Religious. | Affect (Psychology)—Religious
    aspects.
Classification: LCC BL53 .R385 2020 | DDC 200.1/9—dc23
LC record available at https://lccn.loc.gov/2019028490

Printed in the United States of America
22 21 20   5 4 3 2 1
First edition

CONTENTS

RELIGION, EMOTION, SENSATION

❧ Introduction: Mappings and Crossings

KAREN BRAY AND STEPHEN D. MOORE

Free-floating affects lodge in the surface tensions of low-level stress, loneliness, dread, yearning, a sense of innocence, backed up anger, the ins and outs of love.
—KATHLEEN STEWART, *Ordinary Affects*

God is love.
—1 JOHN 4:16

This volume attempts to bring two slippery concepts into contact with each other. *Affectivity*, it seems, is no less elusive a concept than *divinity*. It slides, it shifts, it shimmers. Yet its serpentine, often subterranean, movements are anything but immaterial. They create human worlds even while calling the human into question as a category insulated from the nonhuman. At once transpersonal and prepersonal, affectivity transcends and subtends the human. As such, it has affinity with divinity, but a divinity that is indissociable from materiality. The divinity with which affectivity is intimate dwells particularly in the mundane, the quotidian, the humdrum. Affectivity is always incarnate, then, but not only in human form.

MAPPINGS

The ineffability of affectivity—or, let's just say, of *affect*—comes to eloquent expression in "An Inventory of Shimmers," Gregory J. Seigworth and Melissa Gregg's introduction to *The Affect Theory Reader*, a volume that, by any standard, constitutes a textbook example of a field-consolidating textbook.[1] Unlike other such texts, however, the introduction to this particular text explicates its subject matter by complicating it. To begin with, the opening sentences of this de-introduction administer a rude jolt to any reader predisposed to imagine that "affect" is a mere synonym for "feeling" or "emotion":

How to begin when, after all, there is no pure or somehow originary state for affect? Affect arises in the midst of *in-between-ness*: in the capacities to act and be acted upon. . . . Affect is found in those intensities that pass body to body (human, nonhuman, part-body, and otherwise), in those resonances that circulate about, between, and sometimes stick to bodies and worlds, *and* in the very passages or variations between these intensities and resonances themselves. Affect, at its most anthropomorphic, is the name we give to those forces—visceral forces beneath, alongside, or generally *other than* conscious knowing, vital forces insisting beyond emotion—that can serve to drive us toward movement, toward thought and extension, that can likewise suspend us (as if in neutral) across a barely registering accretion of force-relations, or that can even leave us overwhelmed by the world's apparent intractability.[2]

Affect theory, on this account, might be considered the critical exploration both of what types of acts, knowledge, bodies, and worlds are produced in the capacious,[3] intensely charged spaces of in-betweenness, beneathness, and alongsideness *and* of how we might better attend to affect's roles in such productions. Think, for example, of the exhilarating surge of sensations elicited when you are standing on top of a mountain (whether literal or metaphorical). Think of the incipient, ineffable moment of disquiet that arises when you sense that something is off in your environment. Think of the spark, the electric tingle of expectation, before a first kiss. These and innumerable other similar sensations are all pulsations for which we do not have adequately calibrated language.

This particular concept of affect, it should be noted, is Deleuzian at base. More precisely, Gilles Deleuze's concept of affect, drawn ultimately from Baruch Spinoza, but pressed through a para-poststructuralist sieve in collaboration with Félix Guattari and distilled and further expanded by Brian Massumi, flows into "An Inventory of Shimmers" to shape the version of affect it primarily presents. At its most austere and abstruse, Deleuzian affect is purely processual; it is logically prior to structured sensory perception, conscious cognition, and linguistic representation. It is even prior to feelings. "Affects aren't feelings," Deleuze insisted; "they're becomings that spill over beyond whoever lives through them (thereby becoming someone else)."[4] Neither are affects emotions, according to Massumi, further extending Deleuze's line of thought:

An emotion is a subjective content, the sociolinguistic fixing of the quality of an experience, which is from that point onward defined as personal. Emotion is qualified intensity ["intensity" being a synonym for "affect," for Massumi], the conventional, consensual point of insertion of intensity into semantically and semiotically formed progressions, into narrativizable action-reaction circuits, into function and meaning. It is intensity owned and recognized. It is crucial to theorize the difference between affect and emotion.[5]

Yet the Deleuzian-Massumian trajectory is only one version of affect theory, albeit an extremely influential one.[6] Affect theory is also the investigation of the often unremarkable yet frequently momentous feelings for which we have many names: love, hatred, anger, rage, madness, loneliness, paranoia, depression, despair, envy, anxiety, shame, boredom, joy, happiness, ecstasy, contentment, optimism, pessimism. The study of affect is also about how these feelings get coded within cultures or how they come to stick to certain kinds of bodies, objects, and choices.[7] Consider, for instance, which subjects and objects get coded as *happy* in the hallucinatory landscape of the American Dream. A blonde, white, straight, able-bodied wife accessorized by a whitened smile, a white picket-fenced suburban home, 2.5 smiling white children, and a golden retriever becomes shorthand for happiness. Happiness, in this culturally coded sense, while not unconnected to those ineffable pulsations we feel before that first kiss atop a mountain, takes a very precise shape, one narrowly defined and intimately associated with particular people. These people have other people, tagged with equally stereotypical feelings, as their constitutive others. Over against the Happy (White) Housewife, for example, the culture might set the Angry Black Woman.[8]

How many versions of affect theory are there? More than one, as we have already seen, more even than two. "There is no single, generalizable theory of affect: not yet, and (thankfully) there never will be," Seigworth and Gregg insist. "If anything, it is more tempting to imagine that there can only ever be infinitely multiple iterations of affect and theories of affect: theories as diverse and singularly delineated as their own highly particular encounters with bodies, affects, worlds."[9] Seigworth and Gregg then proceed, however, to delimit that limitless potential, to venture a mapping move that has proved particularly influential, being seized on by many who have wandered about in affect theory, seeking to impose taxonomic order on its eclectic untidiness. Seigworth and Gregg posit "a watershed moment for the most recent resurgence of interest and intrigue regarding affect and theories of affect."[10] That milestone moment amounts to a double origin that is also a dual trajectory: the publication in 1995 of two differently oriented essays on affect, one by Eve Sedgwick and Adam Frank, the other by Brian Massumi.[11] Sedgwick and Frank's "Shame in the Cybernetic Fold" ponders the psychobiological work on affect of Silvan Tomkins, who, indeed, coined the term "affect theory" in 1962, and for whom an affect was the physiological response to a stimulus, whether internal or external, and as such the biological basis of emotion. Sedgwick and Frank recognized, indeed relished, Tomkins's hardwired biologism as being utterly unfashionable in the context of poststructuralist theory and antithetical to certain of its most cherished dogmas.[12] Massumi's "The Autonomy of Affect," meanwhile, elaborated and extended the Deleuzian concept of affect that we outlined earlier. Like "Shame in the Cybernetic Fold," "The Autonomy of Affect" marked a significant moment in the intra-poststructuralist critique of poststructuralism, a post-poststructuralist turning of theoretical attention from language, cognition, and representation to extradiscursive affect and materiality.

Does affect theory come in two flavors only, then, the Tomkins-Sedgwick flavor and the Deleuze-Massumi flavor? Seigworth and Gregg themselves are not content to pitch their own tent between these two streams, settling instead on a multi-trajectory topography of the field. They propose eight "orientations" or "approaches" to affect altogether. The compelling power of their ambitious taxonomy inheres in its capacity to illuminate the relevance for affect theory of bodies of work not normally regarded as being significantly engaged with affect, such as the work encompassed by their "fifth approach":

> The fifth is found in the regularly hidden-in-plain-sight politically engaged work—perhaps most often undertaken by feminists, queer theorists, disability activists, and subaltern peoples living under the thumb of a normativizing power—that attends to the hard and fast materialities, as well as the fleeting and flowing ephemera, of the daily and the workaday, of everyday and every-night life, and of "experience" (understood in ways far more collective and "external" rather than individual and interior), where persistent, repetitious practices of power can simultaneously provide a body (or, better, collectivized bodies) with predicaments and potentials for realizing a world that subsists within and exceeds the horizons and boundaries of the norm.[13]

Elsewhere, however, Seigworth and Gregg's map seems so expansive, so far-flung, as to call the specificity of its professed topic—affect and its critical investigation—into question. The intellectual landscape conjured up by the map is populated by figures as disparate as (early) Sigmund Freud, John Dewey, Walter Benjamin, Frantz Fanon, Giorgio Agamben, Rosi Braidotti, and Elizabeth Grosz. Stretched across such an immense expanse of thought, affect begins to leak meaning as a concept, and affect theory along with it. It is almost as though the editors of *The Affect Theory Reader* are intent on resisting the field-constructing, field-consolidating potential of their enterprise. This would, however, be a defensible stance. As Jasbir Puar remarks of her own capacious account of "the affective turn" in *The Right to Maim*, "These undulating trajectories are arguably more significant than what affect is or what it means."[14]

What other mappings of affect theory are possible? What other mappings are desirable?

In *Religious Affects: Animality, Evolution, and Power*, arguably the inaugural monograph on affect theory and religion,[15] Donovan Schaefer takes a minimalist approach to the cartographic project that contrasts with Seigworth and Gregg's maximalist approach. Schaefer posits two primary currents in affect theory: a Deleuzian current, exemplified by such thinkers as Brian Massumi, Patricia Clough, and Erin Manning, and a phenomenological current, exemplified by such thinkers as Silvan Tomkins, Eve Sedgwick, and Sara Ahmed.[16] (Too) simply put, the Deleuzian approach excludes emotions from its study of affect (as we have already noted), while the phenomenological approach includes them.[17]

Schaefer's streamlined taxonomy of affect is effective in its simplicity, and avoids oversimplification through a nuanced tracing of the complexities within and between its two theoretical currents. We propose, nonetheless, to expand Schaefer's binary to a trinity (this is a volume on affect and theology, after all) by focusing affect theory through three interconnected, yet distinct, lenses: a *psychobiological* lens, a *prepersonal* lens, and a *cultural* lens. The psychobiological lens, employed by such theorists and critics as Silvan Tomkins, Eve Sedgwick, and Elspeth Probyn, looks at how affects, emotions, and feelings complexly intertwine to structure human experience.[18] Psychobiological approaches can, but do not always, cut across histories and cultures. The prepersonal lens, associated with such theorists and critics as Gilles Deleuze, Brian Massumi, Patricia Clough, Erin Manning, Teresa Brennan, Steven Shaviro, and Nigel Thrift, frames affect as a preprocessed force, intensity, or physiological shift.[19] It is important to note, however, that to construe affect as prepersonal is not to conceive of it as inconsequential to the social; rather, it is to understand it as that which perpetually exceeds, and sometimes impedes, the social production of emotional codes. Finally, the cultural lens, most readily found in queer and feminist cultural studies and critical race theory, especially as variously practiced by Sara Ahmed, Lauren Berlant, Ann Cvetkovich, Kathleen Stewart, Jasbir Puar, Mel Chen, and Sianne Ngai, resists categorizing affects as presocial and focuses instead on how they are produced through cultural and historical structures of power.[20] Cultural theorists of affect are interested in how certain feelings and emotions come to be associated with certain bodies and with what consequences.

Among other things and to different degrees, feminist and queer thinkers of affect depathologize and deindividualize "negative" feelings. Instead of viewing such feelings as signs of sickness in the individual, they invite us, whether explicitly or implicitly, to examine the potential of such moods for social diagnosis. How might *envy*, for instance, diagnose a society whose mainspring mentality is a compulsion always to strive—and forever to fail—to "keep up with the Joneses"? How might *depression* diagnose a society that demands we be ever more efficient and productive but systematically denies us the feelings necessary to perform optimally or even adequately? How might *rage* diagnose what it feels like to have your life under threat or your intelligence under suspicion because of your race, gender, or sexual orientation? How might *anxiety* diagnose a society taught to be afraid of anyone who does not worship your God?

CROSSINGS

What (else) might affect theory, in any of the three modes we have distinguished—the psychobiological, the prepersonal, or the cultural—have to say about God or gods, religions or religion, scriptures, theologies, or liturgies? What crossings, what crisscrossings, are possible between affect theory and theology and the study of religion more broadly?

Affect theory seems to make at least four key contributions to religious studies.[21] First, it enables us to resist what Schaefer calls "the linguistic fallacy": the mistaken notion "that language is the only medium of power,"[22] and consequently that religion is a primarily cognitive (and exclusively human) pursuit.[23] For Schaefer, "religion, like other forms of power, feels before it thinks, believes, or speaks."[24] The linguistic fallacy misconstrues religion "as merely a byproduct of language"—of myths, oracles, incantations, rituals, liturgies, creeds, sacred texts, and the like—"and misses the economies of affect—economies of pleasure, economies of rage and wonder, economies of sensation, of shame and dignity, of joy and sorrow, of community and hatred—that are the animal substance of religion and other forms of power."[25] On Schaefer's reading, affects are not only the beginnings of religion but also its ends, for religion is, at base, "a set of embodied practices for the production of affects."[26]

Affect theory confronts us with the ontological, epistemological, and religious significance of the nonlinguistic and the nonrational.[27] Affect theory reminds us that nonrational encounters with both the sacred and the mundane have epistemological force. Affect theory impels us to read sacred texts, other classic religious texts, rituals, and doctrines not only for what they claim to be saying or doing, but also for how they feel, what emotions they reveal—and how such affective capacities might complicate such cognition-heavy scholarly endeavors as biblical scholarship, church history, constructive theology, or philosophy of religion. The queer, feminist, and critical race approaches to affect theory possess particular potential to engage illuminatingly with religion as an extrarational form of power production, because they forcefully interrogate what affects *do* more than what affects *are*. Affect-attuned analyses of what religion does would differ significantly from demystifying analyses of what religion is. Affect theory invites us to put the demystification compulsion, long the driver of so much endeavor in religious studies, in neutral or even reverse. Here Ann Cvetkovich's "outsider" perspective on how religion scholars typically operate is suggestive: "Scholarship in religious studies often remains secular and critical in its perspective, even as it pursues important work in folding religion into culture, but another direction for inquiry would be to hold on to forms of 'enchantment' (and other related feelings) rather than demystifying religion as cultural expression."[28]

Second, affect theory impels us to re-attend to material encounters in the religious sphere. Consider sacred texts, for example, conceived by religious adherents as sites of encounter with the divine. A sacred text is real and material but also incorporeal and virtual, always indeterminately open to be otherwise than it ephemerally is. Even in material terms, however, the "it" that "it is" is not ever one thing. *The* biblical text, for instance, is not, and never can be, *a* general text but is always a finite number of nonidentical textual bodies, each with the capacity to interface with a finite number of nonidentical human bodies, thereby generating a potentially infinite range of religious (and nonreligious) affects. Such affects cannot be adequately comprehended apart from the ineluctable materiality of the intercorporeal encounter. Instead of asking what a scriptural text, a doctrinal document, or missionary tract *means*, we might ask how the sensory encounter with it *felt* to particular bodies in particular places in particular moments in history.[29] Moreover, the intercorporeal dimensions of such encounters are not only interhuman. Approaches to affect theory that employ a New Materialist lens, such as those associated with Mel Chen, Jane Bennett, or William Connolly—a lens that looks to the manifold ways we are also affected by *nonhuman* bodies, both organic and inorganic— further remind us that encounters with nonhuman religious material carry theological *weight* (giving "weight" its full, object-heavy meaning).

Third, reading for affect in contemporary cultural and political movements, and recognizing within them religious sensibilities in certain affectual modes, such as a religious sense of supplication or lament within the moods of certain secular protests, impels us to rethink where ritual and faith are practiced today. For instance, might we not name and analyze as prophetic liturgy the Black Lives Matter protests with their apotropaic, incantatory, gestural chants— "Hands up, don't shoot"; "I can't breathe"; "No justice, no peace"—and other society-convicting elements?

Finally, affect theory might be said to return us to the fourth source of theology, after scripture, tradition, and reason: that of experience. The notion that theology has four sources is commonly credited to John Wesley, the eighteenth-century co-founder of Methodism.[30] But the concept of experience that accords best with affect theory owes more to Spinoza than Wesley. "Nobody as yet has determined the limits of the body's capabilities" is a statement from Spinoza's *Ethics* that has long been canonical for affect theory.[31] Seldom if ever cited by affect theorists, however, is Spinoza's ensuing explication of that formulation: "that is, nobody as yet has learned *from experience* what the body can and cannot do. . . . The body . . . can do many things at which its mind is amazed."[32] The body leads, then, and thought follows in wonder. The body leads and *theology* also follows—or should follow—in awe. But what the body is always leading thought toward is affective encounters with other bodies, both human and nonhuman. What can happen theologically in affective encounters between infinitely capacious bodies is never predetermined, is always open, is ever transforming. Experience, affectively reconceived, constantly cuts escape hatches in the constricting enclosures that scripture, tradition, and reason perpetually threaten to become.

The essays that make up the present volume represent still further crossings and connections between affect theory and the critical study of religion. Donovan O. Schaefer in "The Animality of Affect: Religion, Emotion, and Power" argues that the immensely influential concept of affect as unstructured proto-sensation that is primarily associated with Deleuze and Massumi is insufficient to understand the roles of affect in religion and other formations of power. The Deleuzian approach to affect fails to reckon adequately with the animality of the human body, with its evolutionarily particular bio-architecture that affords it a finitely multiple repertoire of affects. Moving to religion by way of Tomkins, Sedgwick, and Ahmed, Schaefer argues that the felt bodily needs and consequent affective economy of which religion is the product hinge on shame and dignity, and he proceeds to illustrate his claim with reference to Saba Mahmood's analysis of the women's Mosque Movement in prerevolutionary Egypt.

In Gregory J. Seigworth's "Capitalism as Religion, Debt as Interface: Wearing the World as a Debt Garment," we encounter different bodily assemblages, those that sew the threads of Seigworth's "debt garment." A debt garment offers the promise of recognition—that of our worldly belongingness to all other humans and nonhumans—and the threat of burdens that crush some more harshly than others, but whose weight we all must carry. In a semi-secular-theological turn, Seigworth reminds us that credit/debt relationships make and unmake worlds. Threading together insights from a patchwork of sources, including M. T. Anderson's YA novel *Feed*, current advancements in "wearable" technologies, St. Francis, Parrika, Benjamin, Nietzsche, Deleuze and Guattari (to name but a few), Seigworth wraps us in the ethological and ecological web of debt, and ultimately proffers an aesthetics of debt. With Seigworth, debt becomes not merely a garment worn, but both a gesture of promise for, and a threat to, other worlds.

Erin Runions also grapples with interest and debt, but in a different register and a different arena. In "Immobile Theologies, Carceral Affects: Interest and Debt in Faith-Based Prison Programs," Runions examines how the biblically based *theologies* deployed in faith-based prison programs are intertwined with carceral *technologies*, and how the emotional/spiritual objectives of the increasingly theologically supported prison industrial complex are bound up with the affective structures and strategies of (racialized) interest and debt. In effect, Runions brings a range of affect theorists into conversation with critics of the prison industrial complex to tease out the interconnected affective, financial, theological, moral, and environmental components of contemporary carceral technologies. Without such analysis, she argues, prison reform can only ever be a further occluded phase of radical neoliberalism.

Continuing the critical engagement with state terror, this time from a postcolonial perspective, Wonhee Anne Joh's "Affective Politics of the Unending Korean War: Remembering and Resistance" treads the routes and traces the roots of dispossession created by the Korean War. Framing it not as the "forgotten war" but rather as the "unending war," Joh renounces individualized theories of trauma and witnesses to the complex spatiotemporal pulls of transgenerational terror. Through contemporary acts of collective mourning, this essay, which is also an exercise in critical Christian theology, reopens the wounds of the cross to register collective rage, grief, and unending mourning as counters to U.S. imperialism. In making a postcolonial turn to affect, Joh confronts elisions in affect theory and assumes a posture of critical melancholia as an intersubjective act of mourning of and resistance to historical trauma.

Sewol names both the senseless mass drowning of schoolchildren in a 2014 ferry disaster off the southwest coast of South Korea and its abiding affective impact on the South Korean population and diaspora. *Sewol* is also the stimulus for Dong Sung Kim's "Weeping by the Water: Hydraulic Affects and Political Depression in South Korea after *Sewol*." Anchoring himself in the tide of emotion washing from the broadcast images of Pangmok Harbor where families and friends wept and awaited news of lost loved ones, but also reactivating the image from Psalm 137 of earlier weeping by another body of water ("By the rivers of Babylon we sat and wept when we remembered Zion . . ."), Kim explores the affective possibilities of water as an elemental archive or repository of emotion beyond the constricting confines of the national and with a (flowing) eye toward global justice. But affect, too, is a fluid concept in Kim's essay. He notes that a generalized, catch-all concept of affect will not suffice to do justice to *Sewol*. A Korean tragedy evokes a Korean affect, and that affect Kim locates in the Korean concept of *Han*.

The enabling assumption of A. Paige Rawson's "Reading (with) Rhythm for the Sake of the (I-n-)Islands: A Rastafarian Interpretation of Samson as Ambi(val)ent Affective Assemblage" is that the Bible is both a Caribbean text and a rhythmic text. In its illimitable capacity to affect and be affected, moreover, the Bible is also what Gregory Seigworth, Melissa Gregg, and Kathleen Stewart would term an affective bloom-space, an exceedingly fertile concept for Rawson. She proceeds to assemble a Rastafari hermeneutic that effectuates a rhythmic reasoning whereby the resonances of Glissantian orality and Deleuzian affect throb together on the pulsating pages of the biblical Samson story. Orality as musicality meets affect theory in Rawson's reactivation of the Samson story, a reading acutely attentive to rhythm and to the intra-action of narrative and interpretive bodies in/as ambient affective assemblage.

A fragmentary text exhumed from the archives in 1958—or else fabricated that same year—is the fraught subject of Alexis G. Waller's "The 'Unspeakable Teachings' of *The Secret Gospel of Mark*: Feelings and Fantasies in the Making of Christian Histories." *Secret Mark* has been embraced as the earliest surviving version of the Gospel of Mark and denounced as either a second-century forgery or a twentieth-century hoax. The stormy reception history of this controversial text—one that appears to represent a homoerotic encounter between Jesus and an unnamed young man—is an affective history of the first order, as Waller demonstrates. Approaching the scholarly and popular reception of *Secret Mark* as a queer archive of feelings (à la Ann Cvetkovich), Waller explores the ways in which historiographical protocols—even, or especially, in a discipline as austere and affect-challenged as biblical scholarship—act as both medium and cover for affective investments, and she reflects on how we might better handle (our feelings about) the early Christian past, or, indeed, any past.

In "Gender: A Public Feeling?" Max Thornton reframes and reconceives gender as both a public feeling (in Cvetkovich's sense of the term) and an affective assemblage. The latter concept, which extends the former, is designed to accommodate the multiplicity of factors, forces, processes, and agencies implicated in gender in general, but in nonnormative gender in particular. Thornton's affective assemblage is eclectically composed from Deleuzoguattarian philosophy, phenomenology, new materialisms, and affect theory, and enacted in the limit case of nontransitioning transgendered people in online communities. Gender as an affective assemblage assumes its full theological potential in Thornton's concluding section where it counters a territorialized reading of Christ's body, one which seeks to exclude nonnormative genders from the church. Calling for the church's self-deterritorialization, Thornton proposes a corporate body enfleshed by queer affective assemblages that would facilitate gendered exploration and discovery.

Issues of territory and territorialization are also germane to Mathew Arthur's "Writing Affect and Theology in Indigenous Futures." Can affectivity or divinity—or, more precisely, perhaps, affect theory or theology—ever deterritorialize themselves fully from Western citationality? This is the question that drives Arthur's essay. Acutely attuned to the impossibility and importance of this challenge, he implores us to stick with the trouble (à la Donna Haraway) represented by animisms and their indigenous territories: geographical, intellectual, and spiritual. Weaving together indigenous modes of knowing with feminist science studies, Arthur resists the sovereignties of both affect theory and theology. Countering modes of thinking affect and theology that might stake out ground, he instead tracks what each does when they are invoked. He thereby seeks alternate routes for making a world, and finds them most fruitfully in indigenous futurism. Arthur adumbrates a hope for an animist-affect-theology that would create a storied world necessarily rooted in the colonial past/present but also open to indigenous futures and inclusive of other-than-human meanings.

Not inappropriately, the volume ends with death. What does it mean to read and write devoutly, religiously, mystically—even, or especially, if one's reading or writing qualifies for none of these adverbs in any conventional sense? What, in particular, does it mean to read and write about death and dying in these affective registers? These are the questions that animate Amy Hollywood's "Feeling Dead, Dead Feeling," a deeply personal dialogue with selected literary authors that smudges the line between literature and criticism and is less a discourse *on* affect than an immersion *in* affect. Hollywood approaches her chosen literary works—literature with which she has bonded—as both fragmentary inscriptions of the divine and articulations of complex affects that exceed individual subjectivity. Difficult literature, for Hollywood—reading it, writing it—is valuable training for the intractable difficulty of death.

We close with a call for a collective cry. In recent ruminations on religion and resistance in the work of Michel Foucault (not himself an affect theorist, of course, nor a scholar of religion),[33] Mark Jordan asks readers to attend anew to Foucault's meditation on the cry of the raped Creusa in Euripides's *Ion*:

If Creusa's agonized transit from cry to confession was required for the founding of philosophy, the continuance of philosophy requires a series of performances at the edge of sight or of hearing. Truth telling will always demand that someone cry out—and that someone register the cry. What if philosophic writing—or philosophic writing so far as it is resistance—is more like a convulsed cry than voluntary speech?[34]

What, for that matter, if *theological* writing is akin to a convulsed cry, but also a collective cry? What exactly might it mean to register collectively our affectivities and resistances toward religion, toward God, toward gods? On what registers of affect might we find divinity? If this volume tells truths, we hope it does so in convulsions, in cries, in registers divine and mundane, and that its performances run at the edge of thought, undoing territory, and remaking worlds.

NOTES

1. Bailey and DiGangi's claim about "what is now commonly called 'affect theory'" is hardly overstated: It is "a critical moniker given recognizable currency by the 2010 publication of *The Affect Theory Reader*." Amanda Bailey and Mario DiGangi, "Introduction," in *Affect Theory and Early Modern Texts: Politics, Ecologies, and Form*, Palgrave Studies in Affect Theory and Literary Criticism (New York: Palgrave Macmillan, 2017), 1; Melissa Gregg and Gregory J. Seigworth, eds., *The Affect Theory Reader* (Durham, N.C.: Duke University Press, 2010).

2. Gregory J. Seigworth and Melissa Gregg, "An Inventory of Shimmers," in *The Affect Theory Reader*, ed. Gregg and Seigworth, 1.

3. "Capacious" has become something of a charged term in affect theory since the publication of *Capacious: Journal for Emerging Affect Inquiry*, a handsome online journal with a large and illustrious editorial board headed by Seigworth and Mathew Arthur. Introducing the journal's inaugural issue, Seigworth writes of affect theory's "capacities . . . for capaciousness: its mode of attention to the 'more-than,' the 'other-than,' the 'different-than,' its attunements to what exceeds and what seeps from the atmospheres and folds of encounter" ("Capaciousness," *Capacious* 1, no. 1 [2017]: https://doi.org/10.22387/cap2017.7). Yet more expansive—not to say apophatic—is Andrew Murphie's description of affect: "Viewed from a certain (processual) perspective, everything is, beginning, middle, and end, a matter of affecting and being affected. Affect is therefore only impossibly an 'object of study'" ("Fielding Affect: Some Propositions," *Capacious* 1, no. 3 [2018]: https://doi.org/10.22387/cap2018.21).

4. Gilles Deleuze, "On Philosophy," in his *Negotiations, 1972–1990*, trans. Martin Joughin (New York: Columbia University Press, 1995; French original 1990), 137. See also Gilles Deleuze and Félix Guattari, *A Thousand Plateaus: Capitalism and Schizophrenia*, trans. Brian Massumi (Minneapolis: University of Minnesota Press, 1987; French original 1980), 256: "Affects are becomings."

5. Brian Massumi, *Parables for the Virtual: Movement, Affect, Sensation, Post-contemporary Interventions* (Durham, N.C.: Duke University Press, 2002), 28. See also Brian Massumi, *Politics of Affect* (Cambridge, U.K.: Polity Press, 2015), 5: "An emotion is a very partial expression of affect."

6. Deleuzian affect permeates much of Patricia Clough's pivotal collection *The Affective Turn*, for example, while affect theorists as prominent as Lauren Berlant, Kathleen Stewart, and Jasbir Puar also work with concepts of affect that are essentially

Deleuzian (although the projects for which they harness these concepts are differently oriented than Deleuze's, as we shall see). Eugenie Brinkema, meanwhile, begins her book *The Forms of the Affects* with an impassioned critique of the amorphous version of Deleuzian affect that has been so influential in her field of film theory, although her neoformalist counterproposal also draws heavily on Deleuze. See Patricia Ticineto Clough with Jean Halley, eds., *The Affective Turn: Theorizing the Social* (Durham, N.C.: Duke University Press, 2007); Lauren Berlant, *Cruel Optimism* (Durham, N.C.: Duke University Press, 2011); Kathleen Stewart, *Ordinary Affects* (Durham, N.C.: Duke University Press, 2007); Jasbir K. Puar, *Terrorist Assemblages: Homonationalism in Queer Times*, Next Wave: New Directions in Women's Studies (Durham, N.C.: Duke University Press, 2007); and Eugenie Brinkema, *The Forms of the Affects* (Durham, N.C.: Duke University Press, 2014).

7. We borrow the metaphor of "sticking" from Sara Ahmed, as did Seigworth and Gregg in our initial quotation from them above ("those resonances that circulate about, between, and sometimes stick to bodies and worlds" ["An Inventory of Shimmers," 1]). See Sara Ahmed, *The Cultural Politics of Emotion*, 2nd ed. (New York: Routledge, 2015), 11: "The question, 'What sticks?' is one that is posed throughout this study." See especially 89–92, a section titled "On Stickiness."

8. On the Angry Black Woman, see Sara Ahmed, *The Promise of Happiness* (Durham, N.C.: Duke University Press, 2010), 67–69, who acknowledges her own debt to Audre Lorde and bell hooks for her reflections on that cultural stereotype.

9. Seigworth and Gregg, "An Inventory of Shimmers," 3–4.

10. Ibid., 5.

11. Eve Kosofsky Sedgwick and Adam Frank, "Shame in the Cybernetic Fold: Reading Silvan Tomkins," in *Shame and Its Sisters: A Silvan Tomkins Reader*, ed. Sedgwick and Frank (Durham, N.C.: Duke University Press, 1995), 1–28, reprinted in Eve Kosofsky Sedgwick, *Touching Feeling: Affect, Pedagogy, Performativity* (Durham, N.C.: Duke University Press, 2003), 93–121; Brian Massumi, "The Autonomy of Affect," *Cultural Critique* 31 (Fall 1995): 83–109, reprinted in idem, *Parables for the Virtual*, 23–45.

12. "You don't have to be long out of theory kindergarten to make mincemeat of, let's say, a psychology that depends on the separate existence of eight (only sometimes it's nine) distinct affects hardwired into the human biological system" (Sedgwick and Frank, *Touching Feeling*, 94). These eight or nine affects, for Tomkins, are distress-anguish; interest-excitement; enjoyment-joy; surprise-startle; anger-rage; fear-terror; shame-humiliation; disgust; and, related to the latter but subtly distinct from it, "dismell." He works through all of them in his magnum opus, *Affect, Imagery, Consciousness*, vol. 1: *The Positive Affects*; vol. 2: *The Negative Affects*; vol. 3: *The Negative Affects: Anger and Fear*; vol. 4: *Cognition: Duplication and Transformation of Information* (New York: Springer, 1962–92).

13. Seigworth and Gregg, "An Inventory of Shimmers," 7.

14. Jasbir K. Puar, *The Right to Maim: Debility, Capacity, Disability* (Durham, N.C.: Duke University Press, 2017), 18. Puar's sweeping delineation of affect theory includes the following: "The affective turn, alongside the critical deployment of affect as a rubric of analysis and inquiry, . . . potently signals the contestation over the dominant

terms of critical theory itself and the limits of poststructuralist interpretive practices that focus solely on language, signification, and representation. The sites of struggle and their targets include social constructionism (reinvigorated interrogation of biological matter that challenges both biological determinism and also performativity); epistemology (supplemented with ontology and ontogenesis); psychoanalysis (trauma rethought as the intensification of the body's relation to itself); humanism (the capacities of nonhuman animals as well as the durational capacities of inorganic matter are highlighted by scholarship on object-oriented ontology, critical animal studies, and posthumanism); and agency (linked to cognition, perception, emotion, and feeling: an anthropocentric framing of movement challenged by affect, force, intensity, and theories of sensation)" (ibid.).

15. At least from within religious studies. Schaefer himself acknowledges that political theorist William Connolly had already, in such books as *Capitalism and Christianity, American Style*, and in a Deleuzian register, explored the precognitive, affective dimensions of religion. Donovan O. Schaefer, *Religious Affects: Animality, Evolution and Power* (Durham, N.C.: Duke University, 2015), 27–28; William E. Connolly, *Capitalism and Christianity, American Style* (Durham, N.C.: Duke University Press, 2008).

16. Schaefer, *Religious Affects*, 23–34. The phenomenological camp is more populous, in Schaefer's account of it, than the Deleuzian camp. He writes: "Sedgwick and Frank's poststructuralist reading of Tomkins is a major foundation of the phenomenological branch of affect—a canon more or less coextensive with the subfield Sara Ahmed has called 'feminist cultural studies of emotion and affect': her list includes Sedgwick, Teresa Brennan, Elspeth Probyn, Ann Cvetkovich, Lauren Berlant, and Kathleen Stewart" (31–32).

17. Schaefer himself gravitates to the latter approach: "*Religious Affects* . . . trends more toward the approach of Ahmed, Cvetkovich, and Mel Y. Chen in viewing with some suspicion the attempt to compose a hard line between affect and emotion" (ibid., 32).

18. For Elspeth Probyn's appropriation of Tomkins, see especially her *Blush: Faces of Shame* (Minneapolis: University of Minnesota Press, 2005), 18–25. Margaret Wetherell has issued a cautionary note, however, on the Tomkins trajectory of affect theory in general: "It is easy to see the appeal of Tomkins and why Sedgwick and Probyn say that they 'fell for' him. . . . Re-discovery was a lovely thing to happen, but it does feel rather random. Why not take up Magda Arnold who also produced an opus on affect in the 1960s? Arnold was one of the few established women researchers in mid-20th-century psychology. Her work on emotional appraisal . . . is much more congenial to cultural investigation in so many ways." Margaret Wetherell, *Affect and Emotion: A New Social Science Understanding* (London: Sage, 2012), 11; see also Magda B. Arnold, *Emotion and Personality*, vol. 1: *Psychological Aspects*; vol. 2: *Neurological and Psychological Aspects* (New York: Columbia University Press, 1960). For a sweeping survey of psychological, biological, and humanities-based attempts to understand emotions from the post–World War II period to the present, see Ruth Leys, *The Ascent of Affect: Genealogy and Critique* (Chicago: University of Chicago

Press, 2017), which begins with a chapter on Tomkins and ends with a critique of contemporary affect theory.

19. For representative examples of Erin Manning's, Steven Shaviro's, and Nigel Thrift's affect-attuned work, see Manning's *The Minor Gesture*, Thought in the Act (Durham, N.C.: Duke University Press, 2016); Shaviro's *Post-Cinematic Affect* (Washington, D.C.: O-Books, 2010); and Thrift's *Non-Representational Theory: Space/Politics/Affect* (New York: Routledge, 2008), together with Teresa Brennan, *The Transmission of Affect* (Ithaca, NY: Cornell University Press, 2004). Key works by Massumi and Clough have already been listed, although see additionally Brian Massumi, *The Power at the End of the Economy* (Durham, N.C.: Duke University Press, 2015) and Patricia Ticineto Clough, *The User Unconscious: On Affect, Media, and Measure* (Minneapolis: University of Minnesota Press, 2018). For an incisive exposition of Deleuze's expansive and elusive concept of affect, see Gregory J. Seigworth, "From Affection to Soul," in *Gilles Deleuze: Key Concepts*, ed. Charles J. Stivale, 2nd ed. (New York: Routledge, 2011), 181–91. What we are calling the prepersonal lens of affect theory, however, is not entirely Deleuze-driven. Brennan, for example, declares her distance from Deleuze (*Transmission of Affect*, 14); so too does Thrift, although less dismissively (*Non-Representational Theory*, 18, 266–67n18).

20. See Ann Cvetkovich, *An Archive of Feelings: Trauma, Sexuality, and Lesbian Public Cultures*, Series Q (Durham, N.C.: Duke University Press, 2003) and *Depression: A Public Feeling* (Durham, N.C.: Duke University Press, 2012); Mel Y. Chen, *Animacies: Biopolitics, Racial Mattering, and Queer Affect*, Perverse Modernities (Durham, N.C.: Duke University Press, 2012); Sianne Ngai, *Ugly Feelings* (Cambridge, Mass.: Harvard University Press, 2007). Representative works by Ahmed, Berlant, Stewart, and Puar have already been listed. Further manifestations of affect theory's cultural lens, as we define it, include (but are not limited to) Marianne Liljeström and Susanna Paasonen, eds., *Working with Affect in Feminist Readings: Disturbing Differences*, Transformations: Thinking through Feminism (New York: Routledge, 2010); Dina Georgis, *The Better Story: Queer Affects from the Middle East* (Albany: State University of New York Press, 2013); Shaka McGlotten, *Virtual Intimacies: Media, Affect, and Queer Sociality* (Albany: State University of New York Press, 2013); Tyler Bradway, *Queer Experimental Literature: The Affective Politics of Bad Reading*, Palgrave Studies in Affect Theory and Literary Criticism (New York: Palgrave Macmillan, 2017); Elin Diamond, Denise Varney, and Candice Amich, eds., *Performance, Feminism, and Affect in Neoliberal Times*, Contemporary Performance InterActions (New York: Palgrave Macmillan, 2017); Jessica Joy Cameron, *Reconsidering Radical Feminism: Affect and the Politics of Heterosexuality*, Sexuality Studies (Vancouver: University of British Columbia Press, 2018); and Kyle Bladow and Jennifer Ladino, eds., *Affective Ecocriticism: Emotion, Embodiment, Environment* (Lincoln: University of Nebraska Press, 2018).

21. At least four, but surely more. Affect theory, and the critical study of feelings and emotions more generally, has, by now, obtained a firm foothold in religious studies and is beginning to be applied in many different ways to religious texts and phenomena. At the time of writing, the American Academy of Religion hosts a

Religion, Affect, and Emotion program unit; the Society of Biblical Literature hosts a Bible and Emotions unit; and the European Association of Biblical Studies hosts an Emotions and the Biblical World unit. Religious studies volumes devoted to affect, feelings, or emotions (to limit ourselves only to book-length productions) have included, in addition to Schaefer, *Religious Affects*: John Corrigan, *Business of the Heart: Religion and Emotion in the Nineteenth Century* (Berkeley: University of California Press, 2002); idem, *Emptiness: Feeling Christian in America* (Chicago: University of Chicago Press, 2015); idem, ed., *Religion and Emotion: Approaches and Interpretations* (New York: Oxford University Press, 2004); idem, ed., *The Oxford Handbook of Religion and Emotion* (New York: Oxford University Press, 2008); idem, ed., *Feeling Religion* (Durham, N.C.: Duke University Press, 2018); Virginia Burrus, *Saving Shame: Martyrs, Saints, and Other Abject Subjects*, Divinations: Rereading Late Ancient Religion (Philadelphia: University of Pennsylvania Press, 2007); Douglas J. Davies, *Emotion, Identity, and Religion: Hope, Reciprocity, and Otherness* (New York: Oxford University Press, 2011); M. Gail Hamner, *Imaging Religion in Film: The Politics of Nostalgia*, New Approaches to Religion and Power (New York: Palgrave Macmillan, 2011); Jennifer L. Koosed and Stephen D. Moore, eds., "Affect Theory and the Bible," *Biblical Interpretation* 22, no. 4 (thematic issue, 2014); Maia Kotrosits, *Rethinking Early Christian Identity: Affect, Violence, and Belonging* (Minneapolis: Fortress Press, 2015); idem, *How Things Feel: Biblical Studies, Affect Theory, and the (Im)personal*, Brill Research Perspectives in Biblical Interpretation 1 (Leiden, Netherlands: Brill, 2016); Maia Kotrosits and Hal Taussig, *Re-reading the Gospel of Mark amidst Loss and Trauma* (New York: Palgrave Macmillan, 2013); Stephanie N. Arel, *Affect Theory, Shame, and Christian Formation* (New York: Palgrave Macmillan, 2016); Robert Glenn Davis, *The Weight of Love: Affect, Ecstasy, and Union in the Theology of Bonaventure* (New York: Fordham University Press, 2016); Denise Gill, *Melancholic Modalities: Affect, Islam, and Turkish Classical Musicians* (New York: Oxford University Press, 2017); Françoise Mirguet, *An Early History of Compassion: Emotion and Imagination in Hellenistic Judaism* (New York: Cambridge University Press, 2017); Françoise Mirguet and Dominika Kurek-Chomycz, eds., "Emotions in Ancient Jewish Literature," *Biblical Interpretation* 24, nos. 4–5 (thematic issue, 2016); Stephen D. Moore, *Gospel Jesuses and Other Nonhumans: Biblical Criticism Post–poststructuralism*, Semeia Studies 89 (Atlanta: SBL Press, 2017); F. Scott Spencer, ed., *Mixed Feelings and Vexed Passions: Exploring Emotions in Biblical Literature*, Resources for Biblical Study 90 (Atlanta: SBL Press, 2017); Kent L. Brintnall, Joseph A. Marchal, and Stephen D. Moore, eds., *Sexual Disorientations: Queer Temporalities, Affects, Theologies*, Transdisciplinary Theological Colloquia (New York: Fordham University Press, 2018); and Fiona C. Black and Jennifer L. Koosed, eds., *Reading with Feeling: Affect Theory and the Bible*, Semeia Studies (Atlanta: SBL Press, forthcoming).

22. Schaefer, *Religious Affects*, 8.
23. Ibid., 6, challenging Jonathan Z. Smith's highly influential linguistic-conceptual description of religion.
24. Ibid., 8.
25. Ibid., 9–10.

26. Ibid., 146.

27. Cf. Sedgwick, *Touching Feeling*, 5: "[This book] wants to address aspects of experience and reality that do not present themselves in propositional or even in verbal form alongside others that do, rather than submit to the apparent common sense that requires a strict separation between the two and usually implies an ontological privileging of the [propositional over the nonverbal]."

28. Cvetkovich, *Depression*, 199.

29. What we are proposing here has affinities with the New Materialist approaches to history associated with such scholars of religion as John Modern and Sonia Hazard. See, for example, John Lardas Modern, *Secularism in Antebellum America*, Religion and Postmodernism (Chicago: University of Chicago Press, 2011); Sonia Hazard, "The Material Turn in the Study of Religion," *Religion and Society* 4, no. 1 (2013): 58–78. For more on the New Materialism(s) and religious studies (not least theology), see Catherine Keller and Mary-Jane Rubenstein, eds., *Entangled Worlds: Religion, Science, and New Materialisms*, Transdisciplinary Theological Colloquia (New York: Fordham University Press, 2017).

30. For that reason this idea is known as the Wesleyan Quadrilateral.

31. Baruch Spinoza, *Ethics*, in *Spinoza: The Complete Works*, ed. Michael L. Morgan, trans. Samuel Shirley (Indianapolis: Hackett, 2002), 280. Seigworth and Gregg style this statement "one of the most oft-cited quotations concerning affect" ("An Inventory of Shimmers," 3).

32. Spinoza, *Ethics*, 280, emphasis added. Spinoza's status as the patron saint of affect theory derives mainly from his importance for Deleuze. For Deleuze and Guattari, indeed, "Spinoza is the Christ of philosophers, and the greatest philosophers are hardly more than apostles who distance themselves or draw near this mystery." Gilles Deleuze and Félix Guattari, *What Is Philosophy?* trans. Hugh Tomlinson and Graham Burchell (New York: Columbia University Press, 1994; French original 1991), 60.

33. Although the term "queer affect" perfectly captures what Foucault is attempting to describe in *The History of Sexuality: An Introduction*, trans. Robert Hurley (New York: Pantheon Books, 1978; French original 1976), 44–45, and he is also an exceedingly astute commentator on Christianity in much of his later work.

34. Mark Jordan, *Convulsing Bodies: Religion and Resistance in Foucault* (Stanford, Calif.: Stanford University Press, 2015), 191; see also Michel Foucault, *Fearless Speech*, ed. Joseph Pearson (Los Angeles: Semiotext[e], 2001), 52–57.

❧ The Animality of Affect: Religion, Emotion, and Power

DONOVAN O. SCHAEFER

The Center for 21st Century Studies, a research unit at the University of Wisconsin-Milwaukee, puts on an extraordinary series of high-profile annual conferences. Their 2012 conference was on the theme "The Nonhuman Turn." The keynote speakers were an all-star cast of affect theorists, New Materialists, and object-oriented ontologists, including Timothy Morton, Erin Manning, Brian Massumi, and Jane Bennett.

On the ground floor of the concrete tower that housed the center, Manning and Massumi had set up an installation piece, "Weather Patterns," next to the registration area outside the main lecture room. The installation was a mass of black fabric and cables suspended from the ceiling, which conference goers would pass through like a maze of curtains on their way to the theater. There were also speakers embedded in the folds of the cloth. And the cloth wasn't ordinary fabric, but had been wired up to act as a sort of antenna. The fabric was picking up waves of air from the motion of passersby and absorbing the waves as electronic signals. The signals were collated and converted into sound information, which was then emitted by the speakers. The effect was a cascade of whispering, screeching, and clicking emanating from the cloth and rolling through the halls.

The artwork modeled Massumi and Manning's understanding of "affect"—a field of pure potential that circulates between bodies. This version of affect is itself built on the understanding of affect offered by Benedict de Spinoza, as the play of the "infinitely many things in infinitely many modes,"[1] the unfurling of a single substance, what Gilles Deleuze would later call the plane of immanence.[2] As Massumi and Manning wrote of the piece, it was the materialization of "[a] process" that would "register the environmental conditions in a series of relational cross-currents."[3] The art-machine took the whirlpool of affects—understood as abstract processes cross-cutting bodies—and rendered it audible.

At first I would make a point of walking through "Weather Patterns" on the way to sessions. After a few encounters, however, I came to the conclusion that it was better appreciated at a distance. It still looked extremely cool. On the last day of the conference, I left the final session a few minutes early. The registration table still had a grad student working it. She was about twenty feet from "Weather Patterns," still clicking and whispering away. I suddenly realized that she had been effectively embedded inside the installation for hours. She was staring straight ahead with her arms folded. I walked up to her and asked "So has this installation lost its charm for you?" Still staring straight ahead, arms folded, without looking up, she said, "I need a drink."

This essay is about the relationship of bodies to affects, and in particular, the conceptual ambidexterity of the term "affect" itself. Affect theory, as scholars such as Mel Y. Chen, Ann Cvetkovich, Gregory J. Seigworth and Melissa Gregg, Eve Kosofsky Sedgwick, Sara Ahmed, and Eugenie Brinkema have pointed out, is riven by two divergent, and perhaps incommensurable, definitions—*affect*, in the Deleuzian sense as unstructured proto-sensation—the sense reflected in "Weather Patterns"—and *affects* as the emotional textures structuring our embodied experience.[4] My argument is that we need the second—the specified model of affects, rather than a generalized model of affect—in order to understand the relationship between affect and formations of power, such as religion. While the Deleuzian understanding of affect is not irrelevant to accounts of power, it ultimately indexes something so far upstream of bodies that it is oblivious to the way that power interfaces with organisms in their *animal* specificity.

AFFECT AND AFFECTS

Ann Cvetkovich's *Depression: A Public Feeling* opens with an important preface for any discussion of what is now getting called affect theory: that although the term itself is new, attention to affect has been a part of certain scholarly disciplines—including, especially, marginalized disciplines such as feminism, queer theory, antiracism, and postcolonial studies—decades before anyone came up with the phrase "the affective turn."[5] But within the contemporary discussion, Cvetkovich notes two distinct methodological flavors. In one stream is the network of scholars, such as the Public Feelings Collective, who thematize affect as a resource for academic research and political activism. In the other stream are what Cvetkovich calls the "Deleuzians," affect theorists who define affect according to its technical use in the work of Gilles Deleuze. In Cvetkovich's account, the difference between these branches lies in a distinction: Deleuzians tend to rigidly maintain the border between something called "affect," which is "precognitive sensory experience and relations to surroundings," and something called emotion—"cultural constructs and conscious processes that emerge from them, such as anger, fear, or joy."[6] Cvetkovich herself, by contrast, confesses to a less disciplined use of the term "affect," as "encompass[ing] affect, emotion, and feeling, and that includes impulses, desires, and feelings that get historically constructed in a range of ways."[7] Sara Ahmed calls this second perspective—less committed to the differentiation between affect and emotion—"feminist cultural studies of affect."

The Deleuzian approach has been advanced primarily in the fields of poststructuralist philosophy and media studies. One of its most prominent exponents, Brian Massumi, has provided a brilliant exposition of Deleuze's notion of affect, featured in his early works on Spinoza and Bergson and in his later collaborations with Félix Guattari, some of which Massumi himself translated for Anglophone audiences. In Massumi's 1995 essay "The Autonomy of Affect," he argues for a distinction between affects as registers of mobile intensity and emotions as structured, static forms embedded in consciousness. His star witness in this case is an experiment in which German researchers discovered that viewers preferred to watch a very sad film about a melting snowman than a less sad film: "the sadder the better."[8] Massumi's conclusion is that although the emotion "sadness" is bad, the affective preconditions of the emotion are what actually motivate bodies to want to watch the film.

Out of this example Massumi develops an entire ontology of the dynamic between consciousness and affects. Massumi argues that intensity is the pure zone of possibility that forms the background coordinates of experience, but that is in principle undetectable on the register of experience. Intensities—affects—leave traces as emotions as they *escape* bodies, but they can never be absorbed as such. This is because they express the principle of becoming as such: Affect does not exist except inasmuch as it chases the horizon line of the virtual becoming actual. "The autonomy of affect," Massumi writes, "is its participation in the virtual. *Its autonomy is its openness.* Affect is autonomous to the degree to which it escapes confinement in the particular body whose vitality, or potential for interaction, it is."[9] As Ann Pellegrini and Jasbir Puar put it, "This conception of affect poses a distinction between sensation and the perception of the sensation. Affect, from this perspective, is precisely what allows the body to be an open system, always in concert with its virtuality, the potential of becoming."[10] Affectivity is the pastiche of substances that link our motions and gestures to machines to sound waves. True affect is always only obliquely related to experience, but experience is itself directed by this welter of becomings.

This model necessitated, for Massumi, the abandonment of earlier phenomenological research into sensing bodies: "They were difficult to reconcile with the new understandings of the structuring capacities of culture and their inseparability both from the exercise of power and the glimmers of counterpower incumbent in mediate living. [Phenomenology] was all about a subject without subjectivism: a subject 'constructed' by external mechanisms. 'The Subject.'"[11] The subject of phenomenology—what Massumi sees as a rigid, static ontology, the congealed residue of becomings—dissolves and is replaced by an analytics of anti-structure, a chain of terms that are all predicates of the phenomenological subject but are ultimately unavailable to it: "Affect, sensation, perception, movement, intensity, tendency, habit, law, chaos, recursion, relation, immanence, the 'feedback of higher forms.' Emergence, becoming, history, space, time, space-time, space and time as emergences."[12]

This chain of conceptual resonances also becomes the foundation for Massumi's version of the analytics of power.[13] For Deleuzians, the scintillations of affect understood as the streams of becoming function as the currency of power. This is the locus of Massumi's analysis of Ronald Reagan's political effectiveness. Drawing on the research of the neuroscientist Oliver Sacks, Massumi argues that Reagan's ability to marshal a national political network emerged from the particular way that he arranged his bodily gestures and expressions in an oblique relationship to the propositional content of his policy positions. "Reagan politicized the power of mime," Massumi writes. "A mime decomposes movement, cuts its continuity into a potentially infinite series of submovements punctuated by jerks. At each jerk, at each cut into the movement, the potential is there for the movement to veer off in another direction, to become a different movement."[14] Reagan's accomplishment, then, was to configure his pattern of facial expressions as a stream of becomings. He tuned his face to the frequency of pure becoming.

This analysis of power as the unfurling of becoming remains Massumi's priority in his 2014 book *What Animals Teach Us about Politics*. Massumi's project in this book is very interesting to me: He believes, as I argue elsewhere, that the analytics of affect can be advanced by considering animals (and vice versa).[15] But I diverge from Massumi in the execution of the particulars. Massumi reads animality through the prism of Gregory Bateson's notion of "play." He sees animal play as being an outgrowth of a particular version of instinct. Where the conventional understanding of instinct is that it is fixed, Massumi insists that it is better understood as variable.[16] "The form of the gesture is deformed," Massumi writes, "under pressure from the enthusiasm of the body propelling it."[17] Play then becomes a space where actions are shaped by excess intensity—the vitality affect of becoming.[18]

Massumi then takes this notion of play as a field of becoming and transplants it into the analytics of power. He coins a term that, again, I'm very interested in—animal politics—and characterizes it as "a *politics of becoming*, even—especially—of the human."[19] Animal politics is the politics of Reagan and beyond: It's the ensemble of mechanisms circulating power by jump-cutting, distributing becomings and pulling bodies along in their wake. In Massumi's terms, it is "a politics of the performative gesture, alloying itself with practices of improvisational and participative art in the wild."[20] This leads Massumi to a focus on politics in what he calls its "ethico-aesthetic" and "aesthico-political" dimensions. "The main criterion available for the corresponding evaluations," Massumi writes, "is the degree to which the political gesture carries forward enthusiasm of the body."[21] Politics ceases to be about ideological architectures or their corresponding ethical priorities. It is liquidated into a pure stream of affective becoming.

In broad brushstrokes, I think this is the correct approach to analyzing power. As I have argued elsewhere, the model of power that focuses on discourse succumbs to the linguistic fallacy: the fiction advanced by some critical strands in the humanities that humans are fundamentally linguistic-cognitive beings and that the things that move us must also be fundamentally linguistic-cognitive.[22] Like Massumi, I think that power feels before it thinks. I'd go further and argue that even where we see politics moving according to ideological platforms—right or left, authoritarian or egalitarian, militarist or pacifist—those ideological architectures are themselves products of affective configurations. (I'll defend this approach below.) As William Connolly, another affect theorist in the Deleuzian lineage, writes, "Those who continue to think that the existential dimension of life is merely personal, or only private, or unsusceptible to cultural dissemination, or irrelevant to economic life, or wholly determined by other forces, still don't get it."[23] The affective textures of embodied life migrate across the public-private line, determining every aspect of political subjectivities.

But Massumi's approach also encloses an error, one that limits its usefulness for the analytics of power. This error is the exclusive emphasis on the Deleuzian trope of becoming as the currency of power. One way of spotlighting this mistake is to look at the way that Massumi understands the category of instinct. For Massumi, "instinctual movements are animated by a tendency to surpass given forms. . . . They are moved by an impetus toward creativity."[24] From a biological perspective, this is a difficult claim to make sense of. It's not wrong that instinct is more than just stereotyped movement. Many zoologists have seen fit to abandon the notion of instinct altogether; it evokes a modernist notion of animal minds as mechanical, the prereflective other to the glory of human reason.[25] But the most interesting part of whatever-instinct-is isn't that it sometimes varies. It's that it so often remains the same. Instincts—probably better understood as durable learning rules that are embedded in the phenotypes of animal minds—are semi-stable bodily processes that recur with remarkable consistency across populations and generations of a single species. Their locus can't really be explained by an ontology of becoming.

Instead, they diagram a subtle but intransigent tissue of experiential protocols that shape embodied subjectivity. Massumi proposes that the tendency of instincts to exceed themselves is "an evolutionary advantage."[26] But I think this basic adaptationism overlooks the real story, here: If we're going to speculate on fitness benefits, the fixity of certain instincts—stereotyped motions, desires, and forms—is much more likely to be "adaptive" than their flexibility. It is precisely because, at the scale of macro-organisms, we must interact with the world in sophisticated ways—rather than trying to eat and/or mate with literally everything smaller than us as microorganisms do—that we have intransigent learning biases in the first place.[27]

Although cognitive flexibility among some large-brained macro-organisms adds a new dimension to fitness, semi-stable biological and psychological features embedded in organisms at birth—like knowing the smells of certain predators or how to follow the pheromone trail of your cousins or to root for a nipple—are the core survival strategy at the level of every vertebrate organism.[28] From a biological perspective, becoming will kill you. The best prescription for general health is for your intricately structured cells to keep *becoming* to an absolute minimum—leaving enough play in the system for migration, nutrition, excretion, and maybe even a little fun, but by and large being exactly the same boring old *beings* day after day, over and over again. And our highest hope, on any given morning, should be that our neurotransmitters don't start becoming anything other than the highly specific chemical compounds that they are. When they start getting wild ideas and changing into anything even slightly different from what we have now, it will be the functional equivalent of a kill-switch in our brains.

This misunderstanding of the relationship between affects and organisms leads to the problems with Massumi's analytics of power. There are several concerns that come up here. One is that it seems to subsume what we might call ethical intuitions into aesthetic dazzle, producing a politics of spectacle.[29] But I have a more pointed criticism. That is that the model of politics as affect massively limits the analytics of power by reducing power to just one thing, one particular affective template: enthusiasm.

One of the main features of Foucault's analytics of power is that power is "a multiple and mobile field of force relations."[30] My sense is that Massumi sees affect as being the currency at the foundation of this network of relations. I think he is partially correct in this: Power is affect and vice versa. Although Foucault refused to ask after the nature of power itself, the affect approach adds a new level of precision to his picture. But Massumi's model falls apart where he correlates power to becoming. Becoming, as we have seen, is a micro-process that only represents one dimension of embodied life. Massumi's error is Deleuze's error: He takes the micrological register of becoming and elevates it to the existential register. The molecular haecceity is presumed to be the code of the molar. Just as the grad student at C21 probably started out, like me, mildly buzzed by the art installation, she soon grew bored of it, then annoyed, and eventually was driven to drink. If "affect" in the sense of becoming were tantamount to power, then we'd be irresistibly pulled to it like moths fluttering to a lamp. Although "Weather Patterns" materializes Spinoza's notion of affect, it doesn't draw us. Becoming is not sufficient for a model of power.

William Mazzarella characterizes the limitations of Deleuzian affect theory by writing that it "bequeathed to the philosophies it spawned a crudely romantic distinction between, on the one side, all-encompassing form (whose totalizing ambition must be resisted) and, on the other side, the evanescent forms of affective and—it is often implied—popular potentiality (which must be nurtured and celebrated)."[31] But the most pointed criticism, to me, comes in Eve Sedgwick and Adam Frank's 1995 essay debuting Silvan Tomkins to the theory world, "Shame in the Cybernetic Fold," in which they write that the approach that liquidates all response to a single stream of affect is "like a scanner or copier that can reproduce any work of art in 256,000 shades of gray. However infinitesimally subtle its discriminations may be, there are crucial knowledges it simply cannot transmit unless it is equipped to deal with the coarsely reductive possibility that red is different from yellow is different again from blue."[32]

As Eugenie Brinkema points out: "In the end, ethics, politics, aesthetics—indeed, lives—must be enacted in the definite particular."[33] The Deleuzian sense of affect can't capture the real multiplicity of affects, the way that power is channeled through the interplay of specific embodied forms rather than the "pure plastic rhythm" of becoming.[34] Rather than an animal politics, it is a politics of radio static. When an animal body—like the annoyed grad student volunteer at C21—is enfolded in a zone of pure becoming, it is not attracted, but feels itself unraveling.

ANIMAL POLITICS, TAKE TWO

To track the multiple textures of power, we must engage with versions of affect that encounter affect in its animality. There are a number of avenues for doing this. One is Sedgwick and Frank's curated excerpts of the work of Silvan Tomkins. Tomkins, a Princeton psychologist whom Sedgwick brought into queer theory as an alternative to Freudian models of sexuality and emotion, operated in a lineage of psychologists of emotion that incorporated not only Freud but also William James and Charles Darwin. In particular, Tomkins takes Darwin's *The Expression of the Emotions in Man and Animals* as a foundation for his project, deploying a version of what would come to be called the

Basic Emotions hypothesis. In this view, there exists a set of discrete emotional drivers embedded in brains.[35] Sedgwick and Frank use this framework to formulate their counterpoint to the Deleuzian model of affect, the formula *finitely many, n > 2*.[36] Affect is neither singular, nor binary, nor infinite. It is *finitely multiple*, a bricolage of available forms, the product of an evolutionarily particular bioarchitecture.

There's also a second way of encountering animality in affect, and that is to follow the track of phenomenology. Front and center in this conversation is Sara Ahmed, whose training in philosophy has equipped her with the conceptual repertoire of phenomenology going all the way back to its founder, the early-twentieth-century German philosopher Edmund Husserl. Ahmed's 2006 book *Queer Phenomenology* articulates this method: Phenomenology, she writes, "can offer a resource for queer studies insofar as it emphasizes the importance of lived experience, the intentionality of consciousness, the significance of nearness or what is ready-to-hand, and the role of repeated and habitual actions in shaping bodies and worlds."[37] In her earlier work, Ahmed described how the accumulation of impressions from objects in the world shapes the horizon of feeling. The perimeter of the self is not the horizon of agency, but the bricolage of emotional textures that have imprinted themselves on our bodies. "*We need to remember the 'press' in an impression*," she writes. "It allows us to associate the experience of having an emotion with the very affect of one surface upon another, an affect that leaves its mark or trace. So not only do I have an impression of others, but they also leave me with an impression; they impress me, and impress upon me."[38]

Although Ahmed herself never, to my knowledge, makes this connection, the phenomenological tradition is also closely correlated to a set of questions about animality. Part of the imperative of phenomenology as a project was to locate the accumulation of knowledge in experience rather than a metaphysical property of intellect. Whereas intellect was an implicitly or explicitly human feature, Husserl expressly indicated that the perceiving "transcendental ego" was a feature of animal minds no less than human minds. In Chapter 2 of *Ideas 2*, he writes that "the psyche or soul, the identical psychic being which, connected in a real way with the respective human or animal Body, makes up the substantial-real double being: the animal, man or brute."[39] The set of phenomenological subjects of experience therefore includes both human and animal bodies.

This inclusion of animals is fleshed out, quite literally, in the work of a figure who receives insufficient attention in affect theory, other than occasional mention in Elizabeth Grosz and Sara Ahmed: the French phenomenologist Maurice Merleau-Ponty. Merleau-Ponty provided a vital correction to Husserl's core notion of the perceiving transcendental ego: To wit, he detranscendentalized and de-egoized perception, locating the tissues of experience in the specific fleshy architecture of bodies. "By thus remaking contact with the body and with the world," Merleau-Ponty writes, "we shall also rediscover ourself, since, perceiving as we do with our body, the body is a natural self and, as it were, the subject of perception."[40] For Deleuze, phenomenology was anathema because it presupposed the integrity of the perceiving subject. But Merleau-Ponty and other later phenomenologists (including Ahmed) saw the "subject" as not a subject at all, properly speaking, but a sedimentation of forms that enabled a historically particular mode of experience. The constituent parts of the body make up the instrumentation of perception. The deletion of this armature of instruments does not leave us with a transcendental perceiving subject, the homunculus who had been peering through all those telescopes. It leaves us with nothing at all. No body, no plane of perception, no self. And the replacement or reconfiguration of the perceptual apparatus leaves us with a fundamentally *different* self.

Merleau-Ponty expressly understands this in terms of animality, especially in his lectures on "Nature" and "The Structure of Behavior" (which also return to Darwin). Merleau-Ponty, following the early German ethologist Jakob von Uexküll, suggests that animals experience the world in ways that correspond to a set of specific embodied priorities, shaped by both evolutionary lineages and individual learning (not to mention, we now know, epigenetic and ontogenetic factors).[41] What we are left with is not a single faculty of perception, but a range of diverse animal bodies with different architectures of experience and sensation. These architectures become the platforms of our affective encounters with the world. The kind of bodies we are shape how things feel. Each body has a repertoire of affective forms, each of which Tomkins suggests is "like a letter of an alphabet in a language, changing in significance as it is assembled with varying other letters to form different words, sentences, paragraphs."[42] What Derrida calls the "heterogeneous multiplicity" of animal bodies is an efflorescence of assemblages of affective avenues into the world, what I have elsewhere called ontophenomenologies.[43]

None of this is to say, however, that affect in the Deleuzian sense is *not* a formation of power. I think it has simply been located at the wrong level, or rather, that it conflates two different phenomena. The ontology of becoming is an ontology of substance in Spinoza's sense, a picture of matter as always singular and always in flux. At the micro-level, this is correct. The Deleuzian mistake is to assume that this micro-dimension has existential significance at the macro level. Brinkema notes that "affect" elevated to the existential province of macro-organisms is synonymous with "resistance to systematicity, a promised recovery of contingency, surprise, play, pleasure, and possibility."[44] But rather than seeing this as being the core nature of affect, I would argue that it is *one affect among many*, a particular way of encountering the world that orients itself to the *experience of novelty*. This biological enfolding of novelty must be a structured, finite experience. If we were receptive to "becoming" as such, we would explode into glittering dust as the uncountable transformations in the quantum and atomic substrates of our material bodies (not to mention our cells and organs) somehow fed back to our bodies.

Instead, we as organisms have developed certain organic mechanisms for tracking a limited slice of the change, transformation, and novelty in the world. Tomkins and Sedgwick call this the affect of *interest* and situate it on a continuum with shame.[45] The affective neuroscientist Jaak Panksepp calls it the SEEKING system and notes its association with exploratory behavior as well as the dopaminergic system.[46] The existential register of "becoming" is not pure becoming, but a highly refined set of neurophysiological mechanisms that register some of the jolts of novelty that crash against animal bodies—sometimes with excitement, sometimes with terror or shame. Bombard a body with unpredictable noises and it will start out somewhat interested, but eventually take to drink. But some bodies aggressively harvest the affects of novelty and change. When Don Draper's ex-girlfriend Faye says to him after he leaves her for another woman in Season 4 of *Mad Men*, "I hope she knows you only like the beginnings of things," she is describing a body that is fixated on this specific affect: "Affect," the structured phenomenology of novelty.[47]

The animal approach found in feminist cultural studies of affect is necessary in order to produce an account of the multiplicity of power relations rather than a binary of "affective" and "nonaffective" politics. Ahmed's work is again particularly helpful in theorizing this. Ahmed's critique of the Deleuzian sense of affect is that in presupposing a bright line between the "personal" and the "pre-personal," the "analytic distinction between affect and emotion risks cutting emotions off from the lived experiences of being and having a body."[48] Rather than this narrow understanding of affect, Ahmed suggests that we consider the way that the plurality of experienced emotions are configured in political formations, what she calls "affective economies." In her 2004 essay of that title, Ahmed describes how the association of affects with certain objects—including specific bodies—builds those figures into certain political frameworks.[49] For instance, the fear attached to certain bodies—such as refugees—makes them the object of legislative response and violent resistance. If we talk about this only in terms of affect/nonaffect, the political texture of *this particular affect* becomes invisible. The magnetic excitement of a populist campaign appears, but we lose the ability to see how *different* formations of populism play out in *different* power-affect architectures.

In addition to the way that Ahmed diagrams the politico-phenomenological structure of fear, there are multiple examples of the correlation between power and specific affects in the literature. I don't think that it makes sense to talk about the political effects of depression in Ann Cvetkovich's work, for instance, outside the animal framework that identifies it as a specific, bodily grounded affect. What Cvetkovich describes as the depressive phenomenology of the impasse—both its creation against the backdrop of late capitalism and its corrosive effects on individual bodies and political movements—must be diagrammed in its emotional particularity.[50] Similarly, Eve Sedgwick's theory of queer performativity as the reconfiguration of the dynamic of shame necessitates an understanding of the way that shame draws on the same affective currents of excitement. It is precisely because shame and interest are consubstantial that the absorption of shame can be converted into the glorious operatic spectacle of, for instance, drag.[51]

Phenomenological affect, then, attends to animality by enabling a consideration of the biological configurations that articulate bodies to formations of power. The complex, polymorphous biological template of experience is the plane of interface that makes relationality possible, not a pure principle of becoming. Elizabeth Wilson points out that "feminism has thought of biology more as a site of stasis and predetermination, and less as a source of variation, differentiality, and conversion," and proposes that in order to understand, for instance, the political implications of new treatments for depression, we need to focus on the physiological localization of antidepressant medication in the gut.[52] I propose that affect theory enriches the analytics of power by massively expanding this template. How is our world shaped by our biologically potentialized appreciation of rhythm and rhyme, our sensitivity to color, the formulas of our neurochemistry, our susceptibility to other people's laughter, the number of objects we can reliably hold in short-term memory? An analogy: Catherine Keller in *Face of the Deep* proposes that rather than interpreting Genesis through the prism of a macho creatio ex nihilo, we understand creation to be an act of bricolage, a collection of the stuff of the world from the heterogeneous depths of the tehom, "the multidimensional surfaces of heaven-and-earth—its water, earth and atmosphere, its multiple species and societies."[53] The animality of affect is the animality of politics not in Massumi's sense of the politics of pure excess, but a confluence of heterogeneous forms.

AFFECTIVE ECONOMIES AND THE POLITICS OF DIGNITY

This animal understanding of affect also applies to religion. Some philosophers of religion, such as Grace Jantzen, have made becoming a central analytic category in the exploration of religion.[54] My argument would be that seeing religion as fundamentally about becoming is insufficient for understanding religion in its animality. Pure religion, the religion of becoming, the religion of affect rather than affects, risks leaving the body behind, or at least limiting religion to a narrow band of encounters with novelty.

To illustrate the specific relevance of animal affects for religion, I want to conjoin Ahmed's notion of the affective economy to Sedgwick's consideration of the analytics of shame. Rather than aligning directly with Sedgwick's model of queer performativity, though, I want to talk about the way that a dynamic of shame and dignity structures political and religious formations. My contention is that what we can call an economy of dignity is a situation in which bodies make decisions on the basis of the felt need to assert dignity or to repudiate shame—rather than through the liberal tropes of free choice, economic benefit, or political power.

For Tomkins, shame is a labile but profoundly powerful affective configuration. "Though terror speaks to life and death and distress makes of the world a vale of tears," he writes, "yet shame strikes deepest into the heart of man."[55] Already, in this formula, we see that Tomkins is indicating the way in which shame dynamics overrun the cost-benefit calculations of the liberal subject. What Tomkins calls a "shame theory"—a strategy for negating shame—can be so powerful that it overwhelms even core guidelines like survival. "One can frighten the soldier out of cowardice," Tomkins muses, "by making him more afraid of cowardice than death."[56] Honor cultures like the military are nothing less than extremely vivid shame theories. Or, to take the same postulate from the other side, dignity can be such an electrifying affect that it overrules the fear of death. The compulsory force of an economy of dignity can drive bodies to move in directions that are orthogonal to externally assessed standards of flourishing, fitness, or financial benefit.

As a case study for examining economies of dignity, I'd like to consider Saba Mahmood's description in *The Politics of Piety* of the women's Mosque Movement in prerevolutionary Egypt.[57] Mahmood did her fieldwork in Cairo in the mid-1990s with a community of women who were fomenting an Islamic revival out of their mosques. These women discussed Islamic texts and teachings and consumed Islamic media, in particular cassette sermons, analyzed in further detail in the work of Mahmood's colleague, Charles Hirschkind. A particular focus of this expanding network of conversations was the creation of dispositions or habits, embodied practices that were thought to cultivate particular virtues. Building on the last interview of Michel Foucault, "On the Genealogy of Ethics," Mahmood thematizes the way that these embodied practices constituted a set of self-imposed technologies of the self, or "ethics." These technologies—such as the wearing of the hijab—were designed to reshape the landscape of embodied dispositions of ethical agents, transforming them, in this instance, into better Islamic subjects.

As Mahmood writes, however, this project right at the outset played out as "a set of puzzles" inherited from her work in feminist and progressive politics.[58] The central puzzle, from the perspective of a Western liberal feminist, is that the wearing of the hijab would appear to be a patriarchal imposition forced on women in order to constrain their sexuality. The analysis of liberal feminism views the self-imposed practice of veiling as a project of the false consciousness of women who had become so alienated from their own innate thirst for liberation that they had internalized the oppressive coordinates of patriarchy. Women who put on the hijab were zombies for the patriarchy, mindlessly amplifying their own oppression.

The problem, from Mahmood's perspective, is that this approach ended up replicating a colonial political project. It presented a set of Western values as universal and dismissed as deluded or deceived any perspective that did not conform to that project. The ontology of a naturally freedom-seeking agent, Mahmood shows, is a metaphysical presupposition of the Enlightenment.[59] Moreover, the confidence of the Enlightenment posture that it is the only highway to a just society is betrayed by the brutal history of European colonization even after the Enlightenment—even and especially as the Enlightenment was invoked to justify European global sovereignty and numb the response to atrocities committed in its name. From Mahmood's perspective, the critiques of the hijab and Islamism generally by Western feminists unwittingly replicated this oppressive logic, lapsing into the self-serving attempt to "save" brown women from brown men.[60]

Mahmood's argument is that in order to assess the actions of the women in the Mosque Movement in a way that empowers those women, feminism must open itself up to a set of comprehensions of agency that supersede the limited repertoire of Enlightenment liberalism. Foucault, she writes, "encourages us to conceptualize agency not simply as a synonym for resistance to relations of domination, but as a capacity for action that specific relations of *subordination* create and enable."[61] Agency is not a transcendental property, but a dimension of bodily activity embedded within a particular set of material circumstances. By these lights, "what may appear to be a case of deplorable passivity and docility from a progressivist point of view, may actually be a form of agency—but one that can be understood only from within the discourses and structures of subordination that create the conditions of its enactment."[62] The presumed convergence between agency and liberal secular values that structures Western feminist critiques of Islam overlooks the way that Muslimahs devise their own formations of agency within the circumstances of their situation.

I want to suggest another interpretative framing of Mahmood's data. Rather than focusing on individual agency as a good in itself, I argue that religious bodies are embedded in particular affective economies. In this case, the Piety Movement can best be understood as the unfolding of an economy of dignity. This economy guides Muslim women to a set of embodied practices that elicit dignity as a distinct affective structure. Mahmood writes that "according to the participants, the mosque movement had emerged in response to the perception that religious knowledge, as a means of organizing daily conduct, had become increasingly marginalized under modern structures of secular governance."[63] The Mosque Movement tapped into the same affective textures that would eventually play out in the Tahrir Square revolution: a sense that the corrupt Mubarak military government was not only plundering the country economically but laughing at their citizenry as they did it.

Mahmood describes one of her consultants, Hajja Samira, as producing affectively rich narratives that constitute the religious subject as an epic figure avoiding the fires of hell through the diligent cultivation of her own pious self:

> Hajja Samira's audience appreciated her not so much for her scholarly knowledge or argumentative logic, but for her ability to transform moral character through engendering in her audience various emotions associated with the divine. Hajja Samira, it seems, did not simply prescribe fear as a necessary condition for piety, but deployed a discourse and rhetorical style that elicited it as well. In doing so, she punctuated her lessons with evocations of the fires of hell, the trials faced in death, and the final encounter with God after death, all of which served as evocative techniques for the creation of virtuous emotions.[64]

My suggestion is that the virtuous emotions that emerge out of this narrative (a narrative is nothing more nor less than a remarkably effective technology for the distribution of affects) are not a means, but an end—they are "autotelic," in Sedgwick's word, ends in themselves.[65]

The retrieval of a set of religious lifeways that dissociated politically disenfranchised women from a stiflingly aloof ruling class and reconstituted them as religious bodies set apart from the world offered a strategy for affirming dignity in the face of everyday degradation. It articulated their bodies to a set of cultural formations suffused with dignity, majesty, and glory. Moreover, it seems likely to me that this also interlocked with a resistance to the global Euro-American hegemony propping up the Egyptian dictator. Tomkins writes that "we may expect the emergence of counter-terror and counter-humiliation and counter-distress—to repay the former colonial powers for past shame, terror, and suffering."[66] The recourse to Islamism is an expression of defiance, an embodied gesture in a global affective economy that develops the dignity of the religious bodies involved.

Religion often serves this function of a perpetual dignity machine. The doctrinal and moral content of religion operates as a set of struts for building up an embodied sense of dignity.

I see this analysis as, in a sense, an expansion of the register of detail of Mahmood's approach. Where Mahmood affirms that we need an analytics that allows for multiple forms of agency, my suggestion is that "agency" and the seizing of agency is very often an affective maneuver within an economy of dignity. In this case, it is not the individual body that has agency, but the affects moving through the body. Charles Hirschkind interprets the affective registers of the cassette sermons in circulation among Egypt's Islamist subcultures as the affective scaffolding needed to flesh out their conceptualization of what an Islamic society should look like. "As opposed to television," Hirschkind writes, "through which one falls into the 'animality of instincts,' tapes provide a sonorous environment where the nourishing, transformative power of ethical speech works to improve the conditions of one's heart, fortifying the moral sensibilities that, in accord with Islamic ethical traditions, incline toward right actions."[67] I would invert that and suggest that what we're really seeing is a conceptual agenda *driven by affects*. We become religious animals because of the compulsory pressures of an affective economy; we do not coolly select affects in order to become religious.

As Tomkins writes, "shame is an affect of relatively high toxicity. . . . It strikes deepest into the heart of man. . . . It is felt as a sickness of the soul which leaves man naked, defeated, alienated, and lacking in dignity."[68] Dignity is not cosmetic; it is psychological oxygen. Bodies will fight to build affective economies that nurture and sustain dignity and expel shame. Religion seems to be especially well-suited to play this part.

• • •

Affect theory proposes that affects (rather than ideas, will, or discourse) are the raw, jumpy, bullish, quivering matter of subjectivity. The surfacing of affects enables a new level of precision in Foucault's project of the analytics of power. In order to fully capture this precision, affects must be defined in their specificity—as templates emerging out of biological histories that articulate bodies to formations of power in specific ways. In this sense, affects are best understood as animal. They are organic inheritances from our animal genealogies, just as other animal bodies have their own semi-stable affective architectures. At the same time, they are the sovereign engines of our experience and our decision making, inherently multiple, but each advancing a set of intransigent priorities. Affective economies emerge in the tension between these multiple affective priorities, and religion, like other formations of power, is an effect of these dynamics. Religious affects converge or diverge, sow chaos or peace, electrify or devastate, bubble up and boil over, march in lock-step or run wild, always carrying religious bodies on their backs.

NOTES

This chapter is derived from my Cambridge University Press Elements volume, *The Evolution of Affect Theory: The Humanities, the Sciences, and the Study of Power*. The most recent edition of this volume is available here: https://www.cambridge .org/core/elements/evolution-of-affect-theory/46DA7A91839C43541A152EC480 D30942. Versions of this project have been presented in a number of venues. This project was first prompted by a generous invitation from Catherine Keller, Stephen Moore, and Karen Bray to speak at the Drew University Transdisciplinary Theological Colloquium on Affectivity and Divinity, where I benefited tremendously from conversation with an extraordinary group of scholars. Another milestone was a discussion of this research at the Governing by Affect conference at the Freie Universität Berlin in June 2017, during my time as a scholar in residence with the Affective Societies collaborative research center. I thank the conference organizers, Jan Slaby and Rainer Mühlhoff, for the invitation and their thoughtful and sustained engagement with the project, the audience members for a lively discussion, and Christian von Scheve and Yasemin Ural for the invitation to undertake the residency. Other facets of the project have been presented at Syracuse University and the University of the South in Spring 2016 and the Society for European Philosophy conference in at Regents University, London, in Summer 2016. My sincerest gratitude goes to M. Gail Hamner, Sid Brown, and Tam Parker for invitations to speak on those occasions and to their students and colleagues for their comments and criticisms.

1. Benedict de Spinoza, *Ethics*, trans. Edwin Curley (New York: Penguin Books, 1996), 13.

2. Gilles Deleuze, *Spinoza: Practical Philosophy*, trans. Robert Hurley (San Francisco: City Lights Books, 1988), 122.

3. Center for 21st Century Studies, "The Nonhuman Turn" (2012), http://www4 .uwm.edu/c21/pdfs/conferences/2012_nonhumanturn/NHT_Program.pdf.

4. See Mel Y. Chen, *Animacies: Biopolitics, Racial Mattering, and Queer Affect* (Durham, N.C.: Duke University Press, 2012); Ann Cvetkovich, *Depression: A Public Feeling* (Durham, N.C.: Duke University Press, 2012); Melissa Gregg and Gregory J. Seigworth, "An Inventory of Shimmers," in *The Affect Theory Reader*, ed. Melissa Gregg and Gregory J. Seigworth (Durham, N.C.: Duke University Press, 2010), 1–28; Sara Ahmed, "Collective Feelings, or, the Impressions Left by Others," *Theory, Culture & Society* 21, no. 2 (2004): 25–42; Eugenie Brinkema, *The Forms of the Affects* (Durham, N.C.: Duke University Press, 2014); Eve Kosofsky Sedgwick, *Touching Feeling: Affect, Pedagogy, Performativity* (Durham, N.C.: Duke University Press, 2003).

5. Cvetkovich, *Depression*, 3–4. See also Robyn Wiegman, "The Times We're In: Queer Feminist Criticism and the Reparative 'Turn,'" *Feminist Theory* 15, no. 1 (2014): 13.

6. Cvetkovich, *Depression*, 4.

7. Ibid.

8. Brian Massumi, *Parables for the Virtual: Movement, Affect, Sensation* (Durham, N.C.: Duke University Press, 2002), 23.

9. Ibid., 35.

10. Ann Pellegrini and Jasbir Puar, "Affect," *Social Text*, 27, no. 3 (2009): 37.

11. Massumi, *Parables for the Virtual*, 2.

12. Ibid., 16.

13. Ibid., 42.

14. Ibid., 40.

15. See Donovan O. Schaefer, *Religious Affects: Animality, Evolution, and Power* (Durham, N.C.: Duke University Press, 2015).

16. Brian Massumi, *What Animals Teach Us about Politics* (Durham, N.C.: Duke University Press, 2014), 13.

17. Ibid., 12.

18. Ibid., 28.

19. Ibid., 50.

20. Ibid., 40.

21. Ibid., 41.

22. Schaefer, *Religious Affects*, 1.

23. William E. Connolly, *Capitalism and Christianity, American Style* (Durham, N.C.: Duke University Press, 2008), 16.

24. Massumi, *What Animals Teach Us*, 17.

25. Frans de Waal, *Our Inner Ape: A Leading Primatologist Explains Why We Are Who We Are* (New York: Riverhead Books, 2005), 147.

26. Massumi, *What Animals Teach Us*, 18.

27. Lynn Margulis, *The Symbiotic Planet: A New Look at Evolution* (London: Phoenix, 1998), 111.

28. Jaak Panksepp, *Affective Neuroscience: The Foundations of Human and Animal Emotions* (Oxford: Oxford University Press, 1998), 55. See also Keller Breland and Marian Breland, "The Misbehavior of Organisms," *American Psychologist* 16 (1961): 681–84.

29. Massumi, reinventing the notion of transmission of affect named by Teresa Brennan ten years previously (Teresa Brennan, *The Transmission of Affect* [Ithaca, N.Y.: Cornell University Press, 2004]), also suggests that "the ethico-aesthetic paradigm calls for a *politics of relation*" (Massumi, *What Animals Teach Us*, 42). Maybe this would stand as a defense against this challenge.

30. Michel Foucault, *The History of Sexuality: Volume One*, trans. Robert Hurley (New York: Vintage Books, 1990), 102.

31. William Mazzarella, "Affect: What Is It Good For?" in *Enchantments of Modernity: Empire, Nation, Globalization*, ed. Saurabh Dube (London: Routledge, 2009), 301.

32. Sedgwick, *Touching Feeling*, 114.

33. Brinkema, *Forms of the Affects*, xv.

34. Erin Manning, *Relationscapes: Movement, Art, Philosophy* (Cambridge, Mass.: MIT Press, 2009), 6.

35. Silvan S. Tomkins, "The Quest for Primary Motives: Biography and Autobiography of an Idea," *Journal of Personality and Social Psychology*, 41, no. 2 (1981): 310. Tomkins's student, Paul Ekman, has been a major contributor to contemporary conversations in affect science around this template. See, e.g., Paul Ekman, Joseph J. Campos, Richard J. Davidson, Frans B. M. de Waal, eds., *Emotions Inside Out: 130 Years after Darwin's* The Expression of the Emotions in Man and Animals (New York: New York Academy of Sciences, 2003).

36. Sedgwick, *Touching Feeling*, 108.

37. Sara Ahmed, *Queer Phenomenology: Orientations, Objects, Others* (Durham, N.C.: Duke University Press, 2006), 1.

38. Sara Ahmed, *The Cultural Politics of Emotion* (New York: Routledge, 2004), 6.

39. Edmund Husserl, *Ideas Pertaining to a Pure Phenomenology and to a Phenomenological Philosophy, Book 2,* trans. Richard Rojcewicz and André Schuwer (Dordrecht, the Netherlands: Kluwer Academic, 1987), 128.

40. Maurice Merleau-Ponty, *Phenomenology of Perception*, trans. Colin Smith (New York: Routledge, 1962), 239.

41. Jakob von Uexküll, "A Stroll through the Worlds of Animals and Men: A Picture Book of Invisible Worlds," in *Instinctive Behavior: The Development of a Modern Concept*, ed. Claire H. Schiller (New York: International Universities Press, 1957), 49. See also Steven Rose, *Lifelines: Biology Beyond Determinism* (Oxford: Oxford University Press, 1998).

42. Tomkins, "Quest," 321.

43. Jacques Derrida, *The Animal That Therefore I Am*, trans. David Wills (New York: Fordham University Press, 2008), 31. See also Schaefer, *Religious Affects*, chap. 2.

44. Brinkema, *Forms of the Affects*, 30.

45. Silvan S. Tomkins, *Shame and Its Sisters: A Silvan Tomkins Reader*, ed. Eve Kosofsky Sedgwick and Adam Frank (Durham, N.C.: Duke University Press, 1995), 78; Sedgwick, *Touching Feeling*, 97.

46. Panksepp, *Affective Neuroscience*, 144.

47. Matthew Weiner, "Mad Men: Tomorrowland," season 4, episode 13, American Movie Classics, 2010.

48. Ahmed, "Collective Feelings," 39 n. 4.

49. Sara Ahmed, "Affective Economies," *Social Text* 22, no. 2 (2004): 128

50. Cvetkovich, *Depression*, 20–21. See also Jonathan Flatley, *Affective Mapping: Melancholia and the Politics of Modernism* (Cambridge, Mass.: Harvard University Press, 2008).

51. Sedgwick, *Touching Feeling*, 61.

52. Elizabeth A. Wilson, "Organic Empathy: Feminism, Psychopharmaceuticals, and the Embodiment of Depression," in *Material Feminisms*, ed. Stacy Alaimo and Susan Hekman (Bloomington: Indiana University Press, 2008), 374.

53. Catherine Keller, *Face of the Deep: A Theology of Becoming* (New York: Routledge, 2003), xviii.

54. See John D. Caputo, *The Weakness of God: A Theology of the Event* (Bloomington: Indiana University Press, 2006); Grace M. Jantzen, *Becoming Divine: Towards a Feminist Philosophy of Religion* (Bloomington: Indiana University Press, 1999).

55. Tomkins, *Shame and Its Sisters*, 133.

56. Ibid., 57.

57. Saba Mahmood, *Politics of Piety: The Islamic Revival and the Feminist Subject* (Princeton, N.J.: Princeton University Press, 2005).

58. Ibid., ix.

59. Ibid., 14.

60. Ibid., 199.

61. Ibid., 18.

62. Ibid., 15.

63. Ibid., 4.

64. Ibid., 144.

65. Sedgwick, *Touching Feeling*, 19.

66. Tomkins, *Shame and Its Sisters*, 73.

67. Charles Hirschkind, *The Ethical Soundscape: Cassette Sermons and Islamic Counterpublics* (New York: Columbia University Press, 2006), 10.

68. Tomkins, *Shame and Its Sisters*, 148.

ꙮ Capitalism as Religion, Debt as Interface: Wearing the World as a Debt Garment

GREGORY J. SEIGWORTH

. . . how to elaborate debt as embodied; i.e. what could be called, for the lack of a better word, "affective capitalism," where the affect bit refers to the bodily and often non-cognitive states and excitations; of desires and impulsions; whether in the brain or in the gut. Could this be connected to the wider interest in brain sciences in the context of digital culture (interface design)?
—JUSSI PARIKKA, "On Borrowed Time: Lazzarato and Debt"

FIRST THING FELT

In an early scene from M. T. Anderson's young adult sci-fi novel *Feed*, the story's teenage protagonist Titus wakes up somewhere on the moon—the morning after his wireless brain-feed had been hacked at a dance club—to discover that something even more sinister and truly unsettling has transpired. Titus notices:

> The first thing I felt was no credit.
> I tried to touch my credit, but there was nothing there.
> I felt like I was in a little room.
> My body—I was in a bed, on top of my arm, which was asleep, but I didn't know where. I couldn't find the Lunar GPS to tell me.[1]

Credit or, in this case, its absence is a thing to be felt, a point of contact, accessed by touch. Meanwhile, the body as a whole is adrift, and with parts (sleeping arm) out of place. Both of these details—the relation of credit and debt to our sense of embodiment (and disembodiment)—will prove instructive for the aims of this chapter. But to linger for a moment longer over this "first thing felt" . . . why does the seemingly more pertinent matter (where am I? where is the rest of me?) follow *after* the tactile inquiry that Titus makes about his credit? In what kind of future does the contact with credit precede the relation to one's own limbs, to one's entire body, to one's sense of place in the world (even if that world is the moon)?

Meanwhile back on present-day Planet Earth, Bill Maurer—in his book *How Would You Like to Pay? How Technology Is Changing the Future of Money*—investigates the potentials that have arisen at the intersection of mobile money and digital currency. Maurer maintains that the basic factors giving contour and tempo to our everyday experience with money are fairly straightforward: "Existing behavior. Existing infrastructure. Backgrounded technology."[2] For one brief moment though he does wonder about the ways that the emergence of "wearable computing, the so-called Internet of Things, and new distributed [payment] systems" bears on the question "How *should* we like to pay? What are the moral and philosophical aspects of payment that the collision of new technologies and money brings to the fore?"[3] Although answers to these questions are beyond the immediate scope of Maurer's book, it is precisely the moral and philosophical aspects that arise with the intertwining of new technologies, money practices, and the affective capacities of a body that will join up as the prime focus here.

Beginning with a brief excursion through debt and morality, this chapter takes up—through a set of loosely connected sections that I refer to as "threads"—the adaptive behaviors, the algorithmically refined interfaces and infrastructures, and ubiquitous technologies of mundane credit-debt practices that have come to array or drape themselves about and through the body as a kind of garment: what I am calling a "debt garment." Repurposing the words of St. Francis of Assisi who advised that one should *"wear the world as a loose garment, which touches us in a few places and there lightly,"* I will endeavor to show how—through ongoing processes of touch, even if only the barest wisp of a touch or the slightest flourish of a gesture—we find ourselves today wearing the world as a debt garment: a "debt garment" that can offer sometimes a certain element of grace through the recognition of debt as an ongoing reciprocation of worldly belongingness and care-structures (that, as St. Francis continually called into attention, moved between human and nonhuman alike) and, at other times, a debt garment that can weigh heavily upon us through the unforgiving crush of debt burdens as nonbelonging to a world (whether this one or the next). Today this debt garment billows about and binds bodies together through weaves and folds, composed of the soft modulations that Gilles Deleuze claimed were the subtle suturing points and supple guidance mechanisms that contribute to present-day processes of subjectification within "societies of control." Unlike the segmented "molds" and institutional encasements of disciplinary societies, Deleuze argues that, in our era, "control" is much more about the free-ranging undulations and data-sampling derivations of cybernetic meshworks, continuous and unbounded.

As such, Deleuze conjectures that, unlike disciplinary societies, we should speak now "no longer [of] a man confined, but a man in debt."[4] Or, as St. Francis might have reflected, how does contemporary worldliness not only indebt and confine but also offer opportunities to perhaps escape or elude complete capture, to follow what Deleuze, in more emancipatory moments, calls a "line of flight"? A debt garment is always an incorporeal, relational cloak of unevenly shaped potentialities and debilities.

It is through attention to the lived socialities of debt that I hope to gradually pry apart the parentheses in Jussi Parikka's epigraph regarding affective capitalism and its implications with the increasingly fluid ontologies of interface design. At this chapter's close, I return to *Feed*'s Titus and the affective atmospheres that permeate the gestural space of his own body after its full reimmersion in the lived interfaces of credit and debt. But this time, in his renewed awareness of the ways that he is perpetually wearing the world as a debt garment (where even the lightest touch can turn smothering), Titus tears at the hem and seams of the debt garment interface: pushing, feeling, depleting, tracking its system-wide movements, punishing himself all the while. Until there is no credit left to touch.

THREAD #1: A SOMEWHAT BREATHLESS AND MINIATURE GENEALOGY OF DEBT/GUILT

In a previously unpublished writing fragment "Capitalism as Religion" (written in 1921), Walter Benjamin begins by confidently—if not also somewhat breathlessly—enumerating the three (but wait, no, four!) aspects of the religious structure of capitalism: (1) Not simply mimicking the structure of religion but operating in precisely the same practical and conceptual space as religion just more excessively, capitalism is "a purely cultic religion" such that it demands (2) ever greater fealty from each of its worshippers ("no 'weekdays'" in capitalism: every day is Sunday in "all its sacred pomp") and (3) by growing so large in its expansion of despair and guilt that capitalism engulfs even God, "to the point where God, too, finally takes on the entire burden of guilt, to the point where the universe has been taken over by that despair which is actually its secret *hope* . . . until despair becomes a religious state of the world in the hope that this will lead to salvation."[5] Within capitalism's cult, Benjamin continues, (4) God "is not dead; he has been incorporated into human existence" but remains, at the same time, "hidden" and "addressed only when his guilt is at its zenith."[6]

Benjamin readily acknowledges of course that it is Nietzsche, in *On the Genealogy of Morals*, who got there first, proclaiming that his philosophical understanding of the "paradigm of capitalist religious thought is magnificently formulated."[7] In Nietzsche, the whole discourse of indebtedness parasites Christianity, becoming a morality play in parallel: concerned with its own historically particular construction of capitalist subjectivity around guilt and obligation and conscience and interiority (although Benjamin notes that this parasitic relationship of capitalism to Christianity in the West eventually undergoes a reversal). Further, Nietzsche cannot help but call attention to the etymology of the German word *Schuld*; says Nietzsche: "The major moral concept *guilt* [*Schuld*] has its origins in the very material concept *debts* [*Schulden*]."[8] It is a congruence that Benjamin refers to as "the demonic ambiguity of this word."[9] And, to some extent then, Benjamin's fragment efficiently sketches—in miniature—Nietzsche's *Übermensch*, as well as his notion of "the eternal return," to describe how the "intensification and development" of capitalism depends on an ever-accumulating, continually proliferating recirculation of debt/guilt that finally grows "right through the sky," breaking open the heavens.[10]

But almost as soon as Benjamin manages to capture the Nietzschean genealogy in this highly condensed form, his writing fragment sputters out a few short paragraphs later (name-checking Freud and Marx along the way): first writing himself a brief in-text memo about the need to work up a comparison "between the images of the saints of various religions and the banknotes of different states," followed by a long list of references to be further explored. But Benjamin does offer one partially fleshed-out paragraph at the close of the fragment about how "the first heathens certainly did not believe that religion served a 'higher,' 'moral' interest but that it was severely practical" and, thus, "religion did not achieve any greater clarity then about its 'ideal' or 'transcendental' nature than modern capitalism does today."[11] This seems perhaps a slightly off-kilter assertion, one that is at least partially out-of-sync with those more standard readings of Nietzsche's Christianity/capitalism mutual parasitism. It is as if Benjamin is saying: Fealty to or belief in such structures, in the end, has less to do with morality or guilt or conscience or sin (as any manner of interiority or as a trajectory of redemption or transcendence) but, rather, is more intimately connected to more "practical"/practice-able externalizations and sets of outwardly directed acts as found across bodies, gestures, surfaces.

This is not unlike what Deleuze and Guattari, via their own uptake of Nietzsche in their *Anti-Oedipus*, trace out in their genealogy of the debtor-creditor relationship: a ritualized but open-ended process driven by relations of exchange and mutualized states of obligation and reciprocity but, even more, forged through modes of inscription, markings, and codings—capitalist and Christian alike. The prime focus of these inscription-processes is the body (historically, at first, the body as a brute, physical entity but, later, located more within the adjacent atmospheres of a body's capacities/affects). Additionally, like Benjamin, Deleuze and Guattari maintain that, in securing fidelity to the project of capitalism, an inner-dwelling sense of belief is not required:

> The capitalist is merely striking a pose when he bemoans the fact that nowadays no one believes in anything any more. Language no longer signifies something that must be believed, it indicates rather what is going to be done. . . . Moreover, despite the abundance of identity cards, files, and other means of control, capitalism does not even need to write in books to make up for the vanished body markings.[12]

In the historical transitions from sovereign societies to disciplinary societies to control societies, debt, say Deleuze and Guattari, has become "a debt of existence, a debt of the existence of the subjects themselves."[13] From actions taken directly on—marking—a body (sovereign) *to* those enclosures that come to bear on the souls of a citizenry (disciplinary) to the "self-transmuting" weavings that transpire throughout and alongside the real-time movements and habitualized patternings of daily existences (control), we glimpse the dim outlines of making of a debt garment—perhaps growing looser or more intangible over time in some ways (in an era of flexibility, convenience, all-access) and yet tighter in others (with, for instance, the impersonal encroachments of various check-mechanisms, data-gatherings, and profiling machines).

All this to say that more traditional Nietzschean-based conceptualizations of debt that adhere closely to its initiating moralizations are no longer as entirely applicable to contemporary processes of subject-formation; the wages of sin and the bearings of guilt do not hover around and impinge on a body—on any and every "body"—as securely as they once might have. Certainly there are resonating vestiges of persistent forms of morality-as-social-obligation still at work up and down the line of our present-day entanglements with credit and debt (and god), but the affective frissons of guilt and conscience and belief do not quite operate with the same force or along the same vectors as they once (or ever?) did. Brief example: If you want to induce a wave of shivers and shudders that sweeps across a classroom of U.S. university students today, the question to ask is not a socially moralistic one—such as "How does it feel to be a problem?" (with guilt or shame lurking in the background) but, rather, "How does it feel to be a bad investment?" (which addresses most directly the lived consequences of financial responsibilization).[14]

THREAD #2: MATERIALIZING DEBT, OR, DEBT HAS A HAND IN MAKING AND DESTROYING WORLDS

Despite a great deal of (worthy) attention given to the calculative and speculative ambience of today's credit and debt practices, debt is—and always has been—material: affectively so. Long before the time when old materialisms were new again, there was the ancient belief in the matter of our inextricable bindings to each other and to our world through an immanent and mutually constitutive indebtedness. In fact, the earliest known philosophical utterance in the Western world is a fragment credited to Anaximander (610–546 BCE) that, in one translation, reads: "The beginning of all beings is the unbounded and *from there* is the coming to be of all things and *into there* is also their passing away according to necessity and they pay each other their justified debt and penance for their injustice according to the law of time." For Anaximander, every being (human or non-) arises from and returns to undifferentiated matter—what he called the *apeiron*: translated variously as the "unbounded" or the "unlimited" or the "infinite."[15] But in that moment, in the *capacity for* coming to be and of taking—however briefly—consistency of form, each being (and all beings) accrue debts to one another and to an always-more-than-"natural" world.

We then should never forget to remind ourselves that an ontology of debt binds us to the never-less-than inherently social and relational (despite attempts that so often ask each of us to imagine that we must bear our debts responsibly and alone). In his *The Social Life of Money*, Nigel Dodd says matter of factly: "Debt is arguably what makes money social, defining its capacity to be what Simmel called a claim upon society. Or to express this in another way, it is debt's fundamental sociality that makes it possible for money to exist."[16] But I would hasten to add (and Dodd would no doubt agree) that this sociality of debt—a debt that arises at the very moment of one's coming into existence—is never fully sealed up or sealed off from the world as a whole, that debt and the social are never solely constituted by the human.

So although we might primarily think of debt in strictly quasi-moral and monetary terms, debt is likewise always and necessarily *ecological* and *ethological*. Debts arise as the processual or lived relations to the immanence of the world, of a world, of singular worldings, or what Jakob von Uexküll referred to as a creature's *umwelt*: the interleaved milieu where it becomes impossible for a body and its world (or a world and its bodies) to ever be sifted out as fully separable entities. Thus, any critical discourse of debt must endeavor to unfold the variety of ways that relationships of credit/debt can be alternately world-making and unmaking: and, in ways that do, by necessity, always fold the other-than-/more-than-human, even the divine and otherworldly, into their composition.

THREAD #3: DEBT ALWAYS MARKS AN IMBALANCE, A MISMATCH OF RESOURCES AND RHYTHMS

Credit/debt relationships are, by the very nature of their taking-place and by their ensuing trajectories, *asymmetrical*. It probably goes without saying that, around the issues of credit and debt, questions of access, potentials, and precarities are arrayed or distributed unevenly across differently lived spaces and passages of time: operations of power that might be sovereign, disciplinary, or virtual. An all-at-once collective and singularizing arrhythmia—sometimes barely perceptible, while at other times impossible to ignore—has long marked the expansion/contraction of human-nonhuman bonds as relations of credit and debt. And thus the constitutive materialities of credit and debt can never be fully discharged. That is one way to understand what Anaximander might have meant by the rising and falling rhythms (the bindings and dissipations) of "injustice according to the law of time." The cumulative asymmetries/arrhythmias of human indebtedness to the whole matter of each other (and the entirety of impersonal matter that transcends any such intimate relatedness) can offer one way of registering this reciprocating-but-thoroughly-uneven worlding. The anthropocene is, then, the tipping point when the ecological debts owed by humans to the earth have struck an irreconcilable imbalance.

THREAD #4: LIVING DEBT TODAY: A NEW AESTHETICS OF EXISTENCE, OFTEN A TIME OF BARE EXISTENCE

Immediately after Deleuze remarked that "a man is no longer a man confined but a man in debt," he hastened to add that, with so much of humanity "too poor to have debts and too numerous to be confined: control will have to deal not only with vanishing frontiers, but with mushrooming shantytowns and ghettos."[17] The accountings of debt and credit in control societies take on a wider compass here—not merely concerned with biological life or even less cognitive life, but, more precisely, as Maurizio Lazzarato argues, focusing on "existential life": existence as "the force of self-positioning, the choices that found and bear with them modes and styles of life" and, hence, in debt we find a renewed emphasis on the way that "the material of money is [grounded] not in labor time, but the time of existence."[18] Debt long preceded forms of market exchange and wage-labor as the chief means for securing the ties of human beings to the ongoing organization of the social. However, for a brief time—stretching from the late industrial age through the mid-twentieth century Fordist era (when the ascendancy of productive capital and wage-labor served as the foregrounded bases for most efficiently holding social relations together)—the role of debt as a key primer for processes of subjectivation fell briefly into eclipse (in the West particularly). But, once more, the intimacies and abstractions of everyday credit-and-debt management have reemerged with new force, beginning in the mid-1970s and surging more fully into the present. Debt now returns with a vengeance (see: the return of debtor prisons) as an effectively pre-primed and deep-seated suturing mechanism for fastening broken and frayed affective ties to the sub- and suprapersonal conditions of sociality, as a chief marker for the time and tempos of existence itself, and perhaps the beyondings of after-existence as well.

This "renewed emphasis" on "the time of existence" calls for a means of evaluating the felt or sensed values that attend to living with credit/debt as modes or styles of life, as an alternately ruthless and occasionally opportune stylistics of living-on or living-through, as an art of timing and as a perpetual shuffling and transformation of affective-material forces. Thus, it becomes possible to imagine—not just the ethological, ecological, existential, and ethical approach to credit and debt—but an impersonal yet visceral *aesthetics* of credit and debt as well.

Lauren Berlant's writing in *Cruel Optimism*—with its call for a "materialist context for affect theory"—offers one way to glimpse what an aesthetic focus on debt can offer critical analyses. Here Berlant focuses on "how the activity of affective attachment can be located formally in a historical, cultural, and political field in ways that clarify the process of knotty tethering to objects, scenes, and modes of life that generate so much overwhelming yet sustaining negation."[19] How, then, to offer a critical accounting of credit and debt that squares up with the paradoxical nature of those "modes of life" that remain tied optimistically, if not also precariously, to those obstacles that actually impede one's flourishing? What might be revealed through an aesthetic inquiry into modes of living-with-debt that leans more decidedly on the realms of the material and sensory?

Could it be that, at the level of entire populations, the existential bearings of indebtedness—again, what Lazzarato calls "the force of self-positioning"—have never been more (thread)bare, yet more exposed to techniques of aestheticization today, for better *and* for worse, than at any time previously? Indeed, one could plausibly claim that the matters of self-positioning—a blend of locational awareness, of theological anchorings, of relational mappings, and embodied movement—are lived quite differently now than in recent times past and, in part, this ongoing alteration is intimately linked to significant technological, generational, and economic shifts. So many varied alterations in the inhabitations of self-positioning or the visceral sense of affective displacement now initiating vital inflections for living in and through

> displacement, as an embodied verb, a felt fact, a new affect, was something we felt we shared as condition—as condition of possibility as well as shared impasse. We wanted to address the experiences, forms of subjectivity, and material realities generated by displacement within neoliberal capitalism, starting from our own trajectories. As transient subjects—caught between mobility and migration, between precarity and flexibility—. . . displacement sometimes becomes a form of identity for

us. It constitutes a form of subjectivation (production of our subjectivity) and subjectification (capture within a subjective paradigm) we feel ambivalent about, but know we cannot escape.[20]

Or, from a more impersonal angle, Brian Massumi frames this transitional moment in *Power at the End of the Economy* in his own darkly humorous way:

When markets react more like mood rings than self-steering wheels, the affective factor becomes increasingly impossible to factor out. It becomes obvious that the "rationality" of the economy is a precarious art of snatching emergent order out of affect. The creeping suspicion is that the economy is best understood as a division of the affective arts.[21]

Perhaps then it is less the matter and more *the manner* of self-positioning, locational awareness, and embodiment movement that threads through and connects the frayed aestheticized layers and moods (more so than "modes") of social existence. While this particular thread ends here, I promise that I will circle around to rings—"mood" or otherwise—soon.

THREAD #5: DEBT IS WOVEN INTO EVERYDAY LIFE AS A WEARABLE INFRASTRUCTURE OF FEELING

Lived relationships with debt and credit continually configure and are reconfigured by the resonances that rebound or refract around/through the place-positions (as embodied locational awareness) of the particular and the general. There is nothing especially new or somehow wholly unique about this. However, I would argue that the telescoping movements between the particular and the general (between near and far, between singular and generic, between action-at-a-distance and intimacy) are engaged differently in our contemporary era. That is, the material and ambient actualities of debt and credit are less about assembling any kind of perpetually trailing block-by-block, well-delineated spatiotemporal envelopes for subjectivation (i.e., disciplinary societies). Rather, contemporary workings of debt and credit are *more concerned with* how to introduce themselves, more fluidly, into what Nigel Thrift calls "the rate of life itself": as found, for instance, in the ways that the algorithmic, real-time machinic modulations of the corporeal and incorporeal run at first *alongside* and then gradually move *in front of* the rhythms of the increasingly "quantified self," turning predictive and anticipatory, pulling (as the profferings of credit-debt will) the future into the present.[22] Ever more subtle undulations of credit and debt, as garment, move forward and touch lightly (albeit forcefully) across the sure but steady life-streaming extraction of smaller profit-takings via a heightened, densely packed coordination of pinprick pilferings/samplings of the mundane.

The ecologies of twenty-first-century credit-debt capturings—with their various nudgings and tendings—are increasingly coming to function as new forms of everyday *textures* to be engaged with and quite often worn: like a pair of shoes, like a ring, like a cloak, like a patch, like a badge, like a hairshirt, like a halo. The debt garment can be understood as a lively, wearable, mobile texture fitting (loosely) around its in-dwellers as a swath of ceaselessly churning surface-effects strung along in the socially networked/experientially-attentive modes of digitized living and through the multiplying push-feeds of miniaturized, instantaneous self-to-ecosystem relays. A texturizing that is woven through what information-architectural theorist Malcolm McCullough calls "foraging across the abundant facades" of our "ambient commons."[23] Or, along the same lines, one might consider such texturings in the ways that Susan Elizabeth Ryan does, in her illuminating *Garments of Paradise*, when she draws attention to the cultural interface of dress ("skin/dress/tissue/textile" as interconnected interfaces) and how the creation of "affective wearables reflect the biometric information registering on or through the skin, from on or beyond the body, and activate either a remote display or one that is worn as clothing or accessory."[24] And, thus, the arrival of new shapings of intertwined promise and threat as affective wearables (debt garments) and the movements of capital steadily converge along ever-widening circuits of extraction and expressivity.

Nigel Thrift describes this as the rise of an immanently "expressive infrastructure" marking a next phase in the operative logics of capitalism: a logic—one of many, of course—operating as a "new medium [that is composed of] neither time nor space nor time-space but something else, something closer to movement moving."[25] This "movement moving" becomes a means for fashioning a perpetual composition and regeneration of the forces of innovation as distributed among and engaged through the subtlest nestlings of the inanimate, inorganic, and incorporeal with the quite permeable (affectable) human. Thrift ventures that this expressive infrastructure relies perhaps most of all on "a project of channeling and damming affect and imagination through the laying down of technology (and the practices associated with it) that demands more than concentration and acceleration but also reworks the substance of what we regard as the world, down to the smallest grain of interaction, through an architecture of intimacy."[26] And he sums up: "This new kind of massed and yet also individuated land *will feel with us* through its ability to pre-empt and nudge our thoughts [by] placing consciousness everywhere, revealing new means of extracting surplus and thereby turning a profit."[27]

So this is the fresh (and perpetually refreshable, near god-like) mass and individuated terrain where the extractive-conjunctive assemblages of credit-worthiness and indebtedness roam—characterized by what, as Joe Deville observes, are a wide variety of "attachment devices" for debt, each with their own particular "lures for feeling."[28] As such, these mobile and evanescent credit and debt assemblages must always seek the means to knot and weave between the particular and general, the massed and the dividuated, the granular and the planetary into an ongoing process of soliciting and securing debtors' bodily dispositions to their debt devices.

THREAD #6: THE SHIFTING WEIGHT OF DEBT-CARRIAGE IS DISTRIBUTED THROUGH POSTURE AND TOUCH

If this rolling composition of debt's own texturizing intimacy is best conceived as the sensory arrival of a more complexly interwoven, restlessly innovative worlding, then critical analyses of debt might be well-served to consider the sort of roles that *tactility* and *touch* play in the accommodation and adaptation of bodies to the haptic affectivity of everyday indebtedness: along with bodily counter-potentials for resisting, disarticulating, or swerving away from such apparatuses of capture too.

After all, Lauren Berlant argues that a materially based affect theory can be understood as a means of writing a *"proprioceptive history*, a way of thinking about represented norms of bodily adjustment as key to grasping the circulation of the present as a historical and affective sense."[29] And I would likewise claim that the worlding-relationality and extrasomatic sociality that practices and assemblages of credit and debt have always brought into existence—perhaps now more pronounced than ever—are also the primary affective interfaces by which we orient our sense of potentiality and evolving (movement-moving) place or nonplace in the world: at once, existential-ecological-aesthetic-ethological. Always both promise and threat at once. This continually evolving, expressive infrastructure raises fundamental questions about the ways that people—quite literally—*"carry"* debt now and how they (we) will carry debt in the future.

We are all touched by our relationship to debt in different ways. The forms and formattings of this "touch" are varied, complex, and interlaced. How then to consider the very nature—the sensation and the matter—of this *indebted touch* itself? For instance, what roles do mobile/pervasive communication devices play—as key nodes in an always evolving ontology of the day-to-day—in giving tempo, contour, and "feel" to a visceral registering of debt-carriage? Still further, as techniques of perpetual digital connectivity pass from the handheld and into an ambient architecture of built environments with their consumer/debtor captures, how do these real-time coordinations intersect with the more typical and ritualistically sedimented moral, impersonal, and financial calculations of credit-access and debt-opaqueness?

Debt weighs on the matter of bodies and subjectivities and worlds, and this weight is distributed across an expanse of small-scale, up-close interactions while engaging with much more far-flung large-scale calculations. If the ubiquitous nature of "proprioceptive" debt has become one of the defining aspects of our era, then debt's pervasiveness cannot be directly confronted as merely an issue for consciousness-raising and critique. Instead, debt must be met and addressed in its myriad entanglements with matter and the social, in debt's extensions (and overextensions), its sympathies and aggressions, its engagement with bodily potentials and docilities, and combined then as an expressive infrastructure where the techniques and technologies of existence fold and flow in and through our tactile and postural carrying capacities for indebtedness.

THREAD #7: PRACTICES OF LIVING DEBT AND CREDIT WILL COME TO BE NAVIGATED LESS BY TOUCH AND MORE BY GESTURE, LIKE A FIN SLICING THROUGH AIR

Treating touch and tactility as principal points of focus for future-oriented work on issues of credit-debt are, however, not quite on the mark. If we are to begin to address the load-shifting moving-movements in the ways that credit and debt are carried, then we'll need to understand that the hand is *often the final place* where things—like debt—pass on their way toward disappearing: like a new version of a well-worn magic trick, disappearing into the surround, into the ambient umwelt of intimacy and extrusion (even if such a disappearance is rarely complete and can come boomeranging back at you).

That is, to return to the anecdote from *Feed* that opens this chapter, it should be clear that Titus is not actually reaching out to physically "touch his credit"; rather, he is making a credit *gesture.* Titus's body—or, more precisely, the movement space-time of his body's proprioceptive envelope—has become an interface for his credit: part of one continuous surface of credit/debt affordances and bodily affectivity. Here affect and debt have come to operate in the same rhythmic-gestural-conceptual space, occupying the same wedge of existential locational-positioning, and all the while moving at the rate of life itself. In his oft-referenced essay "The Work of Art in the Age of Mechanical Reproduction," Walter Benjamin wrote of the largely unnoticed ways that bodies tactilely appropriate architecture and how the turning points of history are often founded on the gradually altered means of sensory appropriation.[30] Such are our circumstances today with the growing tactile and rhythmically attuned appropriations and expropriations of debt alongside the advent of the gestural interface.

William Bogard, in his essay "Control Surfaces and Rhythmic Gestures," discusses how "haptic research has already discovered ways to diagram the surface of the human skin as a data entry and retrieval system" and how these surfaces are a modulating space between a body's capacity for gesture *and* a technical assemblage's own complex modes of entrainment.[31] As an illustrative example, consider the "Fin" ring. Tagged with the catchphrase "Wear the World," this ring (currently in the midst of product design and early testing) is a kind of wearable expressive interface that turns your palm and fingers into a Bluetooth-mapped numeric keypad and, thus, your entire hand into a gestural interface. One's hand becomes a fin for navigating through thin air.

Although Bogard is not writing about the Fin ring, his argument closely attends to the way that

control is about engineering the human body's interface with surfaces, flesh to glass, then distributing those connections in nested rhythmic figures, timing their onset and decay, and modulating their intensity (amplitude, frequency). How often do you check your email, or scroll through a screen? Tap, double tap, swipe, pinch, wave, hold, drag, blink, utter—a controlled gesture can be any rhythmic movement, including thinking, that connects you to a ubiquitous world of digital screens. . . . Every interface, in effect, is a gesture, a moving diagram that marks the connection of bodies. . . . The control of interfaces is the control of the temporal distribution of gestural figures, the timing of connections, their onset, frequency, repetition, decomposition, and so on.[32]

And so this particular cybernetically inflected historical turning point, as signaled by the gestural interface, unfolds in the capacities for technological assemblages to adjust to bodies, their machinic components, and ongoing events on the fly through "the ability to make minute and flexible adjustments in the timing of events, to produce moving figures, not just fixtures": that is, to move not just at the rate of life itself but to inhabit life's smallest, seemingly inconsequential vibrations, its rhythms and gestures, its postures and existential positionings.[33]

Similarly, in the case of Titus, the credit/debt gesture becomes an open-ended, congealing-and-re-congealing set of rhythmic affectivities continually dovetailing with a real-time access-loop of credit-debt modulations: the infinitely adjustable accretion and replaying of gestural surfacing-contact moments. This is how the matter of indebtedness turns into the affective *manner* of bodily comportments and how the debt gesture becomes an intimately, infinitely (in-)dividualized means of wearing the world. Reach out and touch . . . your credit. Soon enough you will be able to genuflect and gesture debt into existence (it is usually harder to wish away) with as much absent-mindedness or solemn devotion as you can conjure.

THREAD #8: THE MULTITUDE BECKONS: "PANTS SALE"

At the end of *The Making of Indebted Man*, Maurizio Lazzarato holds out some modicum of hope for what Nietzsche called "a second innocence" marked by the moment, as Nietzsche says, "atheism might release humanity from this whole feeling of being indebted towards its beginnings, its *causa prima*. Atheism and a sort of *second innocence* belong together."[34] Lazzarato argues that this would be a

> second innocence [oriented] no longer toward divine debt, but toward *mundane debt*, the debt that weighs in our wallets and forms and formats our subjectivities. . . . We must recapture this second innocence, rid ourselves of guilt, of everything owed, of all bad conscience, and not repay a cent.[35]

But, as we have seen, "mundane debt" is precisely what the gestural interface is set to rhythmically inhabit through the touchless and gestural intimacies of surface control: making our wallets weightless perhaps while continuing to form and format subjectivities in new modulatory ways. It is, you might say, easier to imagine the arrival of worldwide atheism than to somehow imagine the end of mundane debt. (The desirability of canceling [or not] divine debt—as a necessary beholden-ness to one another and to the world—might be another matter entirely.)

In the penultimate scene from M. T. Anderson's *Feed*, Titus—who, by this point in the story, has long been back in touch with his credit—has just arrived at home after leaving the deathbed of his ex-girlfriend Violet. (Violet has been turned down by her insurance company for risky brain surgery that might save her life: in part, because the algorithms that follow and guide her everyday buying behavior are no longer able to construct a reliable consumer profile based on her purchase history and browsing activity.) At the same time, the planet is rapidly falling into environmental catastrophe. People are developing huge weeping lesions (which for a time become a new fashion statement, a new aesthetic). Hair is falling out. Lips are curling back exposing everyone's gums and teeth. Giant cockroaches and rats are roaming in swarms through the ventilation systems of the decaying infrastructure. Forests are being chopped down because "air factories" are more cost-efficient. The oceans are mostly dead. Yes, you won't find a contemporary young teen science fiction story much more bleak. And Titus is no hero in this tale; he loves this world, he lives a life of privilege, and blithely perseveres in the midst of all this decay. He broke up with Violet at the onset of her physical breakdown, but her fate has also stirred something in him: something he cannot quite put his finger on.

Although Titus cannot articulate anything remotely close to resistance or even the vaguest political tactic (whenever Titus tries to narrate a story it always ends up, he claims, sounding like the opening credits of a sit-com or like the voice-over to a movie trailer), he does have the debt gesture, and so he uses it, over and over again, feeling himself at one with the entire expressive infrastructure, its moving movement, its intimately exteriorizing impingements: the living (dis-)embodiment of affective capitalism.

It all begins when Titus notices that there is "a special on draft pants at Multitude" (yes, Multitude):

I ordered the draft pants from Multitude. It was a real bargain. I ordered another pair. I ordered pair after pair. I ordered them all in the same color. They were slate. I was ordering them as quickly as I could. I put in my address again and again. I ordered pants after pants. I put tracking orders on them. I tracked each one. I could feel them moving through the system.

Spreading out from me, in the dead of night, I could feel credit deducted, and the warehouse alerted, and packing. I could feel the packing, and the shipment, the distribution, the transition to FedEx, the numbers, each time, the order number traded like secret words at a border, and the things all went out, and I could feel them coming to me as the night passed.

I could feel them in orbit. I could feel them in circulation all around me like blood in my veins. I had no credit. I had nothing left in my account. I could feel the pants winging their way toward me through the night.

I stayed up all through the early morning, shivering, ordering, ordering, and was awake at dawn, when I put on clothes and went up to the surface, and watched the shit-stupid sun rise over the whole shit-stupid world.[36]

And so Titus's debt-gesture becomes a way too of gesturing toward the process of grieving, a touching but touch-free moment of reaching for what-is-not-there from out of the very midst of a world of indebtedness that you are always already wearing.

NOTES

This chapter is indebted to lots of folks who read or listened to and then responded with insights and suggestions: Jennifer Daryl Slack, Matthew Tiessen, Andrew Murphie, Jussi Parikka, Joe Deville, Jenna Supp-Montgomerie, and Robert Seesengood. Thanks also to Stephen D. Moore and especially Karen Bray for her insightful reading and redirection of several of my theoretical formulations. This essay, now slightly revised, was first published in *Ephemera* 16, no. 4 (2016): 15–31.

1. M. T. Anderson, *Feed* (Somerville, Mass.: Candlewick Press, 2002), 35.

2. Bill Maurer, *How Would You Like to Pay? How Technology Is Changing the Future of Money* (Durham, N.C.: Duke University Press, 2015), 18.

3. Ibid., 28.

4. Gilles Deleuze, "Postscript on Societies of Control," in *Negotiations* (New York: Columbia University Press, 1995), 181.

5. Walter Benjamin, "Capitalism as Religion," in *Selected Writings: Volume 1 1913–1926* (Cambridge, Mass.: Belknap Press of Harvard University Press, 1996), 288–89.

6. Ibid.

7. Ibid.

8. Quoted in Daniel Conway, *Nietzsche's On the Genealogy of Morals* (New York: Continuum, 2008), 61.

9. Benjamin, "Capitalism as Religion," 289.

10. Ibid.

11. Ibid., 290

12. Gilles Deleuze and Felix Guattari, *Anti-Oedipus: Capitalism and Schizophrenia* (Minneapolis: University of Minnesota Press, 1983), 250.

13. Ibid., 197.

14. Borrowing here from Lauren Berlant, quoted in Gesa Helms, Marina Vishmidt, and Lauren Berlant, "Affect and the Politics of Austerity: An Interview Exchange with Lauren Berlant," *Variant: Cross Currents in Culture* 39 / 40 (Winter 2010): 6. Specifically, Berlant says: "It wasn't cruel optimism to think that there would be give in the system, spreading opportunities for living beyond instrumental productivity, and yet we know that even in the good times so many people didn't have enough hours in the day to look each other in the eye and relax. What expanded was fantasy, not time and not a cushion of real-time money. The expansion of the credit economy in Europe and the U.S. once the industrial growth had moved on took care of that, though, purchasing when it couldn't purchase ordinary time, and now that's being revoked too. Plus the revocation of educational democracy, a stand for a public investment in everyone who wanted a shot, is an admission that everyone didn't have a shot, and maybe shouldn't have wanted it. 'How does it feel to be a bad investment?' has substituted itself for 'How does it feel to be a problem?'"

15. Michael A. Gillespie, "On Debt," in *Debt: Ethics, the Environment, and the Economy* (Bloomington: Indiana University Press, 2013), 56–57.

16. Nigel Dodd, *The Social Life of Money* (Princeton, N.J.: Princeton University Press, 2014), 92.

17. Deleuze, "Postscript on Societies of Control," 181.

18. Maurizio Lazzarato, *The Making of Indebted Man* (Los Angeles: Semiotext[e], 2012), 60.

19. Lauren Berlant, *Cruel Optimism* (Durham, N.C.: Duke University, 2010), 51–52.

20. Manuela Zechner and Paula Cobo-Guevara, "Situating Ourselves Collectively and the Problem of Displacement by Way of Introduction," in *Situating Ourselves in*

Displacement: Conditions, Experiences, and Subjectivity across Neoliberalism and Precarity, ed. Murmurae [Paula Cobo-Guevara, Manuela Zechner, and JOAPP (Marc Herbst)] (Brooklyn, N.Y.: Minor Compositions, 2018), 11.

21. Brian Massumi, *Power at the End of the Economy* (Durham, N.C.: Duke University Press, 2014), 2.

22. Nigel Thrift, "The Insubstantial Pageant: Producing an Untoward Land," *Cultural Geographies* 19, no. 2 (2012): 144.

23. Malcolm McCullough, *Ambient Commons: Attention in the Age of Embodied Information* (Cambridge, Mass.: MIT Press, 2013), 161–64.

24. Susan Elizabeth Ryan, *Garments of Paradise: Wearable Discourse in the Digital Age* (Cambridge, Mass.: MIT Press, 2014).

25. Thrift, "Insubstantial Pageant," 151.

26. Ibid., 144.

27. Ibid., 155.

28. Joe Deville, *Lived Economies of Default: Consumer Credit, Debt Collection, and the Capture of Affect* (New York: Routledge, 2015).

29. Berlant, *Cruel Optimism*, 20.

30. Walter Benjamin, "The Work of Art in the Age of Mechanical Reproduction," in *Illuminations* (New York: Schocken Books, 1969), 240.

31. William Bogard, "Control Surfaces and Rhythmic Gestures," *Theory & Event* 16, no. 3 (2013): http://muse.jhu.edu/journals/theory_and_event/v016/16.3.bogard.html.

32. Ibid.

33. Ibid.

34. Lazzarato, *Making of Indebted Man*, 164.

35. Ibid.

36. Anderson, *Feed*, 230–31.

❧ Immobile Theologies, Carceral Affects: Interest and Debt in Faith-Based Prison Programs

ERIN RUNIONS

This essay considers the affective movements of interest and debt as they circulate into the prison-industrial complex through biblical teaching aimed at personal salvation and moral amelioration.[1] My understanding of affect is expansive; it extends to emotion, emotive potential, and that which produces motion, mobility, and importantly for the argument here, immobility—in and beyond the body. I am interested in affect as cognitive and unconscious responses to signification, as well as the affective impact of ideological apparatuses, material/economic structures, and technology.[2] Drawing on theoretical discussions of affect in relation to interest, debt, animacy, and the posthuman, I consider the movements, countermovements, flows, blockages, pools, secretions, and toxicities within a racialized hierarchy of interest and debt, traveling beyond particular subjects and through the many cells and components of the prison-industrial complex. I argue that faith-based prison programs produce a demand for the pursuit of self-interest, countered by the imposition of spiritual and actual debt, thus immobilizing the incarcerated as interested-yet-always-indebted.

Since 2001 there has been an increase in Christian faith-based programming in prisons. Under the direction of Jeb Bush in Florida and George W. Bush in Washington, prisons in many U.S. states have allowed largely privately funded Christian groups to run faith-based programs inside prisons. Michael Hallett and Byron Johnson have called the increase in faith-based programming a shift to a New American Penitentiary.[3] Florida, for instance, boasts of three full faith-based prisons, with twelve more faith-based dorms.[4] These programs take a variety of forms, ranging from weekly Bible study to separate housing units—sometimes called "god pods"—with better food and more freedom. Typically they provide a full schedule of activities, including substantial amounts of Bible study and spiritual accountability. One of the best-known of these programs is Chuck Colson's Prison Fellowship, centrally featured in this

essay. Among other ministries, Prison Fellowship runs InnerChange Freedom
Initiative with residential programs in Minnesota and Texas.[5] Others faith-
based housing units include God of Hope Ministries with dorms in Texas,[6] and
Horizon Communities with dorms in several states, including Florida, Ohio,
and Oklahoma. The Ohio Department of Corrections and Rehabilitation
states its reliance on volunteer faith-based programs to run faith-based housing units and also reintegration units, including "Prison Fellowship, Horizon
Prison Ministry, Gospel Express, Kairos Prison Ministry, Bill Glass Champions
for Life, Promise Keepers, Urban Bible Institute, Wings Ministry, Aleph Institute, Islamic Council, Crossroads Prison Ministry and other local faith-based
volunteers."[7] The Corrections Corporation of America (CCA), now Core-
Civic, one of the largest private prison corporations, partners with a number
of ministries for both residential and reentry services, including Champions
for Life, Prison Fellowship, Purpose Driven Life Ministry, Alpha USA, School
of Christ International, and Trinity Broadcasting Network.[8]

Christian groups take seriously Jesus' gospel exhortation to visit those in
prisons as if they were Christ himself (Mt 25:36). In her ethnography, *God in
Captivity*, Tanya Erzen documents how Christian ministries provide resources,
solace, and meaning for incarcerated people, even as they mask other problems.[9] I do not want to dismiss the genuine concern and care of Christians
ministering in prisons and the significant hope and dignity that these programs
can bring to those held inside prisons. Yet I would like to examine critically, as
Mark Lewis Taylor urges, dominant notions of Christianity that can implicitly
and explicitly feed the prison-industrial complex. The Christian abstraction of
salvation from torture and death, Taylor argues, "sets the stage for a denigra-
tion of matter and bodies, which in turn often yields a toleration of degrad-
ing punishments meted out upon bodies—especially racially marked bodies in
a white dominant society."[10] Following this critique, I explore how Christian
teaching in prisons affectively connects with larger structures of economy and
race to inculcate notions of literal and abstract interest and debt in ways that
can be damaging to those whom Christian programs presume to serve.

Interest and debt stand in immobilizing tension for the incarcerated. Interest operates on two fronts: as actual financial return on the investments
that prisons have become, and as self-interest in personal motivation. These
two meanings of interest may seem unrelated, yet they are, as we will see,
historically, ideologically, economically, and affectively intertwined; further,
they are connected to literal and affective debt to the state, to society, and,
in Christian terms, to God.[11] Those who are able to opt into faith-based programs are encouraged to follow their interests to become "productive" members of society on reentry after serving their time. Yet the incarcerated person

is still one whose indebtedness and lack can only be ameliorated by salvation in Christ and personal reform. The religious language of sin and salvation in these programs is based on an economic model of debt and payment that contributes to racialized structures of oppression in the United States. The push and pull between interest and debt produces a confounded subjectivity, to borrow a line from Saidiya Hartman's analysis of racial discrimination after emancipation.[12] It affectively impacts mobility, and importantly for the argument here, immobility—in and beyond the body. The demand for forward movement and productivity in these programs is thwarted by immobility and criminalization.

The stakes go beyond actual prisons, however; interest and debt are part of a literal and rhetorical economy that circulates through a range of carceral technologies beyond prison walls, with consequences for the nonincarcerated and the environment. As part of a financialized and data-driven security economy, the prison-industrial complex enfolds, shapes, and goes beyond the human as a technology that impacts particularly, but not only, the incarcerated. Multiple systems of financialized economy, corporate power, and securitized governance use logics of surveillance, security, environmental deregulation, and extraction of human "resources" in such a way that they also could be considered carceral technologies. Those, like myself, who want to work against the injustice of prisons need to consider this wider set of carceral economic affects and dynamics so that indebtedness, environmental toxicity, and immobility do not become the new norms of punishment.

ECONOMIC INTEREST, THE PRISON-INDUSTRIAL COMPLEX, AND FAITH-BASED PROGRAMS

The entrenchment of the prison-industrial complex is in large part due to a financialized economy.[13] As Ruth Wilson Gilmore has argued with respect to California, the prison industry was able to solve several problems that emerged within the economic shift to financialization in the United States: Prisons absorbed surplus capital, surplus land, surplus population, and surplus state capacity.[14] Importantly for the emerging financialization, prisons provided financiers ways to lend to governmental borrowers—and earn interest—without feeding into right-wing complaints about public debt and social spending.[15] Politicians generated panic around crime in order to justify these new financial practices. As Gilmore details, beginning in the early 1980s, financiers helped the Californian politicians figure out how to issue bonds to investors—that is, to go into debt—for prison projects without having to ask voters.[16] They did so through what Kevin Pranis and Christopher Petrella have called the "backdoor method" of selling lease revenue bonds, which do not require a vote.[17] In a practice that continues to the present day, the California Public Works Board issues lease revenues bonds to finance prisons. Once built, the California Department of Corrections and Rehabilitation "leases" the prisons from Public Works, thereby paying the interest on the bonds for investors from tax dollars. The amount of money used in this endeavor is enormous; to give an example, in 2007, the California State Assembly passed AB 900 which allocated $7.3 billion as lease revenue bonds for prisons, jails, and reentry programs.[18]

Who earns interest on prisons, then? Investors who buy government issued bonds, or investors in private prisons. Those who profit range from retirees to investment bankers. Government bonds are considered secure investments, because of the political risks of decarcerating. For instance, a 2008 advice article in *Forbes*, written in at the height of the U.S. financial crisis, explains lease revenue bonds for prisons as a secure investment:

> The state creates an entity or agency to build the prison. The agency floats bonds to the public [investors] to cover construction of the facility. The agency then leases the right to use the completed prison to the state. The state pays the entity lease payments. The entity uses the lease payments to service the bond debt. Essentially, the state takes money from one pocket (the general fund appropriations to the prison system) and puts it into another pocket (the agency created for the facility), and then the agency distributes the money to the bondholders. . . . Any state that would stop making lease payments on its correctional facility bonds and set incarcerated offenders out on the streets would have some explaining to do. The stakes are too high for society to permit such default. We think the risk is minimal for prison bonds.[19]

Prisons are secure investments precisely because of the politically generated panic around crime. Underwriters make money too, including Morgan Stanley, J. P. Morgan, Goldman Sachs, and Merrill Lynch, who buy state debt in the hundreds of millions and then profit by selling it at a higher cost.[20]

Other states followed California's lead with similar practices. Counties likewise built jails to make revenue through leasing beds to federal and state corrections for surplus prisoners, as well as to U.S. Immigrations and Customs Enforcement for detention of undocumented immigrants.[21] Government bonds financed not only state agencies but also private corporations, who were contracted to build and run prisons.[22] In turn, corporations cut costs and profit, often at high costs to those incarcerated.[23]

It is not just high-powered investors who profit from prisons, however; regular people do too, perhaps unknowingly, in their investment packages or consumer choices. *Vice* reports that the Vanguard Group and Fidelity Investments, two of the top 401(k) retirement funds, are big investors in private prisons (both with large holdings in TIAA-CREF).[24] At the time of writing, Vanguard Group is the single biggest investor in the two largest private prison companies in the United States—CoreCivic and GEO Group.[25] Additionally, many privatized businesses that find their way into investments provide services to prisons (for example, telephones, transportation, reentry services, surveillance technology) at exorbitant costs to users and with high profits for investors. Then there are the businesses that use prison labor (with wages notoriously at an average rate of 20 cents an hour in state prisons) to make goods sold to consumers.[26]

Faith-based programs feed into this larger production of interest in the prison-industrial complex. Like other kinds of prison programming carried out by volunteers, faith-based programs reform rather than abolish incarceration by lessening the responsibility of the prison to provide programs. Residential faith-based programs are an extreme case, as they take on full-time care and provide a kinder, gentler form of incarceration. They are attractive to states and private prison corporations because although they may receive some grant money from states,[27] they are largely funded by religious groups and staffed by volunteers, so they cut costs substantially. Volunteer programs thus boost the financial stability of public prisons by decreasing costs and lowering the amount of tax dollars needed to pay off the bond debt borrowed to build the prisons. For instance, as Samantha Shapiro documents in her investigative report on a Prison Fellowship InnerChange program in Ellsworth, Kansas (now closed), the program saved the state of Kansas 60–75 percent on programming options.[28] While potentially decreasing use of tax dollars, faith-based programs do nothing to disrupt the financing schemes outlined above, thus leaving the accumulation of interest in place. In private prisons, volunteer programs increase profits. Within these systems, faith-based programs help to maintain order (or more critically, a docile labor force), since they spiritually and physically incentivize good behavior. For these reasons, critics say that faith-based programs are part of a neoliberal move to privatize prisons and privatize social programs.[29]

One might argue, as advocates do, that faith-based programs reduce recidivism, thus decreasing incarceration.[30] Critics have raised the question of how much credit the programs should take, given that there is a question of selection and self-selection in who enters the programs.[31] But even if recidivism levels go down, the race and class injustices of incarceration will not be addressed without interrogation of the system as a whole. Indeed, by lessening the financial burden to states without critiquing the *need* for prisons, these programs may lessen motivation for states to reduce the overall prison population.

Moreover, in private prisons that have occupancy quotas, beds that are not filled through recidivism are simply filled by the newly incarcerated.

INTEREST, AFFECT, CONTROL

The prevailing capitalist demand for financial interest that drives the prison-industrial complex is related to an intellectual history in which self-interest has been considered an affect that can curtail other more harmful passions. Indeed, interest is perhaps *the* affective category driving the development of (neo)liberal policy, or more accurately, an imagined *affect suppressant*. Interest is promoted as something that can control the passions; prisons become interest's affective arm. Like the wider culture in which rational choice theory has become a staple of economic thinking, prisons help cultivate what Michel Foucault calls the "subject of interest" or *homo oeconomicus*, that is, the political subject motivated by the subject's own interests rather than by obligation to collectivity or adherence to a social contract.[32]

Intellectual histories like those of Foucault, Albert Hirschman, and David Grewal argue that interest developed as both a moral and financial concept to constrain passions. Grewal shows that self-interest or self-love first developed as a means to constrain passions in the work of the seventeenth-century French Jansenist, Pierre Nicole. Nicole taught that self-love could help maintain peace and order despite human sinfulness.[33] By the eighteenth century, notions of interest were more narrowly focused on economic gain, in works such as those of David Hume and Adam Smith.[34] Hume, for instance, says, "It is an infallible consequence of all industrious professions, to beget frugality, and make the love of gain prevail over the love of pleasure."[35] Brian Massumi emphasizes that Hume thought of interest as a *passion* that could constrain the other passions, rather than as a rational choice.[36] By the time of the twentieth and twenty-first centuries, as Dean Mathiowetz has shown, neoliberal doctrine has made the rational pursuit of self-interest a central economic and moral concept.[37] The sense of self-interest as affective was lost in the twentieth and twenty-first centuries, so that it is now understood as the epitome of *rational* calculation that tames the passions.

Mathiowetz highlights the work Stephen Holmes, historian and theorist of liberalism, as a clear example of the neoliberal logic of calculating self-regard.[38] Attention to the affective register in Holmes's work is instructive.[39] Holmes calls self-interest a kind of neo-Stoicism that seeks to eliminate the passions.[40] Because self-interest requires rational calculation, it is only possible to pursue it, he argues, after a "strenuous process of self-discipline, a mental therapy in which the unruly passions are not moderated but extirpated."[41] These passions include animosity, enmity, hatred, affection, attachment, love, excessive pride, self-deprecation, spiritlessness, laziness, fear, and more.[42] Within a properly liberal understanding, however, the personal pursuit of self-interest should be within some bounds, says Holmes. As he puts it, interest should be "disciplined by the restraints of social coexistence and justice," that is to say social good and the law.[43]

If affect is considered to be a kind of circulation of bodily movement, within and between bodies and objects, then interest (in this view at least), like rationality, is a kind of sublimatory traffic cop. It prohibits certain movements and tries to direct them to proper capitalist lanes of commerce. There is a sense that true movement forward ("real progress") is only possible if unproductive ("unruly") passions are eradicated in favor of rational financial calculation. But, as Holmes indicates, the movements of interest must be directed and rerouted by law and the common good as well.[44] Interest needs policing, it would seem.

Prisons, are arguably a weapon in interest's affective charge to control passion. They contain and subdue those who are stereotypically disparaged as exhibiting many of the passions excoriated by Holmes: animosity, enmity, hatred, excessive pride, laziness, fear, and so on. As Friedrich Nietzsche says of punishment, we could say of prisons that they aim to produce "an increase of fear, a heightening of prudence, [and] mastery of the desires."[45] Prisons contain the "passions" and their results and at the same time enable financial interest through the construction and management of facilities. Passion becomes racialized in the disproportionate incarceration of black and brown people.[46]

Prison becomes the hyperreal phenomenon (for those not actually in prison) that deflects attention away from the fact that in a political economy driven by scarcity and debt, only some people's interests can be served. Prisons are a way of punishing those whom financial interest apparently has not served as imagined. They provide the literal and figural immobilization of those who cannot be rationalized into the proper pursuit of financial interest or self-interest—cannot be rationalized because no matter what the calculation, the odds are stacked against them so that the usual financial/structural/emotional avenues for following interest are not easily available. It could be said that prisons contain the repressed bodies that allow the fiction of self-interest to function outside of prison walls.

Both interest and prison seek to contain the motion of bodily affects and their bodily impacts, but their end results are starkly different in terms of mobility. Those successful in following and producing financial interests become more mobile, both in terms of actual capacity to move/travel and in terms of what is deemed as "achievement" or "progress." Those who do not have the opportunity or resources to follow their interests or perhaps engage in alternative economies, substances, or violence to meet their interests end up in various states of literal and metaphorical immobility, including limited housing, unemployment, cycles of incarceration, substance use, and so on. This difference in mobility is racialized: Those whom interest fails to serve and who end up with highly restricted movement in prison tend to be black and brown, as so persuasively argued by Angela Davis and Michelle Alexander, among others.[47] As queer theorists and theologians of color have argued, the push to rationality, of which interest is a part, plays out on the bodies of black and brown people who are othered as nonrational, excessive, fleshly, nonnormatively sexualized, differently animated.[48]

But even if prisons open up markets for the pursuit of financial interest and protect the fiction of the unregulated efficacy and mobility of self-interest outside of prisons, they also demand that the incarcerated are socialized to pursue self-interest. Prison programming nurtures hope in the incarcerated that their choices to better themselves will be rewarded by parole boards. Indeed, since the time of Jeremy Bentham (an avid proponent of both self-interest and uncapped financial interest), the idea of rehabilitation assumed that people would be motivated to better themselves and their behavior because of the rewards a change would bring.[49]

Faith-based programming likewise cultivates choices based on the calculation of self-interest. Like other programming inside prisons, faith-based programs implicitly rely on a kind of rational choice theory, by which the incarcerated are meant to make decisions that are good for themselves. There is a notion that self-interest can motivate spiritual change. Programs provide physical perks, on top of the spiritual enticement of moving from lack to plenitude (in God). There are significant rewards for joining. Shapiro highlights the perks offered by Prison Fellowship at Ellsworth prison in Kansas. She writes, "Many prisoners don't join for the ideology. They do it to transfer from other parts of the prison system, and because completing InnerChange amounts to a get-out-of-jail-free card with the Parole Board."[50] She notes the lure of food: "And then there is the pizza. When a new class of prisoners joins InnerChange, the staff orders one hundred large pies, a fact that all 800-plus prisoners at Ellsworth appear to be intimately, obsessively aware of."[51] Life is better inside as well. The ACLU describes "God pods" as having things like comfy chairs, microwaves, and access to a Christian library.[52] Winnifred Fallers Sullivan's account of the Iowa first amendment court case against Prison Fellowship documents the way that the program's unit was more spacious and allowed prisoners keys to their own doors. There was more privacy as well, with toilets outside of cells.[53] People in the programs have a lot more mobility, they have a sense of community, and they have far more reentry programming and support. Almost Benthamite in their approach, faith-based programs offer rewards instead of pain as a motivator, assuming that people might make some calculations about their own interest.

Consistent with a stoic view of self-interest, these programs do try to tame the passions. Spiritual transformation and Bible study are a key part of the programs, which are based on changing people, with the assumption that such change will lead away from crime and reduce recidivism.[54] Emotional control is expected and encouraged. To give an example, Florida's faith- and character-based institutions (FCBIs) list anger management programming under chaplaincy services.[55] Further, as might be expected in conservative faith-based programs, sexual abstinence and heteroconformity are demanded.[56] Passion of any kind other than for the Lord is discouraged. The prison-industrial complex contains and suppresses those criminalized and made-sinful "passions" that get in the way of interest.

LITERAL AND SPIRITUAL DEBT

Everyone has self-interest, or so the story goes, but only some people can actually collect financial interest; some people have to pay up. Debt is more than a large part of this story.[57] Financial interest requires monetary debt, which, as it turns out, is associated with prison in more ways than one. Cultural critics have shown that while financialization has earned interest for the wealthy, for most people it has meant going into debt. Personal debt is meant to increase mobility, and perhaps it often does. As recent work in cultural studies has shown, going into debt has afforded many people around the world the comforts of housing and transportation (that is, mortgages and auto loans) that they may not have had otherwise. For many, it allows actual or illusory social mobility.[58] But as Maurizio Lazzarato has argued, debt is also a form of control, making people infinitely more governable.[59] Although it might provide some social mobility, it also is immobilizing. Debt plays out on actual bodies and their relation to physical environments through austerity measures (think of the contamination of water in Flint, Michigan, to cut costs), pollution burdens, and, as I am discussing here, incarceration. It weighs heavily in social and moral terms as well. If prisons are interest's affective arm of repression, debt is another means of immobilizing.

In her book *Debt to Society*, Miranda Joseph argues that accounting metaphors of indebtedness have become part of the way punishment is conceived, ever since Cesare Beccaria's influential 1764 treatise *On Crimes and Punishment*. Beccaria conceived of the social contract as a kind of debt-producing obligation, for which law-abiding behavior was the credit paid and crime a lapse into social debt.[60] Joseph draws out the way that Beccaria establishes "accounting as the technology through which social standing, social creditworthiness, is to be ascertained."[61] Hence the phrase "debt to society." Joseph helpfully shows the accounting practices (literal and metaphoric) that produce crime as a kind of debt to be paid in time. As social accounting of debt develops in the United

States, Joseph argues, it is historically and presently a technology of racialization, creating a system in which African Americans and other minority and immigrant populations are deliberately indebted.[62]

If paying in time were not enough, prisons also produce literal debt. Not only is there the conceptual "debt" to society, paid in time, that Joseph elaborates, but also, the criminal justice system is increasingly creating monetary debt for people, from restitution fines (up to $10,000 for felonies),[63] to jail fees for those awaiting sentencing, and parole fees once people are released.[64] People go into prison with debts, which are then garnered from their meager wages, and they come out of prison with even greater debts. Indebtedness compounds other financial stress, making it difficult to live without supplementation from alternative economies that may result in additional incarceration. This financial burden can begin in youth. Fees and costs associated with juvenile arrests and detention—including court expenses, fees for public defenders, costs for evaluation, probation supervision fees, treatment costs—result in debt for young people and their families.[65]

The religious language of sin and salvation used in faith-based programs adds moral debt to the burden of debt carried by the incarcerated. The belief in Christ's atoning death is a foundational element in faith statements of many prison ministries.[66] The doctrine of substitutionary atonement, as is well rehearsed by those who adopt it and those who critique it, says that Christ redeems the sinner by paying for the debt of sin with his life.[67] A number of theologians have analyzed how traditional Christian notions of atonement and redemption follow an economic model of debt forgiveness.[68] In the present economic climate that functions on debt, this theology has added impact. As Hollis Phelps has incisively noted, atonement theology "adds theological and moral weight to neoliberalism's own creation of indebted subjects."[69] Linn Tonstad shows that debt closes down futures and future visions, shaping temporalities and "gobbling up the possibilities of *otherwise*."[70] Believers would surely say that all humans carry this same debt to God, yet still crime is said to specially exhibit sin. Prison Fellowship claims, for instance, that "crime is fundamentally a moral problem and a result of man's rebellion against God. It is secondarily a socioeconomic problem."[71] At the same time, this theology arguably reinforces the need for prisons. Greg Carey has looked at how substitutionary atonement theology facilitates tough-on-crime policies, because it positions people to accept a retributive model of punishment.[72] Although prison terms are not always advocated as the retribution required for all forms of crime, punishment is considered morally essential.

If sin is the cause of crime, total surrender to God's love is the solution. Winnifred Sullivan further documents how Prison Fellowship compares itself with traditional therapeutic programs to say that transformation comes through acceptance of biblical truths and encounter with Jesus Christ.[73] There is no interrogation into how people are categorized as criminal and whether or not they should be so named. Such beliefs imply, even if they draw back from explicitly claiming, that those in prison are extra indebted because they are extra sinful.

Redemption is given as the solution to crime, and comes through Christ's atoning work. Listen to this description of a Prison Fellowship Easter Service at Rikers Island:

> We opened our Bibles to Leviticus 16 and visited the celebration of Atonement, where a priest "laid his hands on the goat's head and placed the sins of the people there." We envisioned the walk Jesus made, carrying the sins of every human to the cross and away from us . . . a holy scapegoat, given freely for each and every one of us.
>
> I asked the men if they wished to place their sins upon Jesus, have Him pay for them, and experience real freedom. What a wondrous miracle it was to watch 83 inmates stand up and say, "Yes, I need forgiveness. I will follow Jesus."[74]

The promise of substitutionary atonement is affectively powerful, especially if one is asked to imagine themselves, as the men in this service are asked to do, as narrowly escaping the fate of the goat sent into the desert to die. When combined with the Christian message of redemption, this image could produce a powerful set of emotions for the incarcerated: dread, abandonment, and probable death, followed by relief and hope.

Even if faith-based ministries broaden their view of punishment to include restorative justice, as Prison Fellowship is starting to do, a sense of indebtedness remains for the incarcerated. Following from Christ's atonement and forgiveness, the criminal ought also to pay restitution.[75] Restorative justice focuses on conversations between victims and offenders, and encourages a suitable restitution be decided on, which should bring wholeness and peace. In the words of Daniel Van Ness and Karen Strong—who have developed the particular understanding of restorative justice on which Prison Fellowship relies—restitution should bring shalom, which means "right relationships between individuals, the community and God."[76] Rather than pay a debt to society, restitution is meant to restore relationship with the victim. When restitution is economic, however, it can increase actual debt through payments and fines, as critics of restorative justice have pointed out.[77] Although it does not always have to be monetary, the theology nonetheless draws on the logic of debt and payment. For instance, Van Ness and Strong turn to portions of the Torah (Exodus 22–23; Leviticus 5–6; Numbers 5) that deal with the economics of paying damages (and then some) for stolen or damaged items. They make their argument from the cognates of the Hebrew word for peace or safety, known in English as shalom (*šlwm*). The double meaning of its verbal root *šlm*—to make healthy/complete/safe/whole (in the Qal stem), and to pay or make restitution (in the Piel stem)—suggests to them that *"peace [is] restored through payment."*[78] Although not fully supportable, since the Qal and the Piel uses of *šlm* do not occur in tandem in the Tanakh, the interpretation points to the way that the idea of restitution does not escape the paradigm of indebtedness.

To be sure, there are also other theological articulations of the theology and practice of restorative justice. Howard Zehr, one of restorative justice's foundational Mennonite proponents, and peace studies theologian Ted Grimsrud insist on moving away from the retributive and debt-based theory of punishment.[79] Tracing the development of the theology and its effect on law, they argue that it is manifest in the "punitive practices and person-destroying experiences of prison."[80] Against the idea of God as unchanging holiness that "allows nothing but punishment . . . as recompense for sin,"[81] they look to the many places in both scriptural testaments that exemplify "a God whose mercy is unilateral, whose compassion takes precedence over wrath."[82] God's compassionate love models forgiveness, rather than payment of debt. Along these lines, they suggest that criminal justice should move toward restoration of relationships through compassionate love. It should ask, "Who has been hurt? What are their needs? Whose obligations are they?"[83] expanding obligations to include the entire community. While offenders are held accountable, their needs are also considered.

For many faith-based programs, however, moral debt (to God) is added to time debt (to society) and actual debt (to the victim incurred in the judicial system). Time and monetary debts are not forgiven; they must still be paid. Biblically based theological teaching thus interpellates the incarcerated as figural subjects of debt, who, although perhaps forgiven by God, literally need to pay to make amends, and who, without adequate income, become further indebted financially.

IMMOBILITIES OF INTERESTED YET INDEBTED SUBJECTS

I have been outlining how faith-based prison programming creates what Saidiya Hartman calls a confounded subject position, caught between interest and debt. The incarcerated are triply indebted, yet taught to follow their own interests even as they are harnessed to and immobilized by larger circulations of capital. Hartman's landmark book, *Scenes of Subjection*, illuminates the way interest and debt each have a certain relation to (im)mobility that is historically racialized. Her work points explicitly to the relation between dynamics of self-interest, debt, and mobility as they developed during Reconstruction.

The prison-industrial complex has inherited these dynamics, and faith-based prison programming especially.

Hartman analyzes the way in which former slaves were immediately shaped as socially and financially indebted, even while they were told to pursue self-interest. Following abolition, there was an emphasis on self-interest in advice to former slaves and a contradictory suturing into structures of debt that was a kind of blockage, slowing down, or interruption of interest. She shows how advice manuals to former slaves voice a fear of idleness and counter it with appeals to self-interest, trying "to replace the love of leisure with the love of gain and supplant bawdy pleasures with dispassionate acquisitiveness."[84] Advice manuals, Hartman writes, "aimed at cultivating a rational, dutiful, and acquisitive laboring class."[85] While freed people were expected to be interested and work for interest, they were simultaneously compelled to an indebted subjectivity. They were told, for instance, that their freedom had been paid for in blood and sacrifice—the religious significance of which Hartman notes—so they were symbolically indebted to the nation.[86] More concretely, actual debt was inevitable, since slaves were freed but given no land or capital and given low wages for mandatory contracts. Vagrancy laws meant that former slaves were criminalized if they did not have contracts, forcing people to accept contracts at low wages.[87] With no cash for rent, they became indebted for land and tools in the system of sharecropping.[88]

Hartman importantly highlights the conflicting expectations of movement between interest (keep moving, work hard) and debt (stay put, work for low wages or be arrested for vagrancy). After emancipation, conscientiousness, volition, and will were emphasized as a form of self-interest.[89] Freed people were encouraged to "submission, self-denial, and servile compliance [that] was not considered at odds with autonomy or self-interest."[90] As she writes: "The confounding of the liberty of contract by a compulsory contract system, self-interest by the threat of criminal sanction, and self-fashioning by obligatory conduct delineates the crosscurrents of slavery and freedom that engendered involuntary servitude and the burdened individuality of freedom."[91] Hartman makes clear that it is white landowners who benefit from the cultivation of a self-interested, criminalized, yet indebted workforce.

The account of Reconstruction Hartman gives is eerily similar to current attitudes toward the incarcerated and racially criminalized—attitudes that are often emphasized within faith-based programs. These programs are aimed at producing dutiful, well-behaved citizens, who perhaps have less likelihood of recidivism and are able to move forward. Yet participants are positioned as always-already indebted and lacking. Morals and ethics are assumed to be missing and needed for productivity. Many of these programs speak of building "pro-social attitudes and life skills."[92] The Texas Department of Criminal

Justice website describes Prison Fellowship's mission as able "to create and maintain a prison environment that fosters respect for God's law, the rights of others, and to encourage the *spiritual and moral regeneration* of offenders."[93] The Corrections Corporation of America (now CoreCivic) formerly described their faith-based programs as "a proven way to help *reawaken or develop* a moral and ethical foundation . . . thereby helping inmates serve their time in productive ways as they prepare to lead meaningful lives upon release."[94] When such notions of criminality are combined with a Christian teaching of sin as a permanent state of debt, a discourse emerges that positions people caught up in the prison-industrial complex as always-already indebted, as lacking (grace, morals, "pro-sociality," etc.), and as needing to pay restitution. Moreover, statements such as these suggest that lives prior to prison are not meaningful, productive, social, or with a developed ethics. It is implied that morality is somehow stunted or stopped and that moral movement must be initiated. Difference is turned into lack.

"Antisocial" behaviors are considered to be internal to the participant, rather than reasonable or inevitable responses to external deficits, for instance deficits in economic opportunities or strong support for education. The focus on interiority means that desired outcomes in faith-based programs tend to be spiritual, not practical. A 2011 study that surveyed forty-eight faith-based correctional and reentry programs found that despite any given social services and goals of the programs, the top ranked *outcome* was "deepening personal spiritual commitment" (44 percent of programs), as contrasted with the more obvious social outcomes like "finding steady employment" (4.4 percent of programs), or "improved life skills" (2.1 percent of programs), or "attaining education" (0 percent of programs).[95] This is not to say that the programs surveyed do not facilitate education or job training, but rather that these are not *prioritized* outcomes. Spiritual support may be an important form of support and survival for some, as Erzen shows,[96] but programs that do not prioritize practical skills and education alongside spiritual practice will not likely enable participants to move ahead in the ways expected. The demand for forward movement is undercut not only by a theology of indebtedness and literal debt, but also by a lack of emphasis on practical outcomes.

An analysis of a differential mobility of interest and debt could usefully draw on Mel Chen's discussion of racialized hierarchies of animacy.[97] As Chen points out, U.S. linguistics, cultural structures, and ontological imaginations grant animacy (agency, purpose, activity) to some social actors more than others, with free adult men on the top of the hierarchy.[98] Chen shows how racialized and or colonized people, immigrants, and differently-abled people are objectified and dehumanized by being associated with things considered less animate than humans (animals, vegetable, nonorganic matter). Debt, which is also racialized, might be seen as a cessation of or block to mobility and even *ability*—to move, to grow, and to purchase; in short, to develop in the norms of home and economy. If interest is seen as moving forward, getting ahead, having volition (not being idle), then debt moves differently. Part of the racialized animacy hierarchy, debt slows people down, creates immobility, blockages, pockets of impossibility. Immobility, prison, and debt are of a piece. Significantly, as Andrew Dilts points out in his study of U.S. liberalism and punishment, laws and political discourse around felony and disenfranchisement have figured the U.S. citizen as "white, male, *able*, and innocent."[99]

Debt could be said to pool, or secrete, to think with Gregory Seigworth and Matthew Tiessen.[100] In a highly instructive article that elaborates Deleuze and Guattari's concept of the secret (secret as content, secrecy as form, and secretion as expression), Seigworth and Tiessen show how interest and debt now circulate through the future (futures) in the form of derivatives. They describe the pursuit of financial liquidity in global markets as a kind of secreting plasma, and they analyze the productive market fictions of "expanding credit and endless financial innovation" as "striving for maximum viscosity, striving always to be more fluid and friction-free."[101] Operating out of sight (in secret) are transactions of ever-increasing credit and ever-increasing debt to support it.[102] The production of liquidity—which they explain as the production of forms of capital that can be traded,[103] including "resources and energy from the future"[104]—is a kind of open secret, hidden from the public, but actively producing credit from debt in the present and also for and from the future. (Their discussion of the secrets of the market sound remarkably like the way prisons function: "Inherent and eminent dangers are either publicly disavowed or otherwise secreted away.")[105] As liquidity pools, debt secretes.[106] If liquidity races toward the future—now calculated by computers and algorithms rather than rationally calculating subjects—debt sucks people down into its perpetual swamps.

The force of debt is vastly different for the individual than for the system; within the system it circulates and pools into credit, but for individuals the secretions of debt are like quicksand. Debt operates something like the way that Patricia Clough has described teletechnology: It is a strategy of overexposure and underexposure, aimed in multiple directions and moving beyond any particular subject in a kind of "network imagination" within larger flows of capital.[107] On an individual level, racialized debt is a block to pursuing interest; it is the countermovement to the liberal aspirations of freedom, autonomy, and progress. On a structural level, debt is only a detour for interest; it is directed by racialized interest to congeal around and to be figured through the incarcerated. It is not so much that the debts paid by the incarcerated are contributing to the flows of capital to the 1 percent (although they are), as that the incarcerated are the cautionary tale about what happens if the passions bubble up to prevent the movement of interest. The individual indebtedness of the incarcerated resonates to some degree with Andrew Krinks's analysis of the theological undergirding of criminalization: "The contemporary sin of poverty is bound up with the immorality of refusing participation in the capitalist economy, or in literally transgressing the boundaries of property upon which one's presence can only ever be a contamination and blockage of the moral flow of capital." If the incarcerated are being punished for *not* participating in capital, being brought into debt remedies that supposed problem. Debt is all too necessary to the flow of capital, even as it creates blocks and pooling, sinking secretions.[108]

CARCERAL TECHNOLOGIES BEYOND THEOPOLITICAL SUBJECTS

For those of us who want to see the system changed or abolished, these larger systems must be engaged. The bipartisan push for prison reform in the late Obama era, which most infamously included the backing of the Koch brothers, suggested that there might be some political will for modest changes. Such will for change indicates that the activism and critiques from inside prisons (such as the many hunger and labor strikes since 2010)[109] and also from the outside (including the substantial advocacy of Prison Fellowship and other Christian groups) have an impact. In 2010, Congress passed the Fair Sentencing Act. In 2016, Barack Obama took executive action to end solitary confinement for juveniles. During the Trump era, the proposed Sentencing Reform and Corrections Act of 2015 and 2017 has stalled; it would take some small steps toward reducing prison populations, such as reducing mandatory minimum sentences. The much touted but drastically underfunded First Step Act of 2018 slightly reduces prison time for some federal prisoners (many convicted crimes do not qualify); but it does little to ameliorate sentencing structures and practices that critics have long been calling out as disproportionately affecting black and brown communities.

Legislative reforms might alleviate some of the injustices of the prison-industrial complex; but I join others in wanting to make sure that any reform does not end up expanding the prison-industrial complex in the name of a "better" form of lockup.[110] Prison reform can only become more than a new phase of neoliberalism or oligarchal capital if reformers pay attention to the interconnected affective, financial, theological, moral, and environmental stakes. The pursuit of interest and the collection of debt obviously go far beyond the individual in transnational global capital, circulating through people, goods, and data. Any thinking about prison reform, or better, abolition, must consider carceral technologies that go beyond particular incarcerated persons and even beyond the body-as-organism—via markets, secrets/secretions of interest/debt, new methods of surveillance and data collection, and environmental animacies. Even if prisons were to be abolished, interest and debt could still circulate in ways that allow some people to benefit off the debt and immobility of others. In particular, I suggest we ought to start thinking about what interest and debt might mean in relation to bodies as information, surveillance as data, and environmental animacy.

For one thing, Patricia Clough, Greg Goldberg, Rachel Schiff, Aaron Weeks, and Craig Willse suggest that capitalism is changing; it is moving into a kind of radical neoliberalism that turns all levels of matter and life into capital.[111] Now, they argue, bodies and populations have become a kind of capital as informational matter, data, and as potentiality.[112] If governance is about producing and facilitating capital in neoliberalism, this new form of governance is "radical neoliberalism."[113] Now people, other organic forms, and other types of matter are increasingly understood as information and data, including the "informational substrate of matter"[114] (for example, DNA, gene structure). Governance is no longer aimed simply at the body-as-organism, but at matter and information more broadly, which Clough and her co-authors call "affect-itself." Affect is that which has potential to develop, or that which can be understood as information at all levels of matter.[115] This means that governance and capitalism are concerned with forecasting the emergence of matter as information, controlling it, and also pushing it to emerge. Clough and co-authors propose that "governance is now a matter of pre-emption, but not only to anticipate and control the emergent but rather to precipitate emergence and thereby act on a future that has not yet and may not ever arrive."[116] In Marxist terms, they describe this as "the real subsumption of life itself,"[117] whereby productivity is increased through technology, and in this case through a whole new means of conceiving of matter and information. Clough and co-authors, and others such as Seigworth and Tiessen discussed above, indicate that the market might colonize potentiality and futures, here the potentiality of bodily information and data. If interest expands in these ways, we can imagine that affect-itself can and will also be colonized by relations of debt and immobility.

One might be suspicious, then, paranoid even, about whether prison reform is about ending an unjust system or rather about accommodating to a new mode of capital and governance. The systems of surveillance that are part of the extended prison-industrial complex are also producing data and information that can be colonized. Seigworth and Tiessen take their analysis of secrecy to surveillance and the kinds of data that it seeks to gather—and although they do not discuss it in terms of market speculation, others have done so.[118] If the market, and so governance, is increasingly about the production of potentiality for speculation on data produced by surveillance, and if bodies are taken as information and potential, prisons may no longer be needed for control or the production of interest. We might well ask what debt will look like under radical neoliberalism or oligarchic capital and how we can prevent something worse than prisons from emerging.

One might also think about the relation of prison reform to nonenforcement of environmental regulation and resulting immobilization in and through pollution and toxicity, via illness, disability, and devaluation of homes on polluted land. To give an extended example, critics have argued that the Koch brothers' interest in prison reform stems from their own market interests (which are oil-based rather than informational) and their worry about prosecution of corporate CEOs for environmental damage. The Kochs were prosecuted with felony charges after a number of oil spills and breaches of environmental regulation in several of their refineries. In 2001, after six years of fighting the many charges, they took a plea deal and paid a paltry twenty million dollar fine.[119] Now they seek to reform the prison system, perhaps, as political analysts have argued, in ways that will also decriminalize breaches of environmental regulation.[120] Although the Koch brothers support sentencing reform, they also supported the proposed Criminal Code Improvement Act of 2015[121] that some said would make it more difficult to prosecute corporate crimes.[122] The bill proposed a "default state of mind proof requirement," meaning that in order to prosecute, "the Government must prove that the defendant knew, or had reason to believe, the conduct was unlawful."[123] Along similar lines, Senator Orrin Hatch (R-Utah) suggested additions to the Sentencing Reform and Corrections Act, to require intent for crime (*mens rea*) in ways that would let corporations off the hook.[124] Prison reform may come at the expense of the environment, a fact that will also have deeply racialized results. Environmental justice activists have shown how environmental pollution disproportionally burdens working-class communities of color and immigrant communities.

The momentum of interest moves through corporations and their pollutants into the earth, producing nonhuman animacies, which then, in turn, take their toll on people. As corporations take greater and greater control of the environment, these already overburdened communities are increasingly at risk, now with little legal help to stop the forward march of interest.[125] Worse, as Californians United for a Responsible Budget (CURB), Critical Resistance LA, and No More Jails LA have shown, prisons and jails are themselves being built on sites that have significant environmental problems, including toxic soil, polluted water, and weather patterns that are more likely to produce illness. Take, for instance, the Valley Fever that has killed and debilitated many incarcerated people in the Central Valley of California.[126] Such injustices exemplify what Chen has written about how racialized others are seen as toxic, and are thus made toxic.

TOXICITY AND BEYOND

I have tried to show that interest is conceptualized as a form of rationality that tries to tame affect and to shut down the passions. It is imagined as forward momentum that sublimates bodily desires and excesses, movements that are nonlinear and nonprogressing. What cannot be acknowledged by those who believe in interest's stoic benefits is that interest feeds on debt and that debt works overtime on racialized bodies, often held in prisons. As I have argued, faith-based prison programs amplify a sense of racialized indebtedness by adding moral debt to financial debt and time debt for incarcerated persons through theologies of sin and atonement. The focus on interiority and individual need within these programs occludes the larger movements of interest and debt in which prisons are implicated, including market speculation, bodies and biology as information and potential, and environment as resource-producing animacy or devastated toxicity.

Those thinking about prison reform and abolition need to take seriously the way interest and debt circulate through and beyond human bodies and to consider how the dynamics of interest and debt might (already) be configured in the near future. As indicated above, the rational subject of calculation has been supplemented via methods of surveillance and data collection, computer algorithmic calculation, potentiality, environmental impact, all of which are and can be integrated into the larger prison-industrial complex. Interest has moved beyond the individual body, even as it colonizes, impedes, and confounds particular bodies with debt.

I conclude by invoking Chen's discussion of toxicity as a challenge to think beyond just the danger of contamination to consider how it might operate queerly to trouble the subject-object relations on which interest and debt depend and which they exceed. The dangers of environmental injustice are real and deeply worrying, as Chen's own autoethnography profoundly attests; yet toxicity presents states of being that trouble subject-object relations and usual norms of sociality and "acceptable temporal transit."[127] Toxicity has its own animacy that moves through nonhuman objects and troubles the borders between human and nonhuman.[128] It is an intermaterial "environmental assemblage."[129] As Chen writes, "Toxicity fails over and again to privilege rationality's favorite partner, the *human* subject."[130] Calling toxicity queer is not a form of quietism by any means, but rather—at the risk of oversimplifying Chen's provocative and eloquent disquisition—a call to recognize that toxicity is the constitutive outside of everyday life. It is "a truth of nearly every body and also a biopolitically interested distribution."[131] Debt operates similarly per-haps: Almost everyone has it, and it is also biopolitically distributed, locked down, and intertwined with toxicity. No amount of Christ's atoning work can change these facts. The rational calculation of interest through and beyond the human subject produces forms of toxicity—including debt, lockup, and environmental hazards—that undercut the very notion of human rational cal-culation of interest.

Working toward structural change of the prison-industrial complex will require looking beyond the human subject and beyond the walls of prisons (in partnership with those inside) to the larger system of carceral technolo-gies that are working toward the real subsumption of life itself. One part of the effort of scholars wishing to address the prison-industrial complex—of which there are no small number now—might be further to deconstruct and transvalue the literal and figural toxicities of interest, including debt, passions now made toxic by the criminal justice system, and prisons. Those working in faith-based programs have the added challenge of developing teaching and theologies that do not rely on the immobilizing counterdemands of interest and debt.

NOTES

Thanks to my colleague Anne Dwyer for valuable feedback, as well as my students Peter Chen, Olivia Dure, Pieter Hoekstra, Paolina Siqueira Koo, Kristen Park, Isabella Speciale, Kian Vesteinsson, and Veronica You Wu. I am also grateful to Sagarika Gami for research assistance.

1. A widely cited definition of the prison industrial complex is: "Overlapping inter-ests of government and industry that use surveillance, policing, and imprisonment as solutions to what are, in actuality, economic, social, and political 'problems.'" From the Critical Resistance website: http://criticalresistance.org/about/not-so -common-language/.

2. My approach to affect has been informed most particularly by Baruch Spinoza, *Eth-ics*, in *Spinoza: Complete Works*, trans. Samuel Shirley (1674; Indianapolis: Hackett, 2002), 213–382; Gilles Deleuze, *Spinoza, Practical Philosophy*, trans. Robert Hurley (1970; San Francisco: City Lights Books, 1988); Patricia Ticineto Clough, *Auto-affection: Unconscious Thought in the Age of Teletechnology* (Minneapolis: University of Minnesota Press, 2000); Brian Massumi, *Parables for the Virtual: Movement, Affect, Sensation* (Durham, N.C.: Duke University Press, 2002); Eve Kosofsky Sedgwick, *Touching Feeling: Affect, Pedagogy, Performativity* (Durham, N.C.: Duke University Press, 2003); Sara Ahmed, *The Cultural Politics of Emotion* (New York: Routledge, 2004); Jasbir K. Puar, *Terrorist Assemblages: Homonationalism in Queer Times* (Dur-ham, N.C.: Duke University Press, 2007); Melissa Gregg and Gregory J. Seigworth, eds., *The Affect Theory Reader* (Durham, N.C.: Duke University Press, 2010); Lauren Berlant, *Cruel Optimism* (Durham, N.C.: Duke University Press, 2011); Mel Y. Chen,

Animacies: Biopolitics, Racial Mattering, and Queer Affect (Durham N.C.: Duke University Press, 2012); and Brian Massumi, *Politics of Affect* (Cambridge, U.K.: Polity Press, 2015).

3. Michael Hallett and Byron Johnson, "The Resurgence of Religion in America's Prisons," *Religions* 5, no. 3 (2014): 663–83.

4. The Florida Department of Corrections issued a press release indicating that the full faith-based prisons are: Wakulla CI and Wakulla Annex, Lawtey CI, and Hernando CI. See http://www.dc.state.fl.us/secretary/press/2016/07-15-Missed-It.html.

5. Previously Prison Fellowship ran dorms in Iowa and Kansas as well. Winnifred Sullivan follows a District Court case in Iowa for which she was an expert witness. The court found the activities of Prison Fellowship's InnerChange Freedom Initiative to violate the first amendment of the U.S. Constitution, so it no longer operates in Iowa. Winnifred Fallers Sullivan, *Prison Religion: Faith-Based Reform and the Constitution* (Princeton, N.J.: Princeton University Press, 2009).

6. http://www.thegodofhope.org/programs/faith-based-dorms/.

7. Ohio Department of Rehabilitation and Correction, "Volunteering in Prison," HB 113 Annual Report (October 2012): http://www.drc.ohio.gov/LinkClick.aspx?fileticket=b8g-NqjLiK4%3D&portalid=0.

8. http://www.correctionscorp.com.

9. Tanya Erzen, *God in Captivity: The Rise of Faith-Based Prison Ministries in the Age of Mass Incarceration* (Boston: Beacon, 2017).

10. Mark Lewis Taylor, "Christianity and US Prison Abolition: Rupturing a Hegemonic Christian Ideology," *Socialism and Democracy* 28, no. 3 (2014): 180.

11. For history and analysis of the commonly understood notion of punishment as paying a "debt to society," see Miranda Joseph, *Debt to Society: Accounting for Life under Capitalism* (Minneapolis: University of Minnesota Press, 2014). Multiple articles on the Prison Fellowship website speak approvingly of prisoners paying their debt to society. See Emily Andrews, "Ending a Life Sentence," *Prison Fellowship*, September 20, 2016: https://www.prisonfellowship.org/2016/09/ending-life-sentence/; "Changing Perceptions: A Q&A on Second Chances," *Prison Fellowship*, September 6, 2016: https://www.prisonfellowship.org/2016/09/changing-perceptions/; Steve Rempe, "The Benefits of Hiring Former Prisoners," *Prison Fellowship*, July 27, 2016: https://www.prisonfellowship.org/2016/07/benefits-hiring-former-prisoners/.

12. Saidiya V. Hartman, *Scenes of Subjection: Terror, Slavery, and Self-Making in Nineteenth-Century America,* Race and American Culture (New York: Oxford University Press, 1997), 147.

13. Ruth Wilson Gilmore, *Golden Gulag: Prisons, Surplus, Crisis, and Opposition in Globalizing California* (Berkeley: University of California Press), 30–86; Angela Y. Davis, *Are Prisons Obsolete?* (New York: Seven Stories Press, 2003), 12–17.

14. Gilmore, *Golden Gulag*, 58–86.

15. Ruth Wilson Gilmore, "Globalisation and US Prison Growth: From Military Keynesianism to Post-Keynesian Militarism," *Race and Class* 40, nos. 2/3 (1998–99): 43.

16. Gilmore, *Golden Gulag*, 97–107.

17. Ibid.; Kevin Pranis, "Doing Borrowed Time: The High Cost of Backdoor Prison Finance," in *Prison Profiteers: Who Makes Money from Mass Incarceration*, ed. Tara Herivel and Paul Wright (New York: New Press, 2007), 36–51; Christopher Petrella, "Leasing through the Back Door: The Private Financing of 'Public' Prisons," *Shadowproof*, May 2, 2012: https://shadowproof.com/2012/05/02/leasing-through -the-back-door-the-private-financing-of-public-prisons/.

18. Petrella, "Leasing through the Back Door"; State of California, "Implementation of AB 900," Governor's Budget 2008–09: http://www.ebudget.ca.gov/2008-09-EN/ BudgetSummary/DCR/32270639.html..

19 Alex Anderson, "Hiding Out in Prison Bonds," *Forbes*, October 22, 2008: http://www .forbes.com/2008/10/22/prison-correctional-bonds-pf-ii-in_aa_1022fixedincome _inl.html.

20. For a list of California lease revenue bonds and their underwriters from 1996 until the present, see California State Office of the Treasurer, http://www.treasurer .ca.gov/bonds/os.asp.

21. Pranis, "Doing Borrowed Time"; Lauren Etter and Margaret Newkirk, "How Local Governments Got Burned by Private Prison Investments," *Bloomberg Business Week*, October 1, 2015: https://www.bloomberg.com/news/articles/2015-10-02/how -local-governments-got-burned-by-private-prison-investments; Alice Speri, "Local Jails Profit From Warehousing State Prisoners," *The Intercept* (June 9, 2016): https://theintercept.com/2016/06/09/local-jails-profit-from-warehousing-state -prisoners/.

22. Philip Mattera and Mafruza Khan, "Jail Breaks: Economic Development Subsidies Given to Private Prisons," Good Jobs First (Washington, D.C.: Institute on Taxation and Economic Policy, 2001): https://www.opensocietyfoundations.org/ sites/default/files/jb_complete.pdf; Etter and Newkirk, "How Local Governments Got Burned"; Hadar Aviram, *Cheap on Crime: Recession-Era Politics and the Transformation of American Punishment* (Oakland: University of California Press, 2015), 45–46.

23. Gilmore points out that the private prison industry is only a small fraction of the prison industrial complex; see Ruth Wilson Gilmore, "The Worrying State of the Anti-Prison Movement," Social Justice Blog, *Social Justice: A Journal of Crime, Conflict and World Order*, February 3, 2015: http://www.socialjusticejournal.org/the -worrying-state-of-the-anti-prison-movement/.

24. Ray Downs, "Who's Getting Rich off the Prison-Industrial Complex?" *Vice*, May 17, 2013: https://www.vice.com/en_us/article/whos-getting-rich-off-the -prison-industrial-complex.

25. See "CoreCivic Inc. Institutional Ownership," Nasdaq, https://www.nasdaq.com/ symbol/cxw/institutional-holdings; "GEO Group Inc. Institutional Ownership," Nasdaq, https://www.nasdaq.com/symbol/geo/institutional-holdings.

26. Beth Schwartzapfel, "A Primer on the Nationwide Prisoners' Strike," *The Marshall Project*, September 27, 2016: https://www.themarshallproject.org/2016/09/27/ a-primer-on-the-nationwide-prisoners-strike#.es5iyy77X.

27. Jamie Yoon and Jessica Nickel, *Reentry Partnerships: A Guide for States & Faith-Based and Community Organizations* (New York: Council of State Governments Justice Center, 2008): https://www.justice.gov/archive/fbci/docs/reentry-partnership .pdf.

28. Samantha Shapiro, "Jails for Jesus," in *Prison Profiteers: Who Makes Money from Mass Incarceration*, ed. Tara Herivel and Paul Wright (New York: New Press, 2007), 128–40. InnerChange stopped running programs in Kansas in 2012 and has been replaced by Brothers in Blue Reentry, which teaches values "from a biblical point of view"; they also include practical support, such as G.E.D. programs and substance abuse education (http://www.brothersinbluereentry.org/about).

It is difficult to find a more generalized account of savings attributed to these programs. A DOJ Fact Sheet on Faith-Based Programs, suggests that "U.S. congregations generate an estimated $81 billion annually in revenues, much of which is used to support programs that address social needs." The Fact Sheet goes on to note the high number of volunteers in faith-based institutions. U.S. Department of Justice, Office of Justice Programs, "OJP Fact Sheet: Faith-Based Programs," November 2011: http://ojp.gov/newsroom/factsheets/ojpfs_faith-basedprog.html.

29. Kay Whitlock, "Faith, Inc. and Criminal Justice Reform," *Truthout*, December 11, 2014: http://www.truth-out.org/news/item/27942-faith-inc-and-criminal-justice -reform; Frederick Clarkson, "An Uncharitable Choice: The Faith-Based Takeover of Federal Programs," *Public Eye* 80 (Fall 2014): 12–13.

30. See, for instance, a cost-benefit analysis of the reduction of recidivism for InnerChange participants in Minnesota by researchers from the Minnesota DOC and Baylor University: Grant Duwe and Byron R. Johnson, "Estimating the Benefits of a Faith-Based Correctional Program," *International Journal of Criminology and Sociology* 2 (2013): 227–39.

31. See A. Volokh, "Do Faith-Based Prisons Work?" *Alabama Law Review* 63, no. 1 (2011): 43–96. For an example of how selection might work, Yoon and Nickel (*Reentry Partnerships*, 37–38) caution faith-based organizations against trying to serve individuals with a high risk of reoffense if they are not trained to do so. Likewise, some programs do not accept participants with mental health issues or who are sex offenders; a few, although not many, give preference to those already professing a religious affiliation; see Janeen Buck Willison, Diana Brazzell, and KiDeuk Kim, "Faith-Based Corrections and Reentry Programs: Advancing a Conceptual Framework for Research and Evaluation," National Criminal Justice Reference Service (2011): 23–24, https://www.ncjrs.gov/pdffiles1/nij/grants/234058.pdf.

32. Michel Foucault, *The Birth of Biopolitics: Lectures at the Collège de France, 1978–1979*, ed. Michel Senellart, trans. Graham Burchell (New York: Palgrave Macmillan, 2008).

33. David Grewal, "The Political Theology of *Laissez-Faire*: From *Philia* to Self-Love in Commercial Society," *Political Theology* 17, no. 5 (2016): 417–33.

34. Albert O. Hirschman, *The Passions and the Interests: Political Arguments for Capitalism before Its Triumph* (Princeton, N.J.: Princeton University Press, 1977), 63–66.

35. Ibid., 26; David Hume, "Of Interest," in *Political Discourses* (1752; Edinburgh: Fleming, 1994), 70.

36. Brian Massumi, *The Power at the End of the Economy* (Durham, N.C.: Duke University Press, 2015), 58–65.

37. Dean Mathiowetz, *Appeals to Interest: Language, Contestation, and the Shaping of Political Agency* (University Park: Pennsylvania State University Press, 2011). Mathiowetz's intellectual history helpfully outlines the juridical as the chief site for the formation of interests, thus moving interest into the realm of politics rather than a presumed psychology from which economics seamlessly follows.

38. Ibid., 142–45.

39. Stephen Holmes, *Passions and Constraint: On the Theory of Liberal Democracy* (Chicago: University of Chicago Press, 1995). Holmes was part of a resurgence of attention to interest and its limits in the 1990s. He writes to moderate a notion of interest promoted by twentieth-century economists whom he says are not attentive to the psychological nuances of seventeenth- and eighteenth-century thinkers like John Locke, David Hume, and Adam Smith. Unlike late twentieth-century economics and political theory, says Holmes, these earlier liberal theorists are aware of the varying kinds of motivations for human behavior, and of the varying kinds of self-interest.

40. Ibid., 24.

41. Ibid., 57.

42. Ibid., 57–59.

43. Ibid., 66.

44. Rather neoclassically (Stoically), the movement is away from bodies and emotion and toward the more abstract realm of money and law. Nonetheless, interest is its own affect, its own motion; it has to be held in check. Neoliberals and libertarians would say the market provides its own checks, but Holmes suggests some social contract is still necessary. In his view, it would seem, interest must be held in check so that it does not become tainted by those very affects it should check, including greed and revenge.

45. Friedrich Nietzsche, *On the Genealogy of Morals*, trans. Walter Kaufmann (New York: Vintage, 1967 [1887]), II.15.

46. See also Taylor, ""Christianity and US Prison Abolition," 182.

47. Davis, *Are Prisons Obsolete?*; Michelle Alexander, *The New Jim Crow: Mass Incarceration in the Age of Colorblindness* (New York: New Press, 2010).

48. See, for example, Roderick A. Ferguson, *Aberrations in Black: Toward a Queer of Color Critique*, Critical American Studies Series (Minneapolis: University of Minnesota Press, 2004); Mel Y. Chen, *Animacies: Biopolitics, Racial Mattering, and Queer Affect* (Durham, N.C.: Duke University Press, 2012); Mayra Rivera, *Poetics of the Flesh* (Durham, N.C.: Duke University Press, 2015).

49. Jeremy Bentham "The Panopticon, or The New Inspection House," in *The Works of Jeremy Bentham*, vol. 4 (1787; Edinburgh: William Tait, 1843), 127; note also his famous adage, "Pain and pleasure are the great springs of human action," in "Principles of Penal Law," in *The Works of Jeremy Bentham*, vol. 1 (1775; Edinburgh: William Tait, 1838), 396.

50. Shapiro, "Jails for Jesus," 131.

51. Ibid., 132.

52. Micah McCoy, "God Pods," ALCU of New Mexico, June 11, 2010: https://www
.aclu-nm.org/en/news/god-pods.

53. Sullivan, *Prison Religion*, 36–39.

54. Willison, Brazzell, and Kim, "Faith-Based Corrections and Reentry Programs";
Sullivan, *Prison Religion*.

55. Florida Department of Corrections, "Hernando Correctional Institution": http://
www.dc.state.fl.us/facilities/region3/336.html, and "Lawtey Correctional Institution": http://www.dc.state.fl.us/facilities/region2/255.html.

56. Erzen, *God in Captivity*, 31–34; Andrea Smith, *Native Americans and the Christian
Right: The Gendered Politics of Unlikely Alliances* (Durham, N.C.: Duke University
Press, 2008), 45–47.

57. For recent literature analyzing and critiquing systems of debt, see David Graeber,
Debt: The First 5,000 Years (Brooklyn: Melville House, 2014).

58. See Joe Deville and Gregory J. Seigworth, eds., "Everyday Debt and Credit," a
special issue of *Cultural Studies* 29, nos. 5–6 (2015). For the affective operation and
weight of consumer credit and debt (for example, credit card debt), see Joe Deville,
Lived Economies of Default: Consumer Credit, Debt Collection and the Capture of Affect
(London: Routledge, 2015).

59. Maurizio Lazzarato, *Governing by Debt*, trans. Joshua David Jordan (Pasadena, Calif.:
Semiotext[e], 2015).

60. Joseph, *Debt to Society*, 48–49.

61. Ibid., 48.

62. Joseph points to the predatory lending of the subprime mortgage crisis, in which
Black and Latinx neighborhoods were targeted for loans; she also points to what
Gayatri Chakravorty Spivak names "credit-baiting" on the international scale
(ibid., 25).

63. California Department of Corrections, "Victim & Survivor Rights & Services":
http://www.cdcr.ca.gov/victim_services/docs/AdultFines012004.pdf.

64. Lauren-Brooke Eisen, "Paying for Your Time: How Charging Inmates Fees Behind
Bars May Violate the Excessive Fines Clause," *Loyola Journal of Public Interest Law* 15,
no. 2 (2014): 319–42.

65. Jessica Felerman, *Debtors' Prison for Kids? The High Cost of Fines and Fees in the Juvenile Justice System* (Philadelphia: Juvenile Law Center, 2016): http://debtorsprison.jlc
.org/documents/JLC-Debtors-Prison.pdf.

66. See the mission statements of Prison Fellowship, God of Hope Ministries, Bill
Glass Behind the Walls, Trinity Broadcasting Network, Alpha USA.

67. The classic statement of the doctrine is Anselm of Canterbury's *Cur Deus Homo*
(1094–98; Oxford: John Henry and James Parker, 1865).

68. Kathryn Tanner, *Economy of Grace* (Minneapolis: Fortress Press, 2005); Gary A. Anderson, *Sin: A History* (New Haven, Conn.: Yale University Press, 2009); Nathan
Eubank, *Wages of Cross-Bearing and Debt of Sin: The Economy of Heaven in Matthew's Gospel* (Berlin: De Gruyter, 2013); Devin Singh, "Monetized Philosophy and

Theological Money: Uneasy Linkages and the Future of a Discourse," in *The Future of Continental Philosophy of Religion*, ed. Clayton B. Crockett, Keith Putt, and Jeffrey W. Robbins (Bloomington: Indiana University Press, 2014), 140–53, and "Sovereign Debt," *Journal of Religious Ethics* 46, no. 2 (2018): 239–66; Hollis Phelps, "Overcoming Redemption: Neoliberalism, Atonement, and the Logic of Debt," *Political Theology* 17, no. 3 (2016): 264–82.

Gary Anderson suggests that any elaboration of the doctrine of atonement, as particularly elaborated by Anselm, needs to understand the history of the conceptualization of sin as debt (*Sin*, 202). Anderson argues that in the Tanakh, the primary metaphor for sin is as a weight that must be borne or lifted, but that this metaphor is changed to one of debt in the Aramaic rabbinic texts of the Second Temple period; by the time of the Christian Testament, the notion of sin as debt is well established and elaborated by the early Christian writers. One would certainly want to take issue with his emphasis on the "Semitic" character of this mode of thought as he compares it with Greek thought, especially when it is so fully elaborated in the (Greco-Roman) Christian tradition.

69. Phelps, "Overcoming Redemption," 267.

70. Linn Marie Tonstad, "Debt Time Is Straight Time," *Political Theology* 17, no. 5 (2015): 438.

71. Prison Fellowship, "Biblical Basis for Reentry Ministry": https://www.prison fellowship.org/resources/training-resources/reentry-ministry/ministry-basics/ biblical-basis-for-reentry-ministry/.

72. Greg Carey, "Mass Incarceration and Penal Atonement Theories: Correlation, or Something More?" in *Thinking Theologically about Mass Incarceration: Biblical Foundations and Justice Imperatives*, ed. Antonios Kireopoulos, Mitzi J. Budde, and Matthew D. Lundberg, Faith & Order Commission Theological Series (Mahwah, N.J.: Paulist Press, 2017), 205–16. Carey also notices that in the evangelical community race plays a larger role than theology in determining attitudes toward crime. In other words, African American churches may hold to atonement theology but still take stands against mass incarceration. Notably, support for the death penalty is often present in communities that adhere to atonement theology, especially white communities.

73. Sullivan, *Prison Religion*, 108–17.

74. Jim Liske, "Easter Miracles behind Bars," *Prison Fellowship*, March 19, 2013: https://www.prisonfellowship.org/story/easter-miracles-behind-bars/.

75. A classic, if somewhat harsher than usually articulated, statement to this effect is made in an early restorative justice text by the theonomist Gary North in his *Victim's Rights: The Biblical View of Civil Justice* (Tyler, Texas: Institute for Christian Economics, 1990). North writes: "Double restitution restores the victim's economic position prior to the crime, plus it increases his holdings to compensate him for the trouble the crime caused him. . . . Making economic restitution restores the criminal legally and psychologically. He knows that he has paid his debt, not just to society but to the victim. He is made clean, analogous to the cleansing the

sinner experiences when he accepts Jesus Christ's payment of his sins at Calvary" (180–81).

76. Daniel W. Van Ness, and Karen Heetderks Strong, *Restoring Justice: An Introduction to Restorative Justice*, 5th ed. (Abingdon, U.K.: Routledge, 2015), 6.

77. For a critique of restorative justice, see Annalise E. Acorn, *Compulsory Compassion: A Critique of Restorative Justice*, Law and Society Series (Vancouver: University of British Columbia Press, 2004).

78. Van Ness and Strong, *Restoring Justice*, 19n7, emphasis mine. They rely on R. Laird Harris, Gleason L. Archer Jr., and Bruce K. Waltke, eds., *Theological Wordbook of the Old Testament* (Chicago: Moody Press, 1980).

79. Ted Grimsrud and Howard Zehr, "Rethinking God, Justice, and Treatment of Offenders," *Journal of Offender Rehabilitation* 35, nos. 3–4 (2002): 253–79. Tanner, *Economy of Grace*, 63–67, likewise argues against the kind of transactional view of redemption that sees it as a release from God's punishment or Christ's payment for human sin.

80. Grimsrud and Zehr, "Rethinking," 261.

81. Ibid., 256.

82. Ibid., 262.

83. Ibid., 271.

84. Hartman, *Scenes of Subjection*, 127. That Hartman is thinking explicitly about the intellectual history of interest as a construct is indicated by a footnote (236n10) to Hirschman, *The Passions and the Interests*.

85. Hartman, *Scenes of Subjection*, 145.

86. Ibid., 130.

87. Ibid., 145–58. See also Davis, *Are Prisons Obsolete?*

88. Shirley Hollis, "Neither Slave nor Free: The Ideology of Capitalism and the Failure of Radical Reform in the American South," *Critical Sociology* 35, no. 1 (2009): 9–27.

89. Hartman, *Scenes of Subjection*, 142.

90. Ibid., 134.

91. Ibid., 147.

92. Corrections Corporation of America, "Faith-Based Programs": http://www.correctionscorp.com/inmate-services/inmate-reentry-preparation/faith-based-programs; see also http://www.kairostexas.org; Willison, Brazzell, Kim, "Faith-Based Corrections and Reentry Programs."

93. Texas Department of Criminal Justice, "Rehabilitaton Programs Division: The InnerChange Freedom Initiative": https://www.tdcj.texas.gov/divisions/rpd/inner_change.html, emphasis mine.

94. Corrections Corporation of America, "Faith-Based Programs," emphasis mine.

95. Willison, Brazzell, and Kim, "Faith-Based Corrections and Reentry Programs," A-9, Table 6.

96. Erzen, *God in Captivity*, 17–31.

97. Chen, *Animacies*.

98. Ibid., 24–30.

99. Andrew Dilts, *Punishment and Inclusion: Race, Membership and the Limits of American Liberalism* (New York: Fordham University Press, 2014), 170.

100. Gregory J. Seigworth and Matthew Tiessen, "Mobile Affects, Open Secrets, and Global Illiquidity: Pockets, Pools, and Plasma," *Theory, Culture and Society* 29, no. 6 (2012): 47–77.

101. Ibid., 64.

102. Ibid. See also Tonstad, "Debt Time," 436.

103. Seigworth and Tiessen, "Mobile Affects," 64.

104. Ibid., 67.

105. Ibid., 65.

106. Ibid. 98.

107. Patricia Ticineto Clough, *Autoaffection: Unconscious Thought in the Age of Teletechnology* (Minneapolis: University of Minnesota Press, 2000), 99, 105, 129.

108. Andrew Krinks, "Tracing the Theo-logics of Criminalization," *Religion and Incarceration*, March 3, 2015: http://religionandincarceration.com/2015/03/03/tracing-the-theo-logics-of-criminalization/.

109. Christie Thompson, "Do Prison Strikes Work?" *The Marshall Project*, September 21, 2016: https://www.themarshallproject.org/2016/09/21/do-prison-strikes-work#.oKmtfwNKx; E. Tammy Kim, "A National Strike against Prison Slavery," *New Yorker*, October 3, 2016: http://www.newyorker.com/news/news-desk/a-national-strike-against-prison-slavery.

110. Andrea Smith, *Native Americans and the Christian Right: The Gendered Politics of Unlikely Alliances* (Durham, N.C.: Duke University Press, 2008), 37–39; Kay Whitlock and Nancy Heitzeg, "Moneyballing Justice: 'Evidence-Based' Criminal Reforms Ignore Real Evidence," *Truthout*, March 29, 2015: http://www.truth-out.org/news/item/29818-moneyballing-justice-evidence-based-criminal-reforms-ignore-real-evidence; Whitlock, "Faith Inc."; Gilmore, "Worrying State of the Anti-Prison Movement."

111. Patricia Ticineto Clough et al., "Notes Towards a Theory of Affect-Itself," *Ephemera: Theory and Politics in Organization* 7, no. 1 (2007): 60–77. Of note in relation to interest is their observation that "the value of productive activity is no longer found in conscious and calculated intention, but rather in the play of uncertainty and the direct manipulation of affectivity" (74). In other words, radical neoliberalism no longer requires the rational calculating subject of interest.

112. Ibid., 72–73.

113. Ibid., 72.

114. Ibid., 73.

115. Ibid., 67.

116. Ibid., 63.

117. Ibid., 72.

118. Mark Andrejevic, *iSpy: Surveillance and Power in the Interactive Era* (Lawrence: University Press of Kansas, 2007); Jef Huysmans, *Security Unbound: Enacting Democratic Limits* (Hoboken, N.J.: Taylor and Francis, 2014).

119. U.S. Department of Justice, "Koch Pleads Guilty to Covering Up Environmental Violations at Texas Oil Refinery," Press Release, April 9, 2001: https://www.justice .gov/archive/opa/pr/2001/April/153enrd.htm. See also Steven Rosenfeld, "Exposing the Koch Brothers' Stunning Hypocrisy on Criminal Justice Reform," *Alternet*, July 17, 2016: www.alternet.org/election-2016/exposing-koch-brothers-stunning -hypocrisy-criminal-justice-reform; this latter article also accuses them of, at the same time, backing tough-on-crime politicians and policies.

120. Philip Mattera, "Koch Industries: Corporate Rap Sheet," Corporate Research Project: http://www.corp-research.org/koch_industries; Molly Ball, "Do the Koch Brothers Really Care about Criminal-Justice Reform?" *Atlantic*, March 3, 2015: http://www.theatlantic.com/politics/archive/2015/03/do-the-koch-brothers -really-care-about-criminal-justice-reform/386615/.

121. H.R. 4002, 114th Congress. The bill passed through the House Committee on the Judiciary but has since stalled.

122. Matt Apuzzo and Eric Lipton, "Rare White House Accord with Koch Brothers on Sentencing Frays," *New York Times*, November 24, 2015: http://www.nytimes .com/2015/11/25/us/politics/rare-alliance-of-libertarians-and-white-house-on -sentencing-begins-to-fray.html.

123. Criminal Code Improvement Act of 2015, H.R. 4002, 114th Congress: https://www .congress.gov/bill/114th-congress/house-bill/4002/text.

124. Times Editorial Board, "Pass the U.S. Sentencing Reform Bill to Rein in Mass Incarceration," *Los Angeles Times*, February 17, 2016: http://www.latimes.com/opinion/ editorials/la-ed-criminal-justice-20160215-story.html; Lydia Wheeler, "Hatch Wants Additions to Sentencing Reform Bill," *The Hill*, October 22, 2015: http://thehill .com/regulation/legislation/257729-hatch-calls-for-mens-rea-reform-in-sentencing -bill.

  Hatch's own speeches and writing about *mens rea* suggest that he is concerned about the little guy criminalized by unwitting errors; but his environmental example of the janitor who unknowingly rerouted sewage into the storm drain thinking it went into the sewage system (even though by definition storm drains run out to waterways and are strictly regulated) is an indicator of the kind of defense to which *mens rea* requirements might give rise. Orrin Hatch, "It's Time for Criminal Justice, Mens Rea Reform," U.S. Senator Orrin Hatch, September 21, 2015: http://www .hatch.senate.gov/public/index.cfm/2015/9/hatch-it-s-time-for-criminal-justice -mens-rea-reform.

125. I would not advocate incarceration of corporate criminals, but rather steep fines and reparations that reflect and address financially the harm done to communities.

126. CURB, "We Are Not Disposable: The Toxic Impacts of Prisons and Jails" (2016): http://curbprisonspending.org/wp-content/uploads/2016/10/CURB-WeAre NotDisposableReport.pdf; http://lanomorejails.org/2016/01/05/urgent-submit -comment-now-against-proposed-new-la-county-jail/; Sam Stanton and Denny Walsh, "Lawsuits over Valley Fever Pile Up against California's Prison System," *Sacramento Bee*, July 28, 2014: http://www.sacbee.com/news/politics-government/

article2605061.html. *Mother Jones* reports that "for certain racial groups, the risk of contracting disseminated valley fever is much higher. . . . In California, the quirks of valley fever's pathology have collided with the state's habit of jailing a disproportionately large number of black and brown people"; David Ferry, "How the Government Put Tens of Thousands of People at Risk of a Deadly Disease," *Mother Jones*, January/February 2015: http://www.motherjones.com/environment/2015/01/valley-fever-california-central-valley-prison.

127. Chen, *Animacies*, 219.

128. Ibid., 209.

129. Ibid., 217.

130. Ibid., 221.

131. Ibid., 218.

❧ Affective Politics of the Unending Korean War: Remembering and Resistance

WONHEE ANNE JOH

Open grieving is bound up with outrage, and outrage in the face of injustice or indeed of unbearable loss has enormous political potential. . . . Whether we are speaking about open grief or outrage, we are talking about affective responses that are highly regulated by regimes of power and sometimes subject to explicit censorship.
—JUDITH BUTLER, *Frames of War: When Is Life Grievable?*

Theological inquiry . . . bespeaks a deep affective attitude toward a historical process on the part of the human being.
—WALTER BENJAMIN, *The Arcades Project*

The military empire of the United States can be called the "dynamic engine of American history."[1] The Korean War is an important part of this engine of history. To deny this would be to foreclose and also deny that the American military empire is a global and transnational reality across geopolitical space and time. Recognizing the breadth of this spectrum opens spaces for transnational work to address connective sites of transnational histories, which are generated as a result of U.S. imperial militarism across such sites as Laos, Cambodia, Vietnam, the Philippines, Guam, Hawai'i, Okinawa, and numerous others in Asia, West Asia, and the Pacific.[2]

The Korean War, aka the Forgotten War, aka the Unending War, continues to have a hold on geopolitics that connect the United States to many transpacific places but also continues to have an affective hold especially on Koreans. Whether this affective hold is the force of grief without end or intentionally and incrementally circulated terror through political structures that produce anxiety about potential and possible attack any time, it is no wonder that the affective remainders of the Korean War continue to reproduce terror, anxiety, and grief. It is in the best interest of many to keep the theater of this war open-ended. It is ironic that the brief yet brutal civil war in Korea is named The Forgotten War when in reality the war continues with a formal cease-fire for over seventy years. For many the specter of this war continues to haunt and shape everyday life, relations, and even future possibilities. Although many argue that the Cold War ended and we have moved on to another iteration of it in The War on Terror, the U.S. spectral figure of U.S. military desire continues to pivot around Korea. This is most noticeable in the persistent ways that the threat of nuclear war and the theater of its operation centers on North Korea and thus the necessity of the U.S. militarized presence in the Korean peninsula. Although I will not delve further into various ways in which the U.S. media functions to forge a racist caricature of both North and South Korea as either demonic or dependent, the media performs a critical role in forming our affective registers of terror both within the United States and in the Korean peninsula.[3] Here I'm interested in the ways that affective registers like loss and unresolved grief and terror have been accumulating and transforming for over seventy years in Korea because of various ways that the memory of this war continues to circulate not only in the sense of trauma's belatedness but also how it continues to reconstitute itself in ever new forms because this historical and collective trauma had no end. In this sense there is really no "belatedness" since recursive temporality has been the norm. The Korean War, like any war, fits into the definition of trauma as something that exceeds the range of the ordinary, and yet it also fits into the countercritique that trauma is also an experience of the everyday that is endured indefinitely. Traumas of not only having lived through the "scorched earth" policy of the U.S. military during the Korean War but subsequent historical events like the continued dependent relationship with the United States, the continuing presence of U.S. military bases in Korea, with attempts to build additional bases, the attending growth of military camptowns, the continued racial and gendered relations with the United States, the ongoing sense of loss for those who are still separated from families on the other side of the 38th parallel, as well as migration, which is a form of dispossession and loss. The unending Korean War and its recursive affective power of terror and loss are in no sense "belated" even well into its seventieth year since the onset. The traumas of this unending war continue to circulate affects, yet because of its global political position and ties with the United States, there is no end in sight for this war. This war will remain unending as long as the ties with the United States (especially our policy of preemptive strike) continue, and the affective remainders of this war will continue to circulate, congeal, reproduce, and repeat, making any transformation difficult.

I examine why the past is the present for many war generation Koreans but even among later generations who have no firsthand experience of the

Korean War. I argue that the Korean War as the "unending war"—and not as a "forgotten war"—contributes to the notion of affective politics that may cross time and space to possibly birth collaborative solidarity with other sites and collectives who are at the receiving end of U.S militarized terror. There are implications of this for Christian theologians who may reframe narratives of the cross as a site of trauma terror and unending mourning. This offers one way to engage an affective politics for critical theological studies.

This essay engages U.S. militarism by first turning to the context of the Korean War and its ongoing traumatic aftermath. This requires acknowledgment of loss in the postcolonial plight of contemporary Koreans and Korean Americans.[4] Thus, in subsequent sections, I explore that plight and loss with the aid of trauma theory before bridging into key related notions of affect theory (grief, grievability, mourning). This is no mere trafficking in negativity and despair. It is, as Butler writes in the above quote, "to tap the enormous political potential" unlocked by what she also calls "open grieving bound up with outrage, and outrage in the face of injustice."[5] I will also show how a critical Christian theology engaging U.S. militarism can unlock this "enormous political potential" by theorizing the spectral power of the cross in distinctive ways. In this sense, this essay is an exercise in critical Christian theology, and thus is like the "theological inquiry" that Benjamin describes above, one bespeaking "a deep affective attitude toward a historical process." The essay, then, follows an arc of interpretation of the Korean War and its aftermath, to postcolonial perspectives on collective trauma and affective registers like grief, rage, and mourning, and then to the ways a spectral theory of the cross catalyzes resistance to the ways of the U.S. imperial state today.

THE KOREAN WAR AND AFTERMATH

I begin my commentary on the Korean War with a quote from *Ends of Empire* by Jodi Kim: "What does it mean to want to represent or 'remember' a war that has been 'forgotten' and erased in the U.S. popular imaginary, but that has been also trans-generationally seared into the memories of Koreans and Korean Americans, and experienced anew every day in a still divided Korea?"[6] For Kim, the Korean War signals not only the traumas and arbitrary and violent separations of self, family, and state in addition to other forms of loss, but also displays that the Korean War is a problem of "Cold War knowledge that saturates both American nationalist discourse and Korean America's public or 'admitted' knowledge about the conditions of possibility for its very formation in the post-1945 conjuncture."[7] The significance of Kim's analysis of the Korean War is that it surfaces counternarratives, indeed an entire "unsettling hermeneutic of Korean War" that not only shows a naïve retrieval of glorious war memories, but also inscribes an epistemological project that seeks to foreclose knowledge about how Cold War discourse continues U.S. imperial projects. Kim's analysis questions all this, and in so doing reveals a counterimperial narrative that is radically different from the usual Cold War discourse that privileges imperial power.[8]

Because in the United States the Korean War is often "the forgotten war," let us consider some of its basic features. It is estimated that the Korean War resulted in 4 million casualties, of which 2 million were civilians. The numbers are staggering, and they represent a higher percentage of population lost by Koreans than what the United States lost in World War II. Historian Bruce Cumings notes that a total of 36,940 Americans lost their lives in the Korean War. Some 92,134 Americans were wounded in action, and even now more than 8,176 are still reported missing. South Korea sustained 1,312,836 casualties, including nearly a half-million dead. These are in addition to deaths suffered by other United Nations (UN) allies. Estimated North Korean casualties were approximately 2 million, including 1 million civilians and a half-million soldiers. Another 900,000 Chinese soldiers lost their lives in combat.[9] After three years, in 1953, a cease-fire agreement was signed and brought forth the "demilitarized zone" (DMZ) that separates the Koreas as North and South.

Of course, these numbers do not really point to a more holistic picture of who/what was lost as a result of this war. These figures are premised on discrete identifiable figures but do not account for other unseen, unaccounted, and obscured "side-shows." As Viet Thanh Nguyen notes, there are, "human losses, financial costs, and capital gains," and points to ways that a war neither knows nor respects borders and boundaries.[10] No peace treaty has yet been signed, and Korea is technically still in a state of war.[11] It has been over sixty years now and still no end in sight. In the ruins of devastation, unprecedented economic reconstruction, militarized alliances, and compromises have followed. Further, if it is indeed the case that Korea has now become what Kuan-Tsing Chen refers to as a "sub-imperial" nation in Asia ("sub" vis-à-vis the imperial power of the United States), it is crucial that we explore questions of critical memory and works of mourning and the practices of hope that also often have been foreclosed for South Korea which is given this "subimperial" role.[12]

In 2001 I visited Korea and went to the DMZ after twenty-five years in the United States. Little did I realize then that my visit to the DMZ also was an event of witnessing the traumas of the Korean War. As Suk-Young Kim notes, "The zone between two Koreas stands as a monument to stalemate; an anachronism that memorializes not only the prolonged separation of a once-unified nation but also a longing for the lost other half. . . . For both South and North Koreans, one of the reasons the DMZ figures so prominently as national trauma is that so few are able to cross it."[13] In this, the DMZ figures in the lingering war traumas. While distanced by time and space from the Korean War, it became clear in my visceral response that the Korean War and its subsequent aftermath continue to haunt even those whose formation is in the diaspora.[14] Edwidge Danticat's observation accurately describes my own experiences in the United States and in Korea,

> There are many ways that our mind protects us from present and past horrors. One way is by allowing us to forget. Forgetting is a constant fear in any writer's life. For the immigrant writer, from home, memory becomes an even deeper abyss. It is as if we had been forced to step under the notorious forgetting trees, the *sabliyes,* that our slave ancestors were told would remove their past from their heads and dull their desire to return home. We know we must pass under the tree, but we hold our breath and cross our fingers and toes and hope that the forgetting will not penetrate too deeply into our brains.[15]

To return to Korea and find myself at the DMZ was to witness the persistent wounds of the "scorched earth" policy that had been deployed against the land and its peoples during the Korean War. The visit enabled my better understanding of the flight by many South Koreans to the United States, which some people dismiss as simply a matter of pursuing "the American Dream" and fleeing to the "Promised Land."[16] Not only did the policies during the war indiscriminately scorch the land and leave it in "smoldering ruin" by several players[17] and the peoples, but they also left searing marks indicating the legacy of war's afterlife.[18] Affective life shaped by destructions of war haunt even the generations distanced through space and time from that historical event. I will say more about this later.

The aftermath of my experience at the DMZ and its haunting affective remainder continue to allow me to link both the intimate and the familial with political and historical vectors, and to restore connections suspended by time, place. and politics. I understand this familiar memory that circulates in many Korean and Korean American people as "wounded identification" of which Palestinian American scholar Lila Abu-Lughod speaks. This form of "wounded identification" allows me to enter provisionally into not only the world/s of those who directly experienced the Korean War but also the worlds of its aftermath and also the world that I now inhabit.[19] Perhaps it is *because* of my positioning within the diaspora,[20] distanced by time and space from Korea and the Korean War yet living in the heart of the U.S. empire, that it is possible to begin to articulate the complex interaction "between the affects of belonging and the politics of entitlement in a diasporic world, rethinking and retheorizing the complex interactions between loss and reclamation, mourning and repair, departure and return."[21] It is critical for each of us interested in questions of belonging, of roots and routes, to examine the affective aftermath and the continuing effects of the Korean War as well as the continuous and inextricably intimate relation between Korea, the United States, and Korean America. Only then will we be able to create space for the persistent power of nostalgia and the magnetism of the idea of belonging, and even the obsession with roots in relation, always in relation, to its geopolitical historical convergences. Rather, this dual recognition—the war is simultaneously significant but also not exceptional—forges a way toward an ethical commitment that takes seriously the differential effects of war and dispossession, of migration and the new hegemonies and power structures that are "formed within diasporic communities and gendered and raced conceptions of the relationships between routes and roots in the self conception of displaced peoples."[22] To be sure, each and every experience and event of war is specific, brutal, and with incalculable losses that haunt for generations. To say that a particular war was more brutal than another is a disservice to those who experience war's terror. Just as we challenge the oversimplified notion of "oppression hierarchy" we are also called to be mindful that war/s should not be placed in a hierarchy of terror.

So why does the Korean War still matter today? Why should the Korean War still be significant for the work that remains when it comes to war? Perhaps because the Korean War is what really set in motion the Cold War ideology that morphed into the War on Terror. All the while, the division of Korea and the cease-fire still remain. The Korean War, technically, is still the longest war and may provide a critical lens for understanding the dynamic and complex ways that war makes for alliances that are difficult to disentangle. Although for many Americans it is known as the Forgotten War, for Koreans it is known as the Unending War or the Unforgotten War. This war matters because it has not ended and because of the haunting presence as well as the Obama administration's "Pacific Pivot" or "rebalance" strategy toward the Asia-Pacific region. Beginning in the fall of 2011 the Obama administration issued a series of steps to expand and intensify the already significant presence of the United States and explicitly identified the Asia-Pacific as a geostrategic priority for the United States. By 2020, 60 percent of U.S. naval capacity will be based in the Asia-Pacific, where 320,000 U.S. troops are already stationed. The realignment will entail rebuilding and refurbishing former U.S. facilities in the Philippines, placing 2,500 marines in Australia, transferring 8,000 marines and their families from Okinawa to Guam and Hawai'i, and building new installations like the one on the tiny Pacific island of Saipan. Meanwhile, the U.S. military regularly stages massive joint military exercises involving tens of thousands of troops and nuclear-powered aircraft carriers with its key allies and China's neighbors—that is, with Japan and South Korea.[23] While the previous Obama administration passed one of the biggest military spending bills in the history of the United States, our recent witness of the Trump administration's escalation of threat of nuclear war through the fanning of imaginary terror that is North Korea in the minds of many U.S citizens is yet another instance of seeking an even larger increase in the military budget yet again.

Therefore, the Korean War is hardly a discrete event. It is a geographical and historical phenomenon that calls forth a broader perspective, one, I suggest that is provided by postcolonial studies. Let us therefore look more carefully at how a postcolonial paradigm might shift our understanding of collective trauma amid war and its aftermath.

A POSTCOLONIAL PERSPECTIVE ON COLLECTIVE TRAUMA

In taking up a postcolonial approach to collective trauma, I want to first foreground a problem. Too often, trauma theory texts marginalize "the traumatic experiences of non-western cultures, assume the definitions of trauma and recovery that the West has developed are universal and often favor a distinctively modernist form in order to 'bear witness' to trauma."[24] Consider for example the treatment of trauma in the studies by one of trauma theory's founders, Cathy Caruth. In her influential book, Caruth engages trauma studies through discourses of psychoanalysis and deconstruction to argue that extreme events that defy interpretation and understanding can be represented through a textualist approach.[25] As Stef Craps has critiqued, in this approach "textual 'undecideability' or 'unreadability' comes to reflect the inaccessibility of trauma."[26] What this suggests then is that, for many, history and the material conditions that produce collective trauma are elided in favor of the individual who is trapped in the terrors of unspeakable trauma whose response is loss of articulation. There is a sophisticated theorization of trauma with respect to the individual, but what is missing is a careful examination of the broader political matrix of collective trauma produced by historical and material conditions of colonial and imperial power.

What is not brought forth in many trauma studies is its tendency to be discursively preoccupied with, indeed to "screen" or displace and repress, historical pasts like nuclear warfare, the genocide of Native Americans, slavery, segregation and the many wars the United States wages around the world. The neglect of these issues points to an unexamined Eurocentrism in trauma theory, and a Eurocentrism that conflates the West with the world.[27] This means that interpretations of trauma and following diagnoses such as posttraumatic stress disorder (PTSD) are often rooted in an unexamined universalization of modernist Western paradigms and practices. What is direly necessary are ways to distinguish historical and colonial suffering from other structural forms.

Moreover, counternarratives are needed to make sense of the aftermath of militarized violence and trauma. There is nothing self-evident that justifies any attempts to unproblematically transfer Eurocentric definitions and diagnoses of trauma to non-European contexts.[28] Trauma theories and diagnoses like that of PTSD have been universally applied as if there are no differences across time, space, cultures, and traditions.

Those of us working in Western traditions often feel that when there is a wrong or an injury done to another, then a knowable, calculable, and measurable recompense must take place for the sake of justice. However, what we often have not dealt with is the ambiguous and often heavy weight of nonequivalence. As Judith Butler notes, "No utilitarian calculus can supply the measure by which to gauge the destitution and loss of such lives."[29] There are affective remainders that continue to haunt us even when we think that we have achieved justice.[30] There often remains a loss of language in experiences of trauma so deep and so long that it generates a grief that is unconsciously passed on to the next generation. How shall we interpret this work of grief? Grief resulting from war operates not only in individuals but also in the collective and public unconscious. Precluding possibilities of working through legacies of war is a way in which narratives of memories are often constructed from the dominant perspective and not from the perspectives of victims: "Haunted by memories of pain and suffering, post-conflict communities paradoxically search to 'forget' the horror of war while simultaneously becoming emotionally fixated and constituted by it."[31] Many war victims live in a kind of recursive temporality that defers any sense of temporal belatedness that is often necessary to even engage in any form of trauma articulation.

Because of the limitations of early trauma studies, it is better to inscribe both trauma theory and affect theory within a broader postcolonial studies paradigm. Indebted to earlier anticolonial and decolonial movements taking place in the international arena from the early 1950s and '60s, postcolonial theory examined the complex ways that coloniality and decolonial movements were imbricated in various historical trajectories. In many ways postcolonial theory not only attempts to make sense of the persistent colonial divide but also examines various ways that colonial power gets circulated, generated, recuperated, and so regenerates itself. As a political discourse, then, postcolonial theory critiques and problematizes inherent limits and failures of notions that sustain justification for colonial projects such as democracy, justice, freedom, war, civilization, rights, and even salvation. Addressing not only the colonization of lands, material resources, exploitation of peoples, and production of knowledge—to name a few sites of destruction—postcolonial theories of decolonization also name structural and systematized colonization made legible in the interior psychic space of those who come within the reach of the colonizer and his or her world.[32] This aggressive and unavoidably imperial reach also leaves in its wake worlds in ruins. Although the colonial world may have ended, we continue to live in a world shaped and often overdetermined by the myriad of legacies left through histories of colonialism and ongoing imperialism. A most noticeable continuation of this legacy is the global presence of the U.S. military empire. In the ruins of imperial militarism, imperial war leaves its devastation not only in the lands of peoples but also in their psyches.

It may be that affects circulate and produce what Raymond Williams describes as "structures of feeling."[33] These affects include but are not limited to shame, rage, guilt, and grief. The affective registers of militarized trauma produce grief, terror, and deep loss in postcolonial spaces that often are not mourned or remembered. Or as is often the case, what is remembered is yet another management by the state of selective remembering and forgetting. Affects like unmourned grief are unknowingly transmitted to the following generations. Affects are transmitted intergenerationally despite the overwhelming and often misleading belief that "justice" has been rendered and the assumption that grief has been worked through.[34] In the case of South Korea, the state fabricates if not people's outright denial of the ongoing state of war, then at least a perpetual myth that the two Koreas are only in a perpetual mode of cease-fire. This is perhaps why while a sense of loss circulates, as does a certain terror and fear that now congeals as the new norm, persisting more than sixty years since "the cease-fire" and living as part of the ordinary everyday life of Korean peoples. It is to live with the terror of potential war at any time.[35] Viet Than Nguyen's phrase "vertigo of sorrow and longing"[36] expresses powerfully the incredible weight of both sorrow and longing that are borne by so many traumatized people and which they live with and know so intimately. While vertigo is not a diagnosis, it is often common parlance for the loss of equilibrium, where the ground on which one stands is always tilted, if not spinning out of control—a world turned upside down. There is no anchoring or balancing point, but one must learn to ride the waves of spinning and tossing sensations. With affects like sorrow, grief, shame, and rage, there are no beginning and ending points. They continue to stick and build around one and one's relations. Kelly Oliver notes that "affects move between bodies; colonization and oppression operate through depositing the unwanted affects of the dominant group onto those othered." Thus, affects, especially negative affects, get "deposited into the bones" of the oppressed, and here I would add those whose oppression is marked by experiences of trauma.[37] These affects are not linear or singular but constantly and persistently build and morph into other affects. It becomes difficult to know which affect is operative and whence any of them may originate. Affects not only stick to us and travel from person to person but, as they travel, these affects also build intensity.

When affect is understood only as equivalent to the notion of "feeling," then there can simultaneously occur a reification of a false dichotomy that is so beloved by Western modernity, the binary of feelings/emotions and reason. Often the privileging of the latter is taken for granted. However, against this simplifying reification it should be recalled that affects are also sites of knowledge re/productions. Feelings like terror, for example, are not discrete or without rationale. Affects are somatic and thus affect the entire relations of corporeal bodies and are remembered and even transmitted through generations.[38] For example, we are unable to control the way that shame may make us blush or the way that terror makes our bodies clench and tremble. These trembling vibrations travel to touch and cause other bodies to tremble. Affects thus have long-term mental and physical consequences.[39] Grief, when limited to dynamics pertaining only to individuals, may lose a dialectical or recuperative dimension, that enables a community to acknowledge, hold, and build resilience through loss. In contrast, without this dimension, grief is unending.[40]

Although affect circulates and abounds through diverse scenes of trauma and colonial relationality, here I want to specifically argue that colonization as a sustained source of violent forms of domination and conquest produces what many theorists term collective trauma. Whereas trauma that privileges the individual experience of something "outside the range of the ordinary" breaking into the everyday has been the significant focus of much of trauma studies, my approach in this essay requires exploring the collective experience of historical trauma with particular attention to affective registers like grief and the absence of public mourning especially subsequent to historical and collective trauma. I am here more interested in the social dimension of how affects like grief get transformed into the service of further state-sanctioned violence and in the managing of affects after violence as well as in the ways that affects such as grief are denied public consciousness. For example, after the Korean War, affective registers such as grief, sorrow, loss, shame, and terror did not get experienced as discrete and singular but rather as messily congealed with other affects, such as fear and rage. These affects conceal the ways that state violence continues with the public's complicity facilitated by this concealment. State violence, and here I mean both U.S. and Korean state violence, thus, is left unexamined even while it saturates the collective cultural production of memory. To be sure, these affects at work in the public are intentionally harnessed by the state to reinvigorate the official narrative of potential threat of war. This in turn is used to justify U.S. and South Korean military buildup and presence in Korea. This is not to exonerate Koreans only as victims of the state, of their own or that of the United States. Rather, this points to ways that affective politics manage social and collective feelings such as terror and fear. This is especially evident in the continual demonization of

North Korea by the United States and South Korea. It is no surprise in context, then, that collective trauma "depends on collective processes of cultural interpretation."[41] In an era of perpetual unending wars, most especially those waged by the United States through its War on Terror, there is much at stake in attending to ways that grief and other affects (terror, fear, etc.) saturate many communities traumatized by militarized violence.[42]

Exemplary of the more complex ways of attending to grief that are evident in postcolonial theory is Abraham and Torok's work on "trans-generational haunting." They suggest that trauma[43] does not die out with the person who first experienced it.[44] The aftermath of a traumatic event continues to whisper and hover through to the next generation—thus, in me, my family, our families, immigrant communities in the United States—as it seeks/demands suturing, re-membering. The more we maintain silence, the stronger its whispers grow in the next generations. Although Americans think of the Korean War as the "Forgotten War," it is rather an unending war and not forgotten; it cannot be forgotten by Koreans and all those who had been involved in Korea because the specter of the Korean War is felt to be a threat that "some would like to believe is past and whose return it would be necessary again, once again in the future, to conjure away."[45]

In other words, memories have histories. September 1945 marked the beginning of U.S. military occupation of the Korean Peninsula and thus began Korea's entanglement with the United States, which intensified and became increasingly ambiguous during the Korean War and, as Grace Cho notes, "the subordinate relationship to the United States that was generated on the Korean peninsula through war and imperialism laid the ground on which Koreans could participate in the American dream."[46] What is often not mentioned is the fact that the Korean War is what set Korean migration into motion. War's devastation means displacement and dispossession. Terror and trauma and its affective remainder refuse foreclosure but continue to seek and demand redress and justice and do not forget.

Trauma's affective remainder from the Korean War has been transgenerationally seared into our collective psyche. This affective remainder is the unmourned grief that continues to unmoor those who are dispossessed by the traumas of war from each other. Affective registers such as grief articulate the damaged sense of future that peoples who know dispossession know well.[47] Approaching this unmourned grief is the crucial problem with which this essay wrestles toward its conclusion.

UNMOURNED POSTCOLONIAL GRIEF

What and how do we respond and bear witness to the kinds of loss that hunkers down and sits with us? The kind of grief and loss unbearably so heavy that it refuses to lift and dissipate but rather seeps into one's body and leaks into every cell and every minute of one's life? Grief where consciousness floats between reality and illusion, between form and content, incarnated in the body but disincarnating at the same time? The kind of grief that permeates us, to the very edges of everything we see, the bodily movements of everydayness in which feelings are filtered through the weight of a heavy fog of grief. What do we do with grief so heavy with the gravity of its weight pulling and pressing down on one where one cannot do more than lay prostrate under its weight? What and how do we respond theologically to unthinkable imposed suffering that literally takes one's *breath away or takes one into such darkness that one cannot see anything else?* How do we make sense of grief so shattering that language becomes inadequate and all we are left with are aching keens and fragile and unrelenting anguish of both lament and outrage? How are we to understand the melancholic remainder that stays and sticks to our very being?

Militarized violence leaves in its wake pervasive grief that can be transformed into postcolonial "critical melancholia." A critical melancholia that "cannot be seen as good or bad, because affect is not about judgment, even if it is about a form of demand for justice."[48] There is a "critical" maneuver here in that the heavy ache of melancholia, the weight of loss that persists amid and after war, is harnessed as a way to achieve not only survival and persistence in the aftermath of imperial war, but also a kind of resistance. This "critical melancholia" is what is needed to direct our desire for a better world from the aftermath of militarized terror. How might we understand postcolonial melancholia without claiming it in order to overcome it, pass it, and "get over it" but to claim it and work through and stay in it so that such affect might "annul the multitude of losses continually demanded by an unforgiving social world."[49] As Anne Cheng has argued, "'Getting over' something or 'moving on' is itself symptomatic of the culture's [American] attachment to coercive normality."[50] In many cases in Asia where militarized terror has been experienced, it is more often that remembering and working through the experience of terror, loss, and grief have been managed so that it is not remembered but rather forgotten. Memorialization, if it takes place at all, often celebrates state powers' selected narratives of heroism, heroic sacrifices, and benevolence.[51] In the United States such celebrations are usually focused on the supposed benefits of U.S. interventions. In this regard, state memorialization and practices of remembering are often acts of easy forgetting that dismiss or gloss the injustice done. At the very least, this easy forgetting is a preemptive foreclosure of the mourning that is needed. Such foreclosure is often carried out by a state's continual manufacturing of "legitimate" memories that suppress any and all possible counternarratives to the legitimacy of state power. In contrast, we might consider Butler's suggestion that there is something about tarrying with grief that actually helps us transform our sense of vulnerability in relation to others and in relation to the production of cycles of violence. Butler asks, "Is there something to be gained from grieving, from tarrying with grief, from remaining exposed to its unbearability and not endeavoring to seek a resolution for grief through violence?"[52] It is this sense of "tarrying" with grief that I want to recuperate in later sections of this essay through an interpretation of the cross for our neocolonial times. As George Bonanno argues, "When we live with grief we live with dissonance. . . . In the West, where scientific objectivity rules, we tend to recoil at the thought of communing with the dead. Yet, in many regions around the globe, this idea has long been sewn into the very fabric of people's lives."[53] Grief saturates our world today, yet we rush with too much haste to foreclose the possibility of grieving. The state's preemptive foreclosure of mourning unmoors us from one another and leaves unattended the unbearable loss and the pervasive terror that many in the world bear today. It leaves unnamed the losses and injustices that constitute the ruins of the past and makes endurance of our losses and resistance to the state difficult, if not impossible.

Trauma studies in general contend that traumatic experiences are often the type that are uninvited, outside our control, catastrophic, unexpected, sudden, unrecognizable, and impossible to integrate into ordinary systems of meaning and identity. They cannot adequately be put into words and constitute a fundamentally destabilizing event. Thus bearing witness becomes an often ambivalent and complex process that relies much on intensely fractured or fragmented memory. Here, I want us to consider making a postcolonial turn to affect theory to help us revisit our interpretation of the cross through recognition of the powerful affect of grief. My turn to affect theory to supplement postcolonial theory is due heavily to ways in which affect theory takes as a starting point dimensions such as "feelings" that have often been racialized and "stuck" in negative ways to those who have been colonized. In colonial projects, the binary between reason and emotion has been drawn correlating with other binaries such as mind/body, female/male, light/dark, to give few examples. In this regard, then, I find that thus far much of postcolonial theory has neglected serious examination of the role of affects in the de/colonial process and, of course, that decolonial analysis of affects may serve in a wider and deeper breach of imperial subjugation. We may discover that affects may have been put in service to the imperial projects but that affects can also be a powerful liberating force. Conjoining postcolonial theory with affect theory also provides a kind of corrective to affect theory, which, in general, often fails to acknowledge the role of affects in projects of subjugation. We may find that there is significance to trauma's affect of grief as a force generative of hope in the face of sufferings proffered by the countless crosses of then and now.

Although many people use the terms *grief* and *mourning* interchangeably, strictly speaking, they are not the same. Grief refers to the "feelings of sorrow, anger, guilt, and confusion which occur when one experiences the loss of attachment figure," whereas mourning refers to "the culturally constructed social response to the loss of an individual." Grief is a painful emotion that is looking for a cure, whereas mourning is a ritual that "heals" the pain of grief. Peter Homans writes that grief is an emotion; mourning a grief-infused symbolic action.[54] In what follows, which in some ways begins the work of a critical Christian theology against U.S. militarism, I want to put forth a preliminary exploration on grief, grievability, and mourning, by working at the core of Christian remembrance of the crucifixion and interrogating the limits and failures of mourning that its connection with imperialism may have hindered and compromised. I suggest then that the driving force for all postcolonial resistance work should entail learning rituals of mourning to help us face the overwhelming losses and social suffering meted out in our hypermilitaristic neocolonial world. As Butler notes, "If we are interested in arresting cycles of violence to produce less violent outcomes, it is no doubt important to ask what, politically, might be made of grief besides a cry for war."[55] Moreover, to Christians specifically located with the Western tradition that have also been aligned with projects of colonization, we can be challenged to ask the following: Is grief for us also regulated so much so that we often grieve only for those who are "like us" but do not extend the same grieving or even recognize the grievability of those constructed to be "unlike" us according to the various framing operations in structures of domination? Or as Nguyen frames this, might it be possible to engage in a kind of just memory in which our remembering is inclusive of others, even our enemies? Is it possible to grieve and remember not only ours but others so that there is an "ethics of remembering one's own or remembering others."[56] Butler argues that in today's world even affects are regulated to such an extent that our sense of horror and of outrage in the face of suffering and loss do not run equally for and on behalf of everyone. In fact, because our apprehensions of the world are constructed for us, it is inevitable that our feelings of loss, despair, empathy, and outrage are only directed against a particularly recognizable people who are "like us" while these affects are preemptively closed to those who are apprehended as the "other." Thus, we need ask why the moral horror in the face of violence and loss is differentially experienced.

One way to destabilize the now very familiar interpretation of the cross as a singular event that displaces all other experiences of suffering and loss then and now is to reframe the focus from one singular individual to encompass a broader experience of social suffering. An interpretation of suffering and loss as always already within the matrix of the social allows us to redress the social memory that grief often generates. By expanding and reframing the scene of the cross, we have a broader picture of not only the direct victims of those who suffered torture and terror but also those who participated in carrying out the mandates of the empire as well as those who can make claims to eyewitness status or from a distance and merely heard of what took place. All experienced the overflow of social affect that generates both outrage and grief. So let us look more closely at potential reframing of the scene of the cross.

AT THE CROSS: TRAUMA, TERROR, GRIEF, AND MOURNING

"The central symbol of Christianity is the figure of a tortured man," so writes biblical scholar Stephen Moore.[57] Many scholars from Josephus to Cicero to Martin Hengel note just how horrific and wretched it was to die on the cross. According to Hengel, "Crucifixion was a punishment in which the caprice and sadism of the executioners were given full rein."[58] After going through the many gruesome technologies deployed while one is killed on the cross, Hengel notes that "the earliest Christian message of the crucified messiah demonstrated the 'solidarity' of the love of God with the unspeakable suffering of those who were tortured and put to death by human cruelty."[59] That this cruel mode of execution was a political act of an imperial and dominative state makes the cross a crucial starting place for critical Christian theologies engaging U.S. militarism in Asia or elsewhere.

There are many interpretations of the cross, however, that more particularly turn our gaze away from the horror on the cross. Thus we endorse the much easier alibi of God's love. The most familiar interpretation we have learned is that all this suffering finds equivalence and even justice because God's love exceeds the expanse and depth of suffering, especially that caused by human cruelty evidenced on the cross.

Prominent interpretations of both Abelard's moral exemplar theory of atonement and also of Anselm's theory of satisfaction turn their gaze away from the site of the tortured body, and then they also skitter away from those who witness its slow death and horror. Their gaze and thus our gaze for too long have been directed upward to a God's love that is expected to right the wrongs of such human cruelty. Perhaps the cross bears witness to human capacity for cruelty to another, but God's love neither condones nor stands as alibi to human capacity to impose suffering on another. Mixed with the horrific technology that carries out the tortuous public killing on the cross, I want to call our attention, particularly, to the affect of grief that hovers and thickly saturates the scene of the execution. There is some evidence of rituals of mourning by the tortured body on the cross as well as by those who bear witness to it from near and afar.[60]

What might it mean for us to turn our gaze straight into the horror of what happened before, during, and after the crucifixion and recognize that perhaps while not valorizing suffering in and of itself, such horrific suffering needed to be redeployed. Theorist Rey Chow notes:

> To the Roman officials in occupied Judea, the execution of a political dissenter such as Jesus, too, probably meant little more than the routine extermination of "lice," but for the followers of Christianity, that execution (together with its iconic instrument, the cross) has carried a definitive symbolic significance of sacrifice over the centuries. For these followers, it is the subject that bears the cross, rather than the subject that has been crossed out, that remains noteworthy.[61]

In Chow's take, a suffering subject cannot be glossed, "crossed" out by some other message of "God's love," "divine forgiveness," and so on.

The slow tortuous killing on the cross was one that not only Jesus but countless others before, after, and alongside him experienced. While the numbers make it seem as if dying on the cross might have been "normal" and "routine," we know from historians that such was not the case. Dying on the cross was preserved for a class of people who may have had absolutely no status and sovereign power. However, while their bodies had no value and could thus be easily subjected to one of the most humiliating and painful deaths, it was a form of death that extracted the maximum surplus value in producing terror for all from the perspective of the empire.[62] Again, this makes the cross a key discursive site in a critical Christian theology that arises from the ruins of U.S. imperial wars and empire.

Thus, dying on the cross, or rather getting publicly tortured to a slow death caused lasting trauma to those who bore witness to the event. Jesus' event of torture by crucifixion, any torture, is not just an event for that individual subject. It is a collective subjectivity we must examine. But if, indeed, as Butler notes in the beginning epigraph, "Open grieving is bound up with outrage, and outrage in the face of injustice or indeed of unbearable loss has enormous political potential. Whether we are speaking about open grief or outrage, we are talking about affective responses that are highly regulated by regimes of power and sometimes subject to explicit censorship," is it possible that our open grieving as well as our outrage as affective responses have been censored and regulated by the regimes of power now, just as then in Jesus' time? If open grief and outrage against unbearable loss have political and thus theological potential to transform our world, how might we interpret the cross so that it continues to be the affective space that allows for both grief and outrage? In a world fraught with unbearable grief, what might the Christian tradition offer by way of intersubjective mourning so that we may work through our grief? My focus in this essay has been to examine historical and collective trauma in the case of the Korean War. By doing so, I underscore the significance of collective working through grief and the process of mourning for any work of mourning to be possible. Collective trauma is different from discrete traumas, but rather its composition is grounded in entangled affects that are often knotted up, and the possibility of unknotting congealed and congested traumatic affects is only possible through collective and communal rituals of mourning. Because we are focused on collective historical trauma, any work of mourning must be relational, collective, communal, and intersubjective. In this regard then, Christianity as a tradition rooted in notions of the communal and the collective offers ways for the community to work through grief and mourning together.

CONCLUSION: THE SPECTER OF THE CROSS

I provide here one example of what I mean by reframing our tendency to connect the cross with one singular individual to a more social experience of suffering as well as social memory.[63] My example comes from Nancy Pineda-Madrid's work on the suffering of women, known as femicide in Ciudad Juárez, Mexico, just across the border from El Paso, Texas. While not the DMZ of Korea, Ciudad Juárez/El Paso is yet another borderland fraught with traumas of militarization, state-terror, and gendered violence.[64] Pineda-Madrid writes, "The cross signals a past event, the execution of Jesus, that participants claim holds meaning for them now. It is a central symbol in the life of this gathered community—the event of Jesus and the contemporary execution of Juárez's daughters are linked in the use of this symbol."[65]

This too resonates with Kathleen Corley's work on funerary rituals in the early Christian movements. Corley's work examines the ways in which early followers of Jesus may have followed their elaborate funerary rituals to do the work of mourning with and on behalf of the loss experienced by their communities. However, later resurrection theologies tended to gloss over and even erase the work of lamentation that may have been done by mostly women to help their communities remember the loss of loved ones, as Corley notes that it was women's funerary rituals, or the cult of the dead, "that created community by creating continuity with the living and the deceased, in this case, Jesus. Jesus became the special dead of the community whose presence was memorialized and felt in women's and ordinary people's mortuary and meals and laments."[66] When we put Corley and Pineda-Madrid in conversation, we can do the work of reframing that I mentioned earlier. Notably as the mourning rituals allowed for the process of grieving through remembrance of the loved one, Pineda-Madrid's work with women of Ciudad Juárez clearly shows that the slain daughters too are like Jesus, who draws forth from us both wails of grief and shouts of outrage that such unthinkable acts take place and without the state being able or willing to hold the perpetrators accountable. What is particularly crucial, as Pineda-Madrid shows, is that both the grief and the rage draw forth, too, expression in collective action and organizing by the surviving women for redressive action for the whole of the community. Thus, resurrection in this rising resistance from ruin is evident again.[67]

In thinking of the cross for our neocolonial times, I fear that not much has changed since the Roman Imperial powers executed Jesus to the neoliberal militarized economic engines that solicit degradation and rage that target women in Ciudad Juárez and elsewhere around the world. If we juxtapose the tortured death of the one we have as the central figure of our belief and practices alongside the deaths of women of Ciudad Juárez as one example, Christians must grapple with disturbing and urgent questions: What experiences of suffering are differentially interpreted? Whose bodies really count? Whose sufferings elicit outrage and grief, and whose do not? What theological understanding of being human must be reimagined so that "their" suffering becomes our suffering? How do we theologically understand that the Jesus who ends up on the cross does so precisely because of his affect/ion for the world and for those who suffer with unbearable grief, loss, and outrage after his crucifixion?

Neither in Jesus nor in those who witnessed the vulnerable exposure to death of many in their communities do we find the violative tendencies toward a repressive amnesia. Those who know the terror and trauma of crosses strewn around this world, then and now, know them not simply as implements of torture and trauma, but as specters, continuing to haunt us, generating mourning and a critical melancholia that can produce resistance and counterimperial faith. They return always seeking and demanding that their suffering be remembered, be properly mourned, and that outrage on their behalf is never too late. As Derrida so aptly notes, "In this mourning work in process, in this interminable task, the ghost remains that which gives one the most to think about—and to do. . . . A ghost never dies, it remains always to come and to come-back."[68] The postcolonial spectrality of the cross haunts our time for the times to come, in which we recognize that we are always already vulnerable and undone in the face of the suffering other. In the ruins of colonial and neocolonial death-dealing projects, affects such as grief exceed our attempt to control, regulate, or discipline.

As I wrote in an earlier work, *The Heart of the Cross: A Postcolonial Christology*, there is another "cross"—a torturous yet also spectral border where pain and hope cross, as for Pineda-Madrid in Ciudad Juárez traumatized at the borderline of U.S. imperial, economic, and misogynous hegemony. In

Heart of the Cross, I stood and reflected at the DMZ, where U.S.-backed South Korea borders a demonized North Korea, cycling and recycling a lament and rage among peoples in Korea and which continues intergenerationally into Korean Americans in the United States Yet as I showed in that book, our thinking and feeling from the Korean DMZ—another *es una herida abierta,* "open wound," as Gloria Anzaldúa called the U.S./Mexican border—can generate hope and resistance.[69] The Korean War as the Unending War swings our attention back again to the ongoing effects of both trauma and mourning. That as the war is considered unending, so too is trauma unending and mourning impossible to reach completion. Rather, mourning is perpetual as long as the Korean War continues. It is not only unending affectively but in terms of war policy, Korea is still at a "cease-fire," which means it has been in the state of war for over seventy years to this day. For a collective to live a sustained war for over seven decades is to live with the terrors of war as a normalized condition. Living with the sustained and messy reality that is an "open wound" for a collective means that the conditions of possibility for a life beyond and through trauma is to live with a perpetually deferred sense of hope that is still to come. A hope that is against the hopelessness of living in the state of perpetual war.

For Christians, the cross becomes a critical memory, giving evidence for the spheres of the affective in transforming this world, a world that extracts a "multitude of losses continually demanded by an unforgiving social world."[70] If affect is "sticky" and is what "sticks," then grief and love "stick" intimately.[71] To struggle with grief and let grief bring forth lament and outrage is to be stuck to "love [that] is to struggle, beyond solitude, with everything in the world that can animate existence."[72] For communities living within intimate proximity to historical traumas without end, it may be that crucifixion as well as the hope and reality of resurrection are not two discrete states but rather intricately and inevitably woven together. Perhaps living with unending grief is only possible when living with an even stronger sense, perhaps of hope/threat of resurrection every day.

NOTES

A brief portion of this essay was previously published as "Grief and Grievability: A Postcolonial Spectrality of the Cross," in *Concilium: International Journal of Theology* 2 (Spring 2013): 41–50.

1. Quoted in Maria Höhn and Seungsook Moon, eds., *Over There: Living with U.S. Military Empire from World War Two to the Present* (Durham, N.C.: Duke University Press, 2010), 4.
2. Cf. Catherine Lutz, ed., *The Bases of Empire: The Global Struggle against U.S. Military Posts* (New York: New York University Press, 2009).

3. See Jodi Kim, *Ends of Empire: Asian American Critique of the Cold War* (Minneapolis: University of Minnesota Press, 2010); Chandon Reddy, *Freedom with Violence: Race, Sexuality, and the U.S. State* (Durham, N.C.: Duke University Press, 2011); and Suk-Young Kim, *DMZ Crossing: Performing Emotional Citizenship along the Korean Border* (New York: Columbia University Press, 2014).

4. Much evidence shows that the phenomenal economic growth of Korea is significantly connected to Korea's relation with the United States. Moreover, this relationship is built on mutual militarized desires for not only economic growth but also regional dominance. However, there are fault lines and noticeable points of overreach that are presently evidenced in such works as Jesook Moon, *South Koreans in the Debt Crisis: The Creation of a Neoliberal Welfare Society* (Durham, N.C.: Duke University Press, 2009). See also Katharine H. S. Moon, *Protesting America: Democracy and the U.S.–Korea Alliance* (Los Angeles: University of California Press, 2012).

5. Judith Butler, *Frames of War: When Is Life Grievable?* (New York: Verso, 2009), 39.

6. Kim, *Ends of Empire*, 34. For Kim, "The Korean War appears not simply as a congealed historical episode that is given narrative form after-the-event, but also as a Cold War epistemology in the making." Foremost in this structuring narrative is the production and invention of North Korea.

7. Ibid., 145.

8. Ibid.

9. Bruce Cumings, *The Korean War: A History* (New York: Random House, 2010), 35.

10. Viet Thanh Nguyen, *Nothing Ever Dies: Vietnam and the Memory of War* (Cambridge, Mass.: Harvard University Press, 2016), 7.

11. Of course, this list of deaths does not include other aspects of war's aftermath in Korea such as the deployment of Koreans in the Vietnam War, the growth of military camptowns, and the shadow cast even over the Pacific to the Korean diaspora in the United States. It also does not include the aftermath of war and the emergence of transnational adoption, and because the war did not end and U.S. militarism has continued to be present over six decades, we need to examine another phenomenon, that is, intergenerational circulations of U.S. military soldiers deployed to Korea.

12. Cf. Kuan-Hsing Chen, *Asia as Method: Toward Deimperialization* (Durham, N.C.: Duke University Press, 2010), 63–65.

13. Kim, *DMZ Crossing*, 7.

14. Cf. Michael Rothberg, *Multidirectional Memory: Remembering the Holocaust in the Age of Decolonization* (Stanford, Calif.: Stanford University Press, 2009), 5. Rothberg offers a critique of competitive memory as a "notion of the public sphere as a pre-given, limited space in which already-established groups engage in a life and death struggle." Rothberg proposes instead memory's multidirectionality as "a malleable discursive space in which groups do not simply articulate established positions but actually come into being through their dialogical interactions with others."

15. Edwidge Danticat, *Create Dangerously* (Princeton, N.J.: Princeton University Press, 2010), 65.

16. Ji-Yeon Yuh, *Beyond the Shadow of Camptown: Korean Military Brides in America* (New York: New York University Press, 2002), 37. Not only did the Korean War set in motion the flight of Koreans to the United States, Latin America, and elsewhere, but it also set in motion local economic dependence in its direct relationships with, for example, military camptowns: "The U.S. military presence in South Korea has meant, for example, that whole towns have grown economically dependent on the local U.S. military base, their fortunes waxing and waning with the size of the troops. In short, towns such as Uijeongbu, Songtan are economically dependent on decisions made thousands of miles away by the leaders of a foreign country."

17. For an excellent analysis of various American wars and what he terms as the epistemology of war, see an important work by John Tirman, *The Death of Others: The Fate of Civilians in America's Wars* (Oxford: Oxford University Press, 2010), 91.

18. Cf. Bruce Cumings, *Dominion from Sea to Sea: Pacific Ascendancy and American Power* (New Haven, Conn.: Yale University Press, 2009).

19. For more in-depth discussion on "vicarious trauma" and "empty empathy," see E. Ann Kaplan, *Trauma Culture: The Politics of Terror and Loss in Media and Literature* (New Brunswick, N.J.: Rutgers University Press, 2005). Kaplan notes that there are degrees, spheres, and different positions through which trauma is experienced across time and space.

20. Memory and collective memory, over time and across space, undergo sedimentation and re-presentations and are reconstituted during different times. Cf. Ron Eyerman, *Cultural Trauma: Slavery and the Formation of African-American Identity* (Cambridge: Cambridge University Press, 2001). See also Alison Landsberg, *Prosthetic Memory: The Transformation of American Remembrance in the Age of Mass Culture* (New York: Columbia University Press, 2004), 25: "Prosthetic memories are those not strictly derived from a person's own lived experience. Prosthetic memories circulate publicly, and although they are not organically based, they are nevertheless experienced with a person's body as a result of an engagement with a wide range of cultural technologies. Prosthetic memories thus become part of one's personal archive of experience, informing one's subjectivity as well as one's relationship to the present and future tenses." Cf. Maurice Halbwachs, *On Collective Memory* (Chicago: University of Chicago Press, 1992).

21. Marianne Hirsch and Nancy K. Miller, eds., *Rites of Return: Diaspora Poetics and the Politics of Memory* (New York: Columbia University Press, 2011), 5.

22. Ibid., 6.

23. http://kpolicy.org/open-fire-and-open-markets-the-asia-pacific-pivot-and-trans-pacific-partnership/: "'The hidden hand of the market,' as *New York Times* columnist Thomas Friedman famously wrote in the 1990s, 'will never work without a hidden fist.' The Asia-Pacific Pivot, a one-two neoliberal-militaristic punch, packs both." Accessed September 20, 2015.

24. Gert Buelens, Sam Durrant, and Robert Eaglestone, *The Future of Trauma Theory: Contemporary Literary and Cultural Criticism* (New York: Routledge, 2014), 5.

25. Cathy Caruth, *Unclaimed Experience: Trauma, Narrative, and History* (Baltimore: Johns Hopkins University Press, 1995).

26. Stef Craps, "Beyond Eurocentrism: Trauma Theory in the Global Age," in *The Future of Trauma Theory: Contemporary Literary and Cultural Criticism*, ed. Gert Buelens, Sam Durrant, and Robert Eaglestone (New York: Routledge, 2014), 45.

27. For an excellent and one of the most carefully researched and crafted critiques of Eurocentrism as part of the very structure of the discourse that is trauma studies in general, see Stef Craps, *Postcolonial Witnessing: Trauma Out of Bounds* (New York: Palgrave Macmillan, 2013).

28. Ibid., 48. See also Ethan Waters, *Crazy Like Us: The Globalization of the American Psyche* (New York: Free Press, 2010).

29. Butler, *Frames of War*, 54.

30. Ranjana Khanna, *Algeria Cuts: Women and Representation, 1830–Present* (Stanford, Calif.: Stanford University Press, 2008). In her interrogation of postcolonial Algeria, Khanna offers a critical insight perhaps even for Korea. Her insight is that justice for trauma's "inassimilable remainders" must be sought outside the mechanisms of "virile wars" (242).

31. Emma Hutchinson and Roland Bleiker, "Grief and Transformation of Emotions after War," in *Emotions, Politics and War*, ed. Linda Ahall and Thomas Gregory (New York: Routledge, 2015), 210.

32. I do not examine here the ways that the individual as part of the traumatized collective manages unmourned grief and loss, but suffice it to say that one significant area that needs further critical interrogation is that of the sustained collective culture of addiction. Addiction becomes a collective effort to manage pain and loss for many who have experienced collective historical sense of loss and suffering. Cf. Angela Garcia, *The Pastoral Clinic: Addiction and Dispossession along the Rio Grande* (Los Angeles: University of California Press, 2010).

33. Raymond Williams, *Marxism and Literature* (Oxford: Oxford University Press, 1977), 128–35.

34. Cf. Teresa Brennan, *The Transmission of Affect* (Ithaca, N.Y.: Cornell University Press, 2004). Also, David Eng writes, "Historical traumas of loss, grief, and forgetting are passed down from one generation to another unconsciously" (*The Feeling of Kinship: Queer Liberalism and the Racialization of Intimacy* [Durham, N.C.: Duke University Press, 2010], 167).

35. The way that Koreans have lived in a state of terror and perpetual readiness for the breakout of another war has become a way of life for them. In fact, one may say that it is like living in fear of a potential breakout of terror in a domestic violence context. One is trapped in a scene without end, and thus problematic modes of survival become the new normal.

36. Viet Thanh Nguyen, *The Sympathizer* (New York: Grove Press, 2015).

37. Kelly Oliver, *The Colonization of Psychic Space: A Psychoanalytic Social Theory of Oppression* (Minneapolis: University of Minnesota Press, 2004), xix.

38. For more on how the body becomes the site of memory, see Bessel van der Kolk, *The Body Keeps the Score: Brain, Mind, and Body in the Healing of Trauma* (New York: Penguin Books, 2014).

39. Cf. Arthur W. Frank, *The Wounded Storyteller: Body, Illness, and Ethics* (Chicago: University of Chicago Press, 1995). Also see Arthur Kleinman, *The Illness Narratives: Suffering, Healing, and the Human Condition* (New York: Basic Books, 1988).

40. Eugenia Brinkema, *The Forms of the Affects* (Durham, N.C.: Duke University Press, 2014). For Brinkema, whose focus is on individual loss, grief names "that which resists the relational dimension of loss; the form for that suffering of a general economy in which not everything can be made to mean and things escape systematically without return, labor guarantees no profit. Grief resists mediation and ongoing processual struggle. It takes a different form altogether, and it is undialectical" (71).

41. Jeffrey C. Alexander, *Trauma: A Social Theory* (New York: Polity Press, 2012), 3.

42. For explorations in ways that neoliberal capitalism works against memory and remembering either through erasure or commodification, see various essays in Michael O'Loughlin, ed., *The Ethics of Remembering and the Consequences of Forgetting* (New York: Rowman & Littlefield, 2015).

43. In locating sustained structural trauma as another form of trauma distinct from a singular traumatic event, Dominick LaCapra explores the various ways that understanding a singular event as definitive of trauma needs to be challenged. Dominick LaCapra, *Writing History, Writing Trauma* (Baltimore: Johns Hopkins University Press, 2001). In much of trauma studies, "trauma" has been defined as the event that is beyond the experience of everyday life. A trauma then is an extraordinary event in which the ordinary is breached. However, there are scholars now who offer critiques of this by arguing that some traumas cannot be encapsulated into a singular historical event. A trauma can be a sustained way in which the everyday and the ordinary are violated, as in the reality that many women live within a reality that is saturated with gender-based violence. Many others live with racialized forms of violence that have become routine and the norm that defines and shapes everyday life.

44. Cf. Nicolas Abraham and Maria Torok, *The Shell and the Kernel* (Chicago: University of Chicago Press, 1994).

45. Jacques Derrida, *Specters of Marx: The State of the Debt, the Work of Mourning, and the New International* (New York: Routledge, 1994), 48.

46. Grace M. Cho, *Haunting the Korean Diaspora: Shame, Secrecy, and the Forgotten War* (Minneapolis: University of Minnesota Press, 2008), 13.

47. Judith Butler writes that the "predicament of being moved by what one sees, feels, and comes to know is always one in which one finds oneself transported elsewhere, into another scene, or into a social world in which one is not the center. And this form of dispossession is constituted as a form of responsiveness that gives rise to action and resistance" (*Dispossession: The Performative in the Political: Conversations with Athena Athanasiou* [New York: Polity Press, 2013], viii). How then do those in cultures that uphold the idea of the sovereign self become dispossessed of the sovereign self and enter into forms of collectivity that oppose forms of dispossession that systematically exclude and atomize populations and peoples from collective belonging and justice?

48. Ranjanna Khanna, "Concluding Remarks: Hope, Demand, and the Perpetual," in *Unconscious Dominions: Psychoanalysis, Colonial Trauma, and Global Sovereignties*, ed. Warwick Anderson, Deborah Jenson, and Richard C. Keller (Durham, N.C.: Duke University Press, 2011), 257.

49. David L. Eng and Shinhee Han, "A Dialogue on Racial Melancholia," in *Loss: The Politics of Mourning*, ed. David L. Eng and David Kazanjian (Los Angeles: University of California Press, 2003), 366.

50. Anne Anlin Cheng, *The Melancholy of Race: Psychoanalysis, Assimilation and Hidden Grief* (Oxford: Oxford University Press, 2001), 95.

51. Cf. Erika Doss, *Memorial Mania: Public Feeling in America* (Chicago: University of Chicago Press, 2010).

52. Judith Butler, *Precarious Life: The Powers of Mourning and Violence* (New York: Verso, 2004), 30.

53. George A. Bonanno, *The Other Side of Sadness: What the New Science of Bereavement Tells Us about Life after Loss* (New York: Basic Books, 2009), 203.

54. Peter Homans, Introduction to *Symbolic Loss: The Ambiguity of Mourning and Memory at Century's End*, ed. Peter Homans (Charlottesville: University Press of Virginia, 2000), 2.

55. Butler, *Precarious Life*, xii.

56. Nguyen, *Nothing Ever Dies*, 12.

57. Stephen Moore, *God's Gym: Divine Male Bodies of the Bible* (New York: Routledge, 1996), 4.

58. Martin Hengel, *Crucifixion* (Minneapolis: Fortress Press, 1997), 87.

59. Ibid., 88.

60. Kathleen E. Corley, *Maranatha: Women's Funerary Rituals and Christian Origins* (Minneapolis: Fortress Press, 2010).

61. Rey Chow, *The Age of the World Target: Self-Referentiality in War, Theory, and Comparative Work* (Durham, N.C.: Duke University Press, 2006), 86.

62. For more detailed discussions on the spectacle of torture and killings as terrorizing forms of regulation, discipline, and punishment, see D. G. Kyle, *Spectacles of Death in Ancient Rome* (London: Routledge, 1998); also, Richard A. Horsley, "Prominent Patterns in the Social Memory of Jesus and Friends," in *Memory, Tradition, and Text: Uses of the Past in Early Christianity*, ed. Alan Kirk and Tom Thatcher (Atlanta, Ga.: Society of Biblical Literature, 2005).

63. Cf. Alan Kirk, "Social and Cultural Memory," in *Memory, Tradition, and Text*.

64. Kathleen Staudt and Zulma Y. Mendez, *Courage, Resistance, and Women in Ciudad Juárez: Challenges to Militarization* (Austin: University of Texas Press, 2015).

65. Nancy Pineda-Madrid, *Suffering and Salvation in Ciudad Juárez* (Minneapolis: Fortress Press, 2011), 134.

66. Corley, *Maranatha*, 133.

67. On affective labor of women as a form of biopolitical labor for producing social relations of life, see Michael Hardt and Antonio Negri, *Commonwealth* (Cambridge, Mass.: Harvard University Press, 2009), 131–47.

68. Derrida, *Specters of Marx*, 123.

69. Gloria Anzaldúa, *Borderlands/La Frontera: A New Mestiza* (San Francisco: Aunt Lute Books, 1987), 25.

70. Eng and Han, "A Dialogue on Racial Melancholia," 362–63.

71. Sara Ahmed, "Happy Objects," in *The Affect Theory Reader*, ed. Melissa Gregg and Gregory J. Seigworth (Durham, N.C.: Duke University Press, 2010), 29.

72. Alain Badiou, *In Praise of Love* (New York: New Press, 2012), 104.

❧ Weeping by the Water: Hydraulic Affects and Political Depression in South Korea after *Sewol*

DONG SUNG KIM

*Our bodies and lives are almost a kind of resonating chamber for media-borne
perturbations that strike us and run through us, that strike us and strike beyond us
simultaneously.*
—BRIAN MASSUMI, *Politics of Affect*

By the rivers of Babylon—there we sat down and there we wept. . . .
—PSALM 137:1 (NRSV)

CAN THE SUBMARINE SPEAK? *CAN I WRITE?*

Writing about an event at a place distant from its occurrence, for which the
proximity of the writer or the reader is not warranted, is perhaps an unsafe
thing to do.[1] Gayatri Chakravorty Spivak's poignant question "Can the subaltern speak?" has obstinately challenged the Euro-American academy to
be ethically sensitive to the politics of representation in speaking of others'
disenfranchised positions.[2] This representational concern demands that one
avoid historicizing and totalizing an event, predicament, or atrocity with one's
own perspective, especially when there is geopolitical and cultural distance
between the event and the discourse. Although I am nationally and ethnically
identified as South Korean, the geographical and cultural distance that has
opened up between myself and South Korea during my sojourn in the United
States is neither ignorable nor erasable. My discursive claim to *Sewol* might
take over a space that belongs to the ones who are much more closely affected
by the event.[3] Hence, on this occasion, I feel that what I would like to share
might be much better articulated by others who lived through the pain of the
event more directly.

Moreover, it appears unfeasible in the present moment, or too soon, for
anyone to tell a full-dress story about what happened in and after *Sewol*.
Chronological formulae such as "what happened is X, Y, and then Z" would

reduce the inarticulable event into a singular narrative with artificial closure.[4] *Sewol* is still an ongoing tragic event in South Korea with many questions left unanswered and uninvestigated. The public viewers of the event have been provided with too many conflicting and manipulative stories and reports by government officials and media establishments. For such disturbing reasons, writing about the *Sewol* event is an impossible project for me.

However, it is also impossible not to write about it. The circulated feeling of pain in the public mind refuses both erasure/forgetfulness and closure/ending of the story. The *Sewol* event urges me to write about it, but, simultaneously, it instantly steals the words from my mind, forbidding any forms of description, translation, and representation. Can the submarine speak? The submarine subjects invoked by this question are none other than the drowned victims of *Sewol* themselves. However, their affective lives continue and expand beyond their submergence. The submarine ghosts cannot speak, but they still howl, haunt, and make demands on us in ways that are impossible within the secularized modern definitions of history.[5] To write or not to write . . . ? Caught between the prompting and halting forces of the traumatic event, writing *Sewol* becomes an experience of being haunted.

Writing is an affective practice. It is "affective" in the sense that it begins with an experience of being affected. Writing—conventionally understood as an abstract, cognitive, and reasonable process that is an *ex-pression* of one's interior and immaterial ideas—can be defined, differently, as an outcome of reactive resonance and bodily response (at the level of sensation) to the exterior forces (or *im-pressions*)[6] of one's surroundings. Maia Kotrosits makes a similar point in regard to the bodily susceptibility of knowledge and knowing.

> "Affect" means being *affected*; it suggests being touched, moved. It implies less some kind of internal, personal experience than relationality, physicality, and susceptibility. . . . Even the baldest of facts can be undone by a notion that it just "doesn't feel right," and we may or may not be able to say what exactly about it doesn't quite feel right. In those moments we are forced to encounter the contingencies of our knowing, and it is no coincidence that what *feels* right or wrong is often the kind of knowing most vigorously defended.[7]

The susceptibility of one's knowledge—and the act of knowing—to the surrounding world intimates not only a relational epistemology, but it also suggests that our lives and bodies, in general, are more open to the world than we customarily think. To repeat the first epigraph of this essay: "Our bodies and lives are almost a kind of resonating chamber." If so, we may think of writing as born out of the vibrant resonance of that chamber.

One of the provocative characteristics of the recent theorists of affect and emotion is the turn to the personal and the corporeal, in terms of both the content and style of their writing. Traditionally, academic writing has been considered a different category from other genres of writing, often deemed an intellectual practice with little interest in "writing" per se. As Elspeth Probyn aptly remarks, it appears that most "academic writers do not aspire to be writers."[8] Affect theory interrogates this boundary between research-writing and writing.[9] In her view, writing as an affective and corporeal practice "reworks" our understanding of the body and its relation to the surrounding world.[10] Likewise, Sara Ahmed names her work a "contact writing."[11] In this definition, she suggests that her writing is populated with "everyday forms of contact," including her personal experiences and feelings.[12] It does not simply mean that her feeling is *in* her writing, but the writing/feeling—as a contact zone—shapes *her* and her surroundings.[13] In other words, writing can affect, shape, and transform our bodies and its ways of connection to the social world, that is, other bodies—even or especially when they are submarine bodies submerged in tragedy.

WRITING *SEWOL*, FEELING THE IRREPARABLE

Sewol is the name of the ferry that sank into the water on the 16th day of April 2014, but the name has been turned into a culturally haunting buzzword. The word presses and shakes the body that it gets into. In this regard, I consider *writing Sewol* a bodily and affective response to what the word virulently and violently disseminates in its affectation. The perturbation of emotion and sensation *strikes* my body and *strikes beyond* it, spilling its effects in the form of ink on paper, which profoundly changes the way I understand the relations between my body and that of the submarine.

In my writing that follows, I hope to theorize my experience of being haunted by the event of *Sewol*, interrogating its affective meanings in and beyond the political and religious contexts that I inhabit. Specifically, the ground on which I would like to begin is my personal and embodied reactions to the event. In this regard, I am again reminded by Ahmed and Massumi that emotions are not the products of the interiority of my Self, but they are actually the effects of social distribution and circulation. As Massumi suggests, "We're in affect, affect is not in us."[14] The intense and visceral emotions and reactions I have had in response to the event both paint and simultaneously blur the boundary of representations and discourses. My writing of *Sewol* and *Sewol's* writing on (haunting of) my body take place simultaneously through the eddying affects and intensities gushing out of the event.

To be more precise, however, it is not just general Affect—as a catchall term—that captures what writing *Sewol* is about. As Probyn asserts, difference is a significant matter in dealing with affect and emotion. She states: "A general gesture to Affect won't do the trick. If we want to invigorate our concepts, we need to follow through on what different affects do, at different levels. The point needs to be stressed: *different affects make us feel, write, think, and act in different ways.*"[15]

Categorically speaking, *Sewol*'s affect is a negative one. The negative emotionality of *Sewol* is significant in its relation to writing due to its contrariety to the Euro-American cultural confidence in positive affectivity circulating through cultural media and texts. The dissymmetry in the economic, social, intellectual, and other forms of symbolic capitals between nations, cultures, classes, races, and genders enables—and sets limits to—different kinds of affective responses to social events, especially catastrophic ones. Stories that exalt the courage, decency, humanism, heroism, and competence of an individual or a nation in times of tragedy are not propagated out of cultural/ political vacuum, but are produced and reproduced through cultural and emotive forms of capital that have been gained and accumulated through the society's past triumphs: colonial history, world wars, global economic success, and so on.

Chesley B. Sullenberger III's autobiographical book, *Sully*, subsequently turned into a motion picture directed by Clint Eastwood and starring Tom Hanks, depicts the "miracle on the Hudson" on January 15, 2009.[16] Thanks to Captain Sullenberger's bold and competent maneuver, the bird-stricken Flight 1549 with dual engine loss landed safely on the Hudson River, and all 155 passengers were rescued immediately by first responders. The media's praises for the book not only acclaimed Sullenberger, lavishing due honor upon him, but also celebrated America itself. The *Washington Times*, for example, enthused: "Sullenberger's all-American life story is so compelling that it screams to be required reading for all young people, or anybody else who needs confirmation that courage, dignity, and extraordinary competence can still be found in this land. . . . A remarkable life story." The *New York Daily News* added: "Sullenberger's account of Flight 1549 is a Capra-esque ode to American competence and decency."[17]

Such media texts "work on emotions" to "shape the surfaces" of the national and cultural body of America, to borrow Ahmed's words.[18] The story and its positive affects become essentially *of*, *by*, and *for* American citizens. It creates a specific sense of "we" by suggesting (screaming?) that all deviant young Americans must return to the values it extols and uphold the "decency" of the nation.[19] While the narrative is lifted up and utilized for the construction and control of identity within the society, it simultaneously works outside the national boundary through the effect of "othering."[20] On the one hand, in the global cultural arena, *Sully* is presented as a "good" story of a "good" person who is the product of a society that is also rendered, in effect, as essentially "good." On the other hand, *Sewol* is a "bad" story of a catastrophe caused by "bad" people in an allegedly "bad" society. Juxtaposing the story of "the miracle on the Hudson" with another watery story, that of *Sewol*, virtually and painfully reproduces in the minds of South Koreans the insuperable gap between the two societies. Where was Captain Sully in the *Sewol* story? Why couldn't the first responders rescue the victims? Why isn't the society functioning as it should? Can one possibly lead a "good" life in a "bad," *capsized* society?[21] How can one afford to find a hopeful, reparative, and positive ground from which to write when the moment offers nothing but hurt? Does this bad feeling belong to South Koreans only? Who else is feeling bad? Who else is hurting like I am after *Sewol*?

Ahmed aptly remarks: "Justice is not simply a feeling. And feelings are not always just. *But* justice *involves* feelings, which move us across the surfaces of the world, creating ripples in the intimate contours of our lives."[22] I would like to reflect on, and interrogate, these ripples of negative emotions and their affective, political potentials in and beyond the event of *Sewol*. The singularity of the *Sewol* event must, indeed, be acknowledged in its own particular context and affective register. However, as the reflection that follows seeks to demonstrate, the ubiquity of catastrophic events and the increasing sense of "precarity" in the lives of people under the neoliberal global economic structure cannot be submerged.[23]

To focus on the affective aspects of the *Sewol* event is not to depoliticize it. To do so, indeed, is to effect the exact opposite by deconstructing the boundary between the personal and the political. Deeply personal and embodied, yet thoroughly excessive and pervasive, the emotions that burst out from Pang Mok Harbor on April 16, 2014, resist the neoliberal design and naming of the event as an unfortunate *local accident*. The event and the subsequent political struggle that started out with the protests by the victims' families triggered multifaceted and strong emotional turbulence in those who witnessed them. In my view, the intensity and the duration of affect in and around the *Sewol* event outmatches that of any previous catastrophic events in postwar Korean society. Lingering in the moment of such singular, and yet universally widespread *hurt*, I would like to think about ways to face such bad emotions,[24] and learn how to live, wait, and see what ensues from those ripples of affective forces.[25] Prior to that, however, I must enter the contact zone called *writing* to take the risk of telling my story, sharing my feelings, and opening myself up again to the painful memory that my body wants to forget, in hopes that my readers will feel the resonance and join the affective linkage with others in grief and mourning over our precarious world.

WRITING HURT: CAPSIZED NATIONAL BODY

The commercial ferry *Sewol* is a material symbol of economic disparity and class in South Korea. The group of 325 students from Dan Won High School went aboard it because it was a less costly way than flying for the public-school students to travel to Jeju Island for their school trip. Officials turned a blind eye to the illegally overloaded cargo on the ferry because it served to maximize profits. The official investigation is still bogged down in the political process causing delays in finding out what exactly caused the wreckage. The ship sank quietly into the dark waters of the West Sea, and not one of those who remained in the ship after it was capsized survived. To everyone's astonishment and despair, not a single one of them tried to run or jump into the water for survival. It passed all too quietly and silently. Survivors reported later that the students and other passengers were told by the attendants not to move and to *remain still* (*ga-man-hee yi-ssu-rah!*), while the captain and staff of the capsizing ship fled without being stopped or deterred. Public viewers in South Korea and abroad watched the violently slow and quiet process of this submergence on the media for days and nights.

That duration, I believe, did something profound and disturbing to the bodies of those who were affectively engaged in viewing this event. First, it paused and synchronized the time of the viewers' embodied lives. The different time zones in the Korean diasporic communities were collapsed into a virtually singular temporality as the viewers, including myself, were tuned into the event through the media. We constantly watched, websearched, tweeted, and Facebooked *Sewol*, and could not be stopped doing so for several weeks. What Grace Cho has referred to as the "diasporic machinic vision" was formed across the different time zones.[26] Of course, for those who are in diaspora like myself, such attunement was an entanglement of many sticky feelings and emotions—for example, nostalgia, homesickness, ambivalent feelings about one's cultural origin, nation, and so on.

Second, the duration created a sense of proximity and attachment to the event, which affectively diminished the force of geographical distance. I was not physically standing at Pang Mok Harbor. But, affectively, I was living in the space and time of the *field of attunement* created by the event. Brian Massumi explains the idea of *affective attunement* as a "collective in-bracing" of bodies and lives in what he calls the "field of immediacy."[27] In this field of attunement, Massumi asserts, irreducible differences in the desires and trajectories of the individuals remain, while the event "snaps" them to attention together and correlates their diversity to the affective charging of the space.[28]

But the most important impact of *Sewol* besides its spatiotemporal affect is that it literally broke the bodies of the engaged diasporic viewers. Soon after the tragic event, I discovered that many of my Korean friends and colleagues were experiencing the same symptoms as me. Shock, sorrow, anger, disappointment, and numerous other inarticulable feelings had passed through our bodies in a short period of time leaving us exhausted. Lack of sleep, depression, inertia, and digestive problems kept our bodies from being productive in our individual professions and social and familial relationships. Furthermore, the constant influx of images and news of the event and the scenes of the political struggles it provoked in Seoul made those of us in academia doubt the relevance of the work our bodies were producing. Comprehensive exams, conference presentations, papers, papers . . . and more papers. *Are our bodies made of paper,* we wondered, *since the products of our collective bodily machine materialize in precisely that form?*[29] In this instance, *Sewol's* affect appeared an oozing force that liquefied the printing machines that were our bodies into tears, cold sweats, and diarrhea.

It was painful to watch the families of victims and other citizens of South Korea who protested and yearned for just and humane recognition of their voices by the nation-state, all but begging its acknowledgment of the injustice done to them. The government and the established media tried to turn the narrative around and implant suspicions in the public, demanding that they view the protesters and the families of victims together as potential threats to public security. President Park's approach to the catastrophe was strictly modeled after the commercial insurance policy manuals that structured the event with an "accident-compensation" formula. The media turned the public focus to how much money the families' victims would receive. The politics of emotion in this maneuver was clearly designed to characterize the victims' families as greedy and self-interested protesters. Such responses and moves made by the government officials painfully demonstrated how the country in its hyper-neoliberal state has divested itself from the affective lives of the people, and hence is unable to *feel* what the people *feel.* And those of us who did *feel* were buried in a sense of futility, precariousness, and deep public/political depression.

DEPRESSION'S TEMPORALITY: CVETKOVICH'S *HAN*

In her study of public feelings in the contemporary political landscape, Ann Cvetkovich suggests that depression be approached as a "cultural and social phenomenon rather than a medical disease," hence eliciting the term "political depression."[30] Public/political depression refers to the sense deeply embedded both inside and outside academia in the contemporary world that neither political activism nor critical theory is "working either to change the world or to make us feel better."[31] In this redefinition, Cvetkovich refuses pathological, "pastoralizing," or "redemptive" approaches to depression, while envisaging negative feeling as a force that is generative of affective "foundations" for social, political transformation.[32] She does not propose to "convert" the negative feeling into something immediately action-inciting or "positive," but she asserts that public depression as social theory understands positive/negative not as a binary but as a continuum, and it thus "embraces categories such as utopia and hope."[33] She elaborates on this approach in her book, *Depression*:

> In investigating the productive possibilities of depression, this book aims to be patient with the moods and *temporalities* of depression, not moving too quickly to recuperate them or put them to good use. It might instead be important to *let depression linger*, to explore the feeling of remaining or resting in sadness without insisting that it be transformed or reconceived.[34]

The dimension of time or temporality seems significant in Cvetkovich's recalibration of negative affect for social change. That is to say, depression has *temporality*. We are pushed into that temporality through, say, 9/11, subsequent militarism and wars, economic disparity, the Occupy movement, Black Lives Matter, gender inequality, refugee crises . . . and *Sewol*—events summed up as a growing sense of futility and failure. However, inhabiting and lingering in that temporality steadily and resiliently can be a willful and necessary response that may foster persevering anticipation for transformation. For that purpose, Cvetkovich turns to the religious concept of *acedia* (spiritual despair) and is impelled by it to advocate ordinary habit or creative practice in order to sustain and channel negative feelings into the present everyday circuits of life, pulling ordinary and spiritual dimensions of life into academic and political endeavors.[35]

Cvetkovich's theory of depression resonates strongly with the notion of *Han* in Korean Minjung theology, in my view. Putting the two concepts in dialogue cross-fertilizes both concepts and provides deeper contents for the affective meaning of life after *Sewol*. In his book *The Wounded Heart of God*, Andrew Sung Park describes *Han* as follows:

> Han can be . . . defined as the collapsed pain of the heart due to psychosomatic, interpersonal, social, political, economic, and cultural oppression and repression. The reality of han is the emotional, rational, and physical suffering of pain rooted in the anguish of a victim. . . . Like a black hole, when suffering reaches the point of saturation, it implodes and collapses into a condensed feeling of pain. . . . In the life of han-ridden people,

the mode of han overwhelms the other types of human emotion and becomes a domineering spirit. This collapsed feeling is more than a psychological phenomenon. Such a feeling encompasses all dimensions of human existence.[36]

Park goes on to explain the two aspects of *Han*. One is its acquiescent nature, denoting the passive feeling of pain, frustrated hope, wounded heart, and so on. The other side is its aggressive potential, which appears in the form of "resentful bitterness."[37] Thus, to harbor *Han* in one's heart is to experience both potential aspects—active/bitterness and passive/helplessness.

The two affective aspects of *Han* do not operate in an either/or category, but the alteration between them is a processual change or passage in both directions, which has a temporal character. Thus, it can be said that both *Han* and public depression have temporalities that are neither linear nor unidirectional. Neither of them leads directly to action. Rather, their affective nature challenges our agency and control over them, requiring that we rethink the relationship between feeling and praxis. We cannot simply pick up and use these affects and emotions for political actions or transformation. Rather, *Han*/depression *is* a temporality that we enter without fully knowing what is to come—which is why Cvetkovich's formulation is so effective: *Let depression linger.*

Although *Han* and public depression bear similarities in their affective, embodied, and temporal natures, they have different foci. Or, let's just say, they are the two different aspects of the political negative affect: the synchronic and the diachronic. Whereas Cvetkovich's theory of public depression focuses on the sustained, synchronic present (entailing a lingering and tarrying with the emotions of the now), *Han* is diachronic in its affective movement. That is to say, the idea of *Han* constantly finds itself connected to past generations. Due to theological investments in the word, *Han* has been understood in a parallel and antithetical relationship to the concept of "original sin," and hence has been dubbed "original han."[38] Original sin, in Minjung theology, refers to the violence of the oppressor, while original *Han* is the pain and resentment of the victims and the oppressed.[39] Minjung theology understands the original human condition as the "intertwining" and repetitive cycle of "sin and han," understanding history in turn as the continuing vicious cycle of the two.[40] Therefore, Park describes *Han* as a prehistory of the world including the human and the natural world. He states:

Below all the diversity of han lies *world han*, a common denominator of all world sorrow and grief. The world han is the dark side of the world soul. It is the world grief which *recollects all the tragic memories of the past.*

No single tragic event is lost forever, all are related in the world of grief that is the han of the world.[41]

As an "archival"[42] concept, *Han* thus recollects and stores memories—the past experience of violence and victimization—and interconnects different times and generations in empathy and solidarity. If the concept of public depression anticipates community formation in contemporary societies—that is, across the boundaries of *space*, the idea of *Han* exposes, and invites, one to distant and fluid past temporalities. The retrospective power and desire of *Han* invoke what Elizabeth Freeman has called "the relationality across *time*."[43]

To recapitulate, I have tried to articulate and theorize the despair and sorrow emerging from the *Sewol* event with two interrelated concepts: public depression and *Han*. Both concepts exert a certain temporality. That is, both affective forces are experienced as a *lived* time and moment in which various connections can be made for social and individual transformation. Specifically, I distinguish the temporal foci of the two concepts, synchronic and diachronic, in order to suggest that public depression's ethical potential is in community formation across the boundaries of space (that is, spatial/social relationality), whereas *Han*'s retrospective and theological investments draw one to engage temporal/spiritual relationality. Reading an ancient religious text, as I will now attempt to show, may be considered a search for contact zones of affective emotions such as *Han* across time, across the boundary between text and life, and across the line between past and present.

PSALM 137 AND THE AFFECTIVE WE/I ASSEMBLAGE

A famous deictic phrase "By the rivers of Babylon . . ." opens Psalm 137. Such a spatial introduction appears to suggest an unambiguous time frame and context within which the song must be understood. However, as recent studies of this psalm have demonstrated, its setting is, in fact, difficult to determine. Karl A. Plank notes that the repeated use of *sham* ("there") in verses 1–4 indicates the psalmist's distance from Babylon.[44] However, the second section (vv. 5–6) implies contrarily that the psalmist's location is also distant from Jerusalem since the psalmist feels compelled to *remember* Jerusalem.[45] With Babylon and Jerusalem standing as the two poles, the spatial and temporal location in the final form of the psalm appears indeterminate. Plank remarks:

> If the first section identifies Babylon as "there," the second resists marking Jerusalem as the implied "here" and encourages us to perceive the exile's "there" as the psalmist's "here." . . . The difficulty in the psalm's spatial map lies not in a lack of simple deictic clarity, but in the tension between two spatial orientations.[46]

James L. Mays aptly describes this unstable location as follows: "The soul of the singers *moves* between Babylon and Jerusalem."[47] I would add: The souls of the *readers* also move between these two cities in the psalm. What does this spatiotemporal polyphony have to do with the psalm's affectivity?

Imagine a song leader speaking to you in fifth century BCE Jerusalem. A place is invoked: "By the rivers of Babylon. . . ." And the song leader's introduction begins:

> You and I are invited to sing together about the place. Get the rhythm and rhyme: Nine-fold repetition of the sound nu. You and I share the meaning of this nu if you can remember that place. That place is in our memory. It is the canals of Babylon, where our parents, our grandparents, and all our kinfolk worked—where "we" worked hard under the oppression of the Babylonians. It is not only them but we, living in the present, who have sat there, wept, and remembered Zion. You were there even though you are here now! On the poplar trees, right there, did we not hang up our instruments? Our lighthearted oppressors derided us: "Sing for us from the songs of Zion!" We yelled, we shouted in our silent reply: "How can we sing a song of YHWH on foreign soil? If I forget you, O Jerusalem, my right hand shall lose its function. My tongue shall cling to the roof of my mouth, if I do not remember; if I do not lift Jerusalem over the head of my gladness!"[48]

A sort of psychic time-travel would have been required for singing this song. The use of perfect tense verbs indicates that it is a past event. However, the inescapable designation "we" makes the singers identify with those who sat and wept by the canals of Babylon. Thus, the "I" in the present Jerusalem merges with the "they" in the past by the river of Babylon, and becomes a "we." The singers sing and relive the past in the present. The present and the past meet and collide. A deliberate *touch* is desired and effected in order to make a particular connection with the past in this performative act of singing. The psalm's mnemonic device, visceral bodily language, and interchange between the identities of the singers (between the communal "we" and the single-person "I") work together to generate strong affective connection among the singers.[49]

"By the rivers of Babylon—there we sat down and there we wept," sings the psalmist. The river as a site of exilic memory is where the fall of Jerusalem was experienced physically and emotionally. "There *we* sat." In the space of hurt and shame, the Israelites, singers, and audiences sit. *Let depression linger. . . .* Sitting and waiting, people enter grief and mourning, which other *Han*-ridden subjects are invited to share. "And there we wept." The water of the river commingles with the water of the body of "we." In this "we/I" as an affective assemblage of grieving souls, I envision a nonidentitarian subjectivity[50] based on affective response to one's suffering, empathy, and solidarity. Feeling and experiencing the pain of the current world in deeply personal and embodied ways, and yet also experiencing the in-bracing of the affective force with others, we may be able to endure another week in hope for a better world.

OUTRO: HYDRAULIC AFFECTIVITY/DIVINITY

Inspired by Cvetkovich's promotion of ordinary spiritual practice as a strategic response to political depression, I have made it an ordinary habit to sit by the Hudson River just a block away from my apartment in College Point, New York. This secret altar is where I can keep myself attuned to the bodily experience of Spring 2014. Sitting by the river helps me feel virtually closer to *Sewol* as experienced by so many of my Korean brothers and sisters. But the locational difference, since it is the Hudson River not a Korean river, invites me to connect to other kinds of hydraulic affects and memories in addition: Not only the lucky survivors in 2009 who landed safely on this river, but also Aylan Kurdi, the boy who was found dead, washed ashore in Turkey; thousands of other dead refugees in that Mediterranean Sea and their capsized boats—not only the contemporary ones but also the past ghostly ones of memory, extending to the slave ships of the Middle Passage and other capsized boats in history that did not find Noachian deliverance. My attempt to connect to the spectral presence of *Han* archived in the water points me to its primordial affectivity and divinity. The contact in grief between myself and this body of water is the contact between the water within (my tears) and the water without (the river). Derrida's claim, "I mourn therefore I am"[51] is, in my theological view, a manifestation of hydraulic affectivity that moves between the I and the Thou—myself and the submarine.

O water, voice of my heart, crying in the sand,
All night long crying with a mournful cry,
As I lie and listen, and cannot understand
The voice of my heart in my side or the voice of the sea,
O water, crying for rest, is it I, is it I?
All night long the water is crying to me.

Unresting water, there shall never be rest
Till the last moon droop and the last tide fail,
And the fire of the end begin to burn in the west;
And the heart shall be weary and wonder and cry like the sea,
All life long crying without avail,
As the water all night long is crying to me.[52]

NOTES

1. My choice of the term "event" is intentional. It is to avoid the much-politicized categorical term "accident."

2. Gayatri Chakravorty Spivak, "Can the Subaltern Speak?" in *Marxism and the Interpretation of Culture*, ed. Cary Nelson and Larry Grossberg (Urbana: University of Illinois Press, 1988), 271–313. For more detailed and engaged discussion on Spivak and postcolonial theory as it pertains to religion and especially theology, see Stephen D. Moore and Mayra Rivera, eds., *Planetary Loves: Spivak, Postcoloniality, and Theology*, Transdisciplinary Theological Colloquia (New York: Fordham University Press, 2011).

3. This concern for the ethics of representation is impelled by Katherine Doob Sakenfeld's 2007 presidential address to the Society of Biblical Literature, which was published as "Whose Text Is It?" *Journal of Biblical Literature* 127, no.1 (2008): 3–18.

4. The Wikipedia article titled "Sinking of MV *Sewol*," for example, begins: "The sinking of MV *Sewol* (Hangul: 세월호 침몰 사고; Hanja: 世越號沈沒事故), also referred to as the *Sewol Ferry Disaster*, occurred on the morning of 16 April 2014, en route from Incheon to Jeju in South Korea. The ferry capsized while carrying 476 people, mostly secondary school students from Danwon High School (Ansan City). . . ." And it ends: "On the first anniversary of the disaster, as part of commemorations for the victims of the sinking of *Sewol*, 4,475 people held electronic candles to form the shape of the ferry in an attempt to set a Guinness World Record for the largest torchlight image."

5. Exemplary uses of the ideas of spectrality and hauntology in the study of affect, emotion, and history can be found in Avery Gordon, *Ghostly Matters: Haunting and the Sociological Imagination* (Minneapolis: University of Minnesota Press, 2008) and Carla Freccero, *Queer/Early/Modern* (Durham, N.C.: Duke University Press, 2006), as well as their antecedent, Jacques Derrida, *Specters of Marx: The State of the Debt, the Work of Mourning, and the New International*, trans. Peggy Kamuf (New York: Routledge, 1994).

6. Sara Ahmed's discussion of the meaning of "impression" is implied here. By highlighting the effect of the subject/object formation caused by the circulation of various emotions, she urges readers to focus on the "press" of the word "impression." See her *The Cultural Politics of Emotion*, 2nd ed. (New York: Routledge, 2014), 6–7.

7. Maia Kotrosits, *Rethinking Early Christian Identity: Affect, Violence, and Belonging* (Minneapolis: Fortress Press, 2015), 4.

8. Elspeth Probyn, "Writing Shame," in *The Affect Theory Reader*, ed. Melissa Gregg and Gregory J. Seigworth (Durham, N.C.: Duke University Press, 2010), 73.

9. Ibid. In Probyn's terms, "writing up research" and "writing." Although she critiques the "pretense of academic writing as purely objective," she nonetheless challenges the binary of writing/academic-research by introducing the affective domain of shame into her own academic/affective writing.

10. Ibid., 74.

11. Ahmed, *Cultural Politics of Emotion*, 14.

12. Ibid.

13. Ibid.

14. Brian Massumi, *Politics of Affect* (Malden, Mass.: Polity Press, 2015), 124. Ahmed's detailed definitions of emotion, affect, and feeling can be found in *The Cultural Politics of Emotion*, 8–12.

15. Probyn, "Writing Shame," 74, emphasis added.

16. Chesley B. Sullenberger III with Jeffery Zaslow, *Sully: My Search for What Really Matters* (New York: HarperCollins, 2009).

17. From the book's preface (ibid., 1).

18. Ahmed, *Cultural Politics of Emotion*, 1.

19. Cf. ibid.

20. Ibid. For many Korean and Korean American viewers of the film, the comparison between the two events (Sully vs. *Sewol*) was inevitable. A Korean American film critic states in his online review of the film: "I want to tell you one interesting thing I observed during my viewing. While I and my parents watched 'Sully' during last Sunday morning, the rescue sequence in the movie touched my parents a lot in a bitter way, and I heard their audible responses during the screening. They and many other South Koreans still remember well the sinking incident of *MV Sewol* in 2014 April, and they are also well aware of how its enormous human tragedy was caused by the sheer incompetence and ignorance of our government, which, to our dismay, remain same as before as shown from its clumsy response to the recent earthquakes in this year. Watching how everything could be worked out so wonderfully for Sullenberger and others on the plane, we could only envy what made that miracle on the Hudson River possible" (Seongyoung Cho, "Sully (2016): He Simply Did His Job . . . ," in *Seongyoung's Private Place* [blog], October 5, 2016, https://kaist455.com/2016/10/05/sully-2016, accessed July 20, 2017).

21. The question is drawn from Judith Butler's chapter, "Can One Lead a Good Life in a Bad Life?" in her *Notes toward a Performative Theory of Assembly* (Cambridge, Mass.: Harvard University Press, 2015), 193–220.

22. Ahmed, *Cultural Politics of Emotion*, 202.

23. Much of Judith Butler's recent work has been focused on this theme. See especially her *Precarious Life: The Powers of Mourning and Violence* (New York: Verso, 2006).

24. Ann Cvetkovich discusses and theorizes depression in nonpathological and political terms. She suggests that one must see "negative feelings of failure, mourning, despair, and shame" as emotions that are "already political" and that transform "our understandings of what counts as political." See her *Depression: A Public Feeling* (Durham, N.C.: Duke University Press, 2012), 2–3, 5–7, and 110–11.

25. See Cvetkovich's discussion of public/political depression and its possible construal as "ordinary" and hence as residing in the daily art of living (*Depression*, 161).

26. Grace Cho, "Voice from the Teum: Synesthetic Trauma and the Ghosts of the Korean Diaspora," in *The Affective Turn: Theorizing the Social*, ed. Patricia Ticineto Clough with Jean Halley (Durham, N.C.: Duke University Press, 2007), 157.

27. Massumi, *Politics of Affect*, 115.

28. Ibid.
29. Cvetkovich shares similar emotions in regard to the depressed conditions of academics in the present capitalistic state of academia. See her discussion in *Depression*, 18–19.
30. Ibid., 1.
31. Ibid.
32. Ibid., 2.
33. Ibid., 5–6.
34. Ibid., 14, emphasis added.
35. Ibid., 197.
36. Andrew Sung Park, *The Wounded Heart of God: The Asian Concept of Han and the Christian Doctrine of Sin* (Nashville, Tenn.: Abingdon Press, 1993), 17.
37. Ibid., 31.
38. Ibid., 69.
39. Ibid.
40. Ibid.
41. Ibid., 41–42, emphasis added.
42. Theorization of the concept of archive has been a thriving topic in multiple interdisciplinary venues for some time. Reflections inspired by Derrida or Foucault, feminist and/or postcolonial/decolonial theories, or various cultural memory projects are the most prominent examples. For an overview, see Marlene Manoff, "Theories of the Archive from across the Disciplines," *portal: Libraries and the Academy* 4, no. 1 (2004): 9–25. Most relevant to my own discussion is/are queer theory's approach(es) to archive: see Charles E. Morris, "Archival Queer," *Rhetorics & Public Affairs* 9, no 1 (2006): 141–51, and Ann Cvetkovich, *An Archive of Feelings: Trauma, Sexuality, and Lesbian Public Cultures* (Durham, N.C.: Duke University Press, 2003).
43. Carolyn Dinshaw et al., "Theorizing Queer Temporalities: A Roundtable Discussion," *GLQ: A Journal of Lesbian and Gay Studies* 13, nos. 2–3 (2007): 184.
44. Karl A. Plank, "By the Waters of a Death Camp: An Intertextual Reading of Psalm 137," *Literature and Theology* 22, no. 2 (2008): 181.
45. Ibid., 182.
46. Ibid., 183.
47. James L. Mays, *Psalms*, Interpretation series (Louisville, Ky.: John Knox Press, 1994), 422.
48. Psalm 137:2–6, my translation.
49. However, the slippage in the psalm's ending (vv. 7–9) must also be acknowledged. The subjectivity of "we" at the end of the psalm slips into identity politics and boundary mechanism and turns to militarist nationalism: "A blessing on him who seizes your babies and dashes them against the rocks" (Psalms 137:9, JPS). Like the *Sewol* event, Psalm 137 ends with dead children and highly questionable ethics.
50. The meaning of this term echoes what Namsoon Kang has named "solidarity-in-singularity." See her *Cosmopolitan Theology: Reconstituting Planetary Hospitality, Neighbor-Love, and Solidarity in an Uneven World* (St. Louis: Chalice Press, 2013), 147–48.

51. Jacques Derrida, *"Istrice 2: Ick bünn all hier,"* in *Points . . . : Interviews 1974–1994*, ed. Elisabeth Weber, trans. Peggy Kamuf et al. (Stanford, Calif.: Stanford University Press, 1995; French original 1992), 321.

52. Arthur Symons, "The Crying of Water," in *Poems*, vol. 2 (South Yarra, Victoria, Australia: Leopold Classic Library, 1914), 218. This poem is also quoted, famously, in W. E. B. Du Bois, *The Souls of Black Folk* (Chicago: A. C. McClurg, 1904), 1.

❧ Reading (with) Rhythm for the Sake of the (I-n-)Islands: A Rastafarian Interpretation of Samson as Ambi(val)ent Affective Assemblage

A. PAIGE RAWSON

The book has become the body of passion. . . .
—GILLES DELEUZE AND FÉLIX GUATTARI, *A Thousand Plateaus*

Yes, as the (eye)land plays with itself, the sea, the horizon, and a vast beyond, should you pursue the pull, another (eye)land appears. . . . The drum beats a ready rhythm, the (eye)land transmoots its undulating seaing, w(e)aving.
—ALTHEA SPENCER MILLER, "Creolizing Hermeneutics: A Caribbean Invitation," in *Islands, Islanders, and the Bible: Ruminations*

THE BIBLE AS BLOOM SPACE

How are we *moved* by the Bible and why? What is it about this text that is worthy of an entire field of academic study, more commentaries than any other book ever written, and billions of devotees around the world? Just what is it about the Bible that (like Reggae) "moves" some bodies and not others? It draws or disgusts, but sometimes only amasses dust. Yet innumerable bodies, like my own, experience an ambi(val)ent affective resonance that binds us to the Bible in an inextricable[1] relationship of cruel optimism.[2] I hate it, I love it, I always find myself wanting more of it. And it is from this precarious positionality that I offer my ruminations on (the *in-between-ness* of) affectivity and divinity within the Bible through a reading (with) rhythm. Interpreting the story of Samson as affectual archetype, I propose that this *special something* about the Bible—that which matters to us and has the capacity to move us—is somatic and spiritual, sympathetic and structural. It is a body without organs, an ambi(val)ent affective assemblage. The Bible is bloom space.[3]

Reading the Bible as bloom space can actually resemble listening to music, and Reggae music in particular. In each we encounter a narrative, a history, and a particular structure—one that I will call *rhythm*—characterized by distinctive and distinguishing formal features that make *this* text the Bible and not some other work of literature and make *this* tune Reggae and not some other musical genre. Everyday human engagements with both the Bible and Reggae, while most often conscious, are typically nonconceptual and pre-propositional: We *feel* them rather than analyze them structurally or exegete them formally. This holds particular valence when one considers those who are affectively drawn to the Bible as God's Word because they take it to be God's words. These particular interpretive communities understand the Bible to be more than an amalgam of theologies—God-talk or words about God—from particular historical communities, and even more than a literary medium through which God has and might continue to reveal Godself to humanity. For these folks the Bible is a spiritual emollient, literally God's mouth speaking—to them, their community, and at times the entire world—directly, personally, and intimately. This perception of and relationship to the Bible evinces the ways in which the Bible, in common with all sacred texts, holds affective intensities or resonances—and with as much significance in and for affect theory as for biblical and religious studies.[4]

The Bible is oral literature, *oraliture* (Glissant) and *oraliterary* (Jones), in sundry ways, and, as such, reading the Bible from and with perspectives, hermeneutical lenses, and/or cultures that privilege orality (as epistemology) over the literary can benefit our interpretation of this sacred text.[5] The Rastafari are, in fact, prototypical in this way, for their oraliterary interpretation, "citing up," of the Bible is a bold example of the Bible's re-membering and (re)definition as a Caribbean text, and I contend that their approach has the capacity to facilitate a new-old, avant-garde hermeneutical approach with the potential to push us further in our interpretive endeavors.[6] Reading the Bible for the Rastafari, orchestral architects of Reggae music, requires a profound reverence for and resonance with (its) *rhythm*—an expression of the intimate interconnection between Jah, *I-n-I*, and creation embodied in the(ir) reasoning of the biblical "text."[7] In this way, Rastafari biblical hermeneutics necessitates an apprehension of orality as musicality, birthed of the creativity that is their *"hermeneutical privilege* as a once oppressed group."[8] Just as in Édouard Glissant's *oraliture*, in which *the written becomes oral* only to expose the literary as inherently oral, the Rastafari orality erupts in a melody of meaning amid the persistent—and at times perilous—rhythms and resonances of livity and language. According to Glissant, in fact, Rastafari is "an irruption into modernity" and, I would add, Eurocentric biblical interpretation.[9]

Rastafari biblical interpretation is the embodiment of and "the upsurge of the oral into the written."[10] Through the creation of a musical medium that is but one manifestation of their biblical interpretation, and/as the aesthetic expression of "the imposition of lived rhythms," the Rastafari enact an ambient affective assemblage in and by which they are able to incorporate (through resonance and resistance) a "reality," or text as it were, that previously appeared to restrain them.[11] It is for these reasons and more that I engage Rastafarian hermeneutics to reinterpret the biblical story of Samson. I do so, not as a representative of the Rastafari movement, a representation of a ubiquitous or even a common Rastafarian interpretation, nor as a reading characteristic of a particular Rastafari community, mansion, or house, but in order to proffer a re-presentation, a re-membering, of Samson. Engaging concepts and conversations from Afro-Caribbean and continental philosophy with significant affective resonances, in this essay I perform an exegesis inspired and animated by a Rastafari biblical hermeneutics in an effort to advocate for the necessity of reading the Bible with rhythm in order that it might be re-membered entirely otherwise, that is, as ambi(val)ent affective assemblage and archipelagic bloom space.[12]

For Glissant, the oral-musicality of Caribbean peoples in general, and the Rastafari in particular, is inextricably linked to their relationship to history and to landscape—to the rhythm of the islands.[13] The rhythmic repetition of the undulating and unceasing waves on the shore, surrounding as a resounding reminder of all that these waters, as rhythm, represent: both enslavement and liberation, motion and inertia, order and chaos, establishment and its undoing.[14] Glissant understands rhythm, then, as a means of accessing (Caribbean) memory and of understanding and recuperating history. Rhythm is "a lever of awareness,"[15] integral to our understanding of ourselves as always already in relation to other bodies—of land, water, and knowledge, human, divine, textual, and otherwise—bodies comingling, converging, and diverging, in and across time and space. As integral as rhythm is to a *poetics of relation*, it is equally indispensable to the affective aesthetics of oral-musicality as a biblical hermeneutic. The rhythmic oralizing of the Bible, which the Rastafari embody in their citing up of scripture, invigorates my interpretation, as does the(ir) desire to *find expression in the imposition of lived rhythms*. Rhythm is lived, imposing upon, accepting, resisting, moving with, against; forging new identities in refusal; always risking the threat of reification. Rhythms delineate and define, yet always already exceed the bindings of the book and the bounds of our all-too-porous encasement, this weak flesh, this thin veil of skin. To be a body, according to Bruno Latour, is to learn to be moved.[16]

And so, it is here—in the rhythms enfleshed, encasing, and exceeding the boundaries of textual and corporeal bodies—that I find resonance, in the in-betweenness of affectivity and divinity that is (reading) the Bible; in fact, it is within the very concept of resonance.[17] According to Silvan Tomkins, resonance is a central characteristic of affect. It refers to a person's (bodily) capacity to experience the same affect in response to viewing an affectual display by another; it is a sort of *contagion*.[18] Tomkins understood *affective resonance* to be the origin of and, therefore, foundation for all human communication (as embodied expression precedes verbal).[19] Affective resonance, however, is not simply personal or prepersonal, as Deleuze and Guattari point out: It is conceptual.[20] In *What Is Philosophy?* they assert that concepts (in distinction from propositions) are "centers of vibrations, each in itself and every one in relation to all the others. This is why they all resonate rather than cohere or correspond with each other."[21]

One might also think of concepts as the islands of an archipelago, such as the islands of the Caribbean. Glissant, in fact, challenges Eurocentric epistemologies and "continental thinking" through what he deems "archipelagic thinking," and what I have come to call *archipelogics*.[22] He explains this type of creative cognition as unique to archipelagic peoples, and in distinction from continental thought, since "in the Caribbean each island embodies openness. The dialectic between inside and outside is reflected in the relationship of land and sea. It is only those who are tied to the European continent who see insularity as confining. A Caribbean imagination liberates us from being smothered."[23] Like the Caribbean islands, Deleuzoguattarian concepts are connected according to their relationship to one another. Although the bridges from one concept to another may at times form a wall, Deleuze and Guattari assert, "Everything holds together along diverging lines"—even the traverses from one concept to another are movable, more aqueous than concrete; they are "junctions, or detours, which do not define any discursive whole."[24] They are archipelogical.

In Deleuzoguattarian terms, affects correspond to art, to aesthetics and poetics rather than science or philosophy, without, of course, precluding their interbreeding.[25] Affective resonance, then, as affect, is ineluctably prepersonal, prediscursive, and proprioceptive[26] as well as peripersonal, emerging in the encounter of human and nonhuman bodies (with internal consistency and exoconsistency) and impelling a vibrancy that is both convergent and divergent.[27] In both the Tomkinsian and Deleuzoguattarian iterations of affect, *resonance*, like waves and wave frequencies in physics, is defined by the affect of one body upon another—*movement* in/of one body producing some sort of corresponding response (amplification) in another body. Resonance is *sympathetic vibration* establishing a significant or meaningful relationship in the *movement* between two or more bodies: concepts, objects, or sentient beings.[28] As human body-beings, to state that we *resonate* is to say we relate, we connect, we understand, that we are in some way *moved*. This movement, this *force, in the midst of the in-betweenness*[29] of bodies, might even be conceptualized in terms of musicality.[30] And although this affective quality may be present in all music, the rhythm of the Rastafari—the irie[31] *island vibe*[32] of Reggae music—unequivocally conveys the "I feel ya" vibe of resonance.[33]

Eric Shouse, in his essay, "Feeling, Emotion, Affect," acknowledges that music is but one medium through which affect is transmitted. Shouse asserts that "every form of communication where facial expressions, respiration, tone of voice, and posture are perceptible" is capable of transmitting affect.[34] He then proceeds to list every mode of mediated communication *but* reading texts. Shouse's omission reflects a prevalent and pervasive error in judgment. In fact, one need only look to Eugenie Brinkema's affective interventions in *The Forms of the Affects* to grasp the gravity of this omission. Brinkema's critique of affect's allergy to textuality and subsequent solipsistic slip into sterility—as it reproduces the same sappy omphaloskeptic sentiments ad infinitum, ad nauseam—is incisive.[35] The film theorist announces in her introduction to *Forms* that "close reading" alone can save affect (from it*self*).[36] Many a Lit Crit might agree, but this is particularly "good news" *(euangelion)* for the Bible wonks among us, who are the Steve Urkels of academia—arguably the *least* sexy of all scholars(hip). While biblical scholarship is still considered a requisite interlocutor within religious studies, it is often difficult to know just where or how to fit us into the conversation. In light of the precarity and plight of the biblical scholar, then, Brinkema's (altar) call for close reading is an event, whereby the Bible wonk who *reads* her words, *feels* her words.

Those of us who, having so deeply resonated with the Bible, have devoted our lives to its study, know that it is not only possible but of absolute necessity to read (biblical) texts *so closely* that we are able to *see, hear,* and *feel* them, both structurally and sympathetically. Unfortunately, although we are aficionados of its formal, rhythmic analysis, many of us have yet to *feel* the Bible's rhythms. Although there are scholars who have begun this important work, biblical studies can only benefit from the increased acknowledgment and engagement of the rich entanglement that make up the various conceptual, and entirely movable, bridges between affect, orality, musicality, and textuality. It is in this space that biblical studies rescues and is rescued by affect,[37] where rhythm is both felt and formally exegeted. Not because this is their first encounter but because they have always been intimately intertwined comrades meeting again for the first time, each new time. Multifarious and diverse texts, voices, and hermeneutics always already converge in-and-as we approach the Bible. This is a text constructed by and, in its *in-betweenness*, inhabiting and inhabited by such profoundly human, nonhuman, and divine affective intensities, resonating throughout time, and around the world.

READING THE BIBLE WITH RHYTHM

And so, in this concrescence,[38] I now move into my own "close reading" of the Bible, an interpretation of the story of Samson and the Philistines in Judges 16. Although Samson is one of the more well known biblical characters in popular culture, a brief summary of his story may serve as a refresher to some and an introduction to others. Samson (if he ever actually existed) was a judge over the people of Israel (c. 1200–1000 BCE) and a Nazirite. As a Nazirite, he was a special class of Israelite, designated by a more prohibitive consecration to God at birth. This vow and his status forbade the cutting of his hair, so he wore seven locks on his head. (All of these are reasons the Rastafari revere him.) There are a host of other things Samson was required to refrain from in order to remain pure, holy, and "set apart" as a Nazirite.[39] His repeated failure to do so, however, is so unfortunate, not to mention hyperbolic, as to be comical.[40] Arguably the most critical biographical information about Samson is (1) that his locks are (ostensibly) the source of his divine strength and (2) that his life is constituted in and by *in-betweenness* and especially in relation to the Philistines: He is incessantly and passionately embroiled with Philistine women and men. Samson is plagued by ambivalent affective resonance throughout the story and particularly in chapter 16, a bind resulting from the imposition of lived rhythms that his inevitable entanglement with the Philistines engenders.

In addition to the particulars of Samson's story, I would like to offer a word about what I mean by "reading (with) rhythm." In order to acknowledge more formally and honor the text's orality as musicality, I quite literally (philologically) foreground and follow the *beat* within the text. Judges, like all other books in the so-called Old Testament, was originally penned in Hebrew and the Hebrew word for "beat," *pa'am*, occurs on seven occasions in the Samson saga (Judges 13–16). Upon a closer reading of the biblical text and after much deliberation, I realized that, like Reggae music, the locations of the beats and their spatial relationship to one another defined the text: The timing of the beat appeared to determine the rhythm and, therefore, meaning of and in the medium.[41] The Bible so profoundly yearns to be read with rhythm that the repetition of the very Hebrew signifier for beat becomes the rhythmic medium and a mediator bridging all these bodies in order that we might feel the rhythm and be moved toward (a new understanding of) what the Bible means and what it means to read the Bible.[42] This interpretation of rhythm is actually quite Deleuzian, for according to Deleuze (and Spinoza before him), affect is achieved through the relationship of *rhythms and pauses* rather than in reference to concepts or objects—where the sense of absence, hesitation, holding back, or even halting creates the affective experience, and particularly affective resonance.[43] My exegesis, then, is guided by the structural placement of the beat (*pa'am*) and in terms of this sort of relational understanding of rhythm's affect, which functions as both structural and sympathetic framework for my Rastafari interpretation.

Pa'am's first occurrence in Judges is just after Samson's birth in 13:25. In its verbal form *pa'am* can mean "to move, thrust, impel, stir, trouble, agitate or disrupt."[44] Thus, in this instance, the verse reads, "The *ruach* (or spirit) of Jah began moving [Samson]." As a noun, *pa'am* not only signifies "beat" but may also be translated "step, pace, foot, time, once, now, again, anvil or hammer."[45] The remaining six times *pa'am* appears in the folktale it is in this form.[46] As the story nears its conclusion, *pa'am*'s presence becomes more prevalent: We find it four times in 16:15–20—twice in verse 20 alone—and is then surprisingly entirely absent for another seven verses until it finally resurfaces in Samson's penultimate statement (16:28). One might, then, read this repetition as a *refrain*, *ritournelle*, or even *anaphora*—where the repetition of *pa'am* gives *prominence to the concept, rhythm to the passage*, and even *appeals to our emotions* in order to not only *move* the narrative and its protagonist but also us, its readers.[47] Without understanding *pa'am*'s context or linguistic signification in each of its occurrences, simply by identifying its appearances and their proximity to one another, we are able to interpret what it is *doing* (even as it is *undoing*).[48] It is as if the space between each subsequent *beat*—how the text's rhythm *and* affective resonance is established—is communicating with the audience, before and beyond cognition. As if the words become pauses that mean in excess of conscious activity. As if the beat of the rhythm is slowly and deliberately *moving* (Samson and us) forward, toward some dramatic end, yet simultaneously harkening back to the story's beginning and the first time Jah's *ruach moved*, stirring Samson. As if the rhythm is teasing the reader, gingerly, yet relentlessly luring us—the beat builds, heightens, and ceases altogether, then, it rests (for seven counts), only to *pound* (us), yet again, one last time.[49]

Now, when we read the narrative attentive to these rhythmic cues, we notice the beat becoming more vigorous at one of the most climactic and erotically charged moments in the narrative. We find the passage's first *pa'am* as the Philistine Delilah begs to know Samson's "whole secret," thereby proving his love for her, and—after hours of what is now assumed among queer Bible folk to be light bondage or edgeplay—Samson concedes.[50] Once he has proven himself by sharing his secret/strength, we encounter the next *pa'am*, and, then, out of sheer exhaustion Samson falls asleep on Delilah's lap. The actual Hebrew terminology in Judges 16:19 is *'al birkeyhâ*, which means "between her knees" and is an oblique reference to her genitalia.[51] So while the sleeping head of a sapped Samson is nestled there betwixt her legs, Delilah has a nameless man shear his seven locks and then rouses Samson just before her Philistine co-conspirators enslave him and gouge out his eyes.[52] When Samson awakens "helpless" in verse 20, his shock is palpable as one beat immediately follows the next, in rapid succession, *pa'am* pulsating: *k'pa'am b'pa'am*. Up to this point in the narrative Samson has been inextricably bound *to* the Philistines, now, however, he is bound *by* them and in this encounter, Samson experiences an unprecedented inertia.[53] We watch as the protagonist emerges not from but into a nightmare that becomes his reality. Possibly assuming himself to be in a hypnopompic state, Samson is unaware his strength has left him as he struggles to shake free. Samson fails. And yet this is not the end of the story; there must be one more beat.[54]

The entire folktale resonates with affective force but never more than in the denouement. Shackled by the Philistine "lords," now fashioning themselves as his masters, Samson is led down to Gaza and summoned to "entertain" them. He is then stationed between and bound to the pillars of the Philistine's temple.[55] Chained, imprisoned, incarcerated, in an entanglement that bears no resemblance to the in-betweenness, the liminality, which has previously characterized his livity, Samson implores the young boy leading him *by the hand* to release him. "Let me *grasp* and *feel* the pillars upon which the temple is established."[56] While the text proceeds without complication, reading with rhythm has led us to intuit otherwise. Awaiting, anticipating; the story is not over—there must be one more beat! Waiting, we watch a sightless Samson *embrace* and *feel* the pillars, *lean* into them. Our *eyes* follow the one whose *eyes* cannot see the crowd of 6,000 *eyes* all on him. And the beat returns, it re-sounds—*pa'am*—as Samson enacts *an active discharge of emotion* directed right at Jah.[57] In verse 28, Samson screams. "Oh Jah! Please. Re-member me!" He then demands strength just this one last time (*pa'am*) in order to be avenged.[58] Now, while Samson emphatically exclaims that he wants revenge, he does not implore that he be avenged for the Philistines' shearing his locks, enslaving, or ridiculing him. Samson proclaims that he desires vengeance "if only . . . for (one of) my *two eyes*." That is, for the sake of I-an-I.[59]

"At their most philosophical," Patrick Taylor writes, "the Rastafari are the bearers of relational thinking in its fullest."[60] Incorporating the ambient and all-pervasive divinity of Jah through the acknowledgment of and reverence for Pan-Divinity *and* a profound livication (dedication) to self-awareness, through affirmation and assertion, I-an-I simultaneously represents personal agency and collective interdependence[61]—what I would identify as the divine assemblage, the plurality of God, *elohim* in all and through the all.[62] Like Plato's chaosmic *khora* and Keller's tehomic *many-one*, I-an-I is the one exploding into many: "out of many, one."[63] *We can seek the unity of rhythm only at the point where rhythm itself plunges into chaos, into the night, at the point where differences of level are perpetually and violently mixed.*[64] In the final scene of Samson's story, the rhythmic wave of Jah's *ruach* (spirit) as I-an-I su(bme)rges Samson, who is surrounded and engulfed by sensation and imbued with affective force: understanding to overcome.[65] In his last (scream)breath,[66] Samson cries out: "If the Philistines die, my livity will cease!"[67] In I-an-I we are many-one. "*A body is as much outside itself as in itself.*"[68] Samson violently pushes and pulls down the pillars of his captivity[69]—the boundaries of body as "organism . . . [which]

imprisons life."[70] He obliterates the strongholds of an edifice built to construct and constrict identity according to the downpressing dyad of either/or, in accordance with the relentless rhythms of Babylon, Western European imperialism's insidious apparatus.[71] Can the machines and machinations of war somehow bring peace? In a moment, death triumphs over (and in a distance of incremental) difference, bearing new possibility, generating life. The cycle begins again. The beat goes on. But (we are) never quite the same. A reading with rhythm redefines bodies interpreting and interpreted and their difference as ambient affective assemblage of divine multiplicity. This mass slaughter-suicide, aggregate annihilation, then, betrays undeniable affective resonance *when read with rhythm for the sake of the I-an-Islands*—engulfed as we all are in the waves of relatedness and *in-betweenness* amid ostensibly discrete and divergent (converging) bodies of land, of text, and of human and other-than-human beings; we are, as Glissant asserted, the world becoming archipelago.[72] And somehow, Samson's affective *undoing* becomes bloom space and a site of indefinite do-overs and perpetual becomings.[73] And so it is with the entire biblical corpus.

THE BIBLE IS ARCHIPELOGICAL; THE BIBLE IS BLOOM SPACE

An allegedly "closed" canon haunted and haunting by its excess of meaning, the Bible is itself bloom space—a gathering place always already open and opening in its capacity *to affect and be affected*, enduringly instantiating an event of innumerable incontrovertible (and irrepressible) reiterations in its capacity for illimitable interpretations of the human, the nonhuman, and the divine. Jewish, Christian, Muslim, Buddhist, Hindu, atheist, agnostic, anyone who has ever spent the night in a hotel since 1908, and even if you have never laid a finger on it—the Bible affects us all, human and nonhuman alike. Since its endorsement and promulgation by the cleaving (and collaboration) of the crown and the cross (and later capitalism), it has permeated, saturated, and supplied the planet with language, imagery, and/as a system and structure of meaning. In short, the Bible has (in)formed our world beyond and before consciousness—conditioning us to unconsciously collaborate in and corporealize these (binary) constructs as originary. The Bible's ubiquity (as imperial machine), in fact, makes it an ideal bloom space for interdisciplinary, cross- and counter-cultural, as well as transmediary, encounters—which is precisely why it must remain an integral interlocutor for affect studies (and the theorizing of affect) writ large. This bloom space opens limitless opportunities to consider how novel and otherwise unorthodox relationships of affective resonance might inaugurate avant-garde and effectual hermeneutical approaches (formalist and otherwise).[74] Reading the Bible with rhythm is but one of these affectual approaches, as it reads for the resonances betwixt and between bodies, in the in-betweenness of livity (orality) and (biblical) literature, affectivity and divinity. And so . . . we are *moved* into the Spinozan "not yet-ness" of these diverse dancing bodies, "forward toward the next encounter of forces, and the next, and the next, and the next."[75] Our affective engagement with the porous and pulsating pages of the Bible makes these tales more than stories, these words more than God's—the Bible is connective, a corpus of corpuses, a body of bodies, touching each other touching us, tasting, retching, dancing, sweating, swooning, quivering, consuming, imbibing, expelling, aching, enjoining, forcing, receiving, holding, releasing, exploding, emerging, converging, coming, diverging, kissing, laughing, crying, syncing, and screaming in a multisensory, archipelogical, transtemporal, and always already intertextual interpretive orgy.[76] We—as *one* as we are *many*—*feel* the Bible and are *moved*. Reminded in its rhythmic resonances and in its archipelogical re-membering(s), that the Bible is bloom space, an ambi(val)ent affective assemblage, and that close reading (and biblical interpretation)—while at times insipid, and, yes, even soporific—can also be very sensual.

NOTES

1. That is, complicated, complex, tricky, involved, knotty, tangled, indissoluble, inseparable, indivisible, and anything but simple.
2. See Lauren Berlant, *Cruel Optimism* (Durham, N.C.: Duke University Press, 2011).
3. See Gregory J. Seigworth and Melissa Gregg, "An Inventory of Shimmers," in *The Affect Theory Reader*, ed. Melissa Gregg and Gregory J. Seigworth (Durham, N.C.: Duke University Press, 2010), 9. Also see Kathleen Stewart, "Worlding Refrains," in *The Affect Theory Reader*, 339–53. Stewart writes that "all the world is a bloom space now" and proceeds to define bloom space as "a promissory note. An allure and a threat that shows up in ordinary sensibilities of not knowing what compels, not being able to sit still, being exhausted, being left behind or being ahead of the curve, being in history, being in a predicament, being ready for something—anything—to happen, or orienting yourself to the sole goal of making sure that nothing (more) will happen. A bloom space can whisper from a half-lived sensibility that nevertheless marks whether or not you're in it. It demands collective attunement and a more adequate description of how things make sense, fall apart, become something else, and leave their marks, scoring refrains on bodies of all kinds—atmospheres, landscapes, expectations, institutions, states of acclimation or endurance or pleasure or being stuck or moving on. . . . Anything can be a bloom space" (340, 341).
4. This acutely personal, sympathetic, and invested view of and relationship with the Bible is, incidentally, one important reason that others are so disgusted by it. Applying Derrida, Barthes, and Kristeva, Dale Martin addresses this issue which has plagued the church and biblical interpretation for decades if not centuries, asserting that "texts don't speak" (Dale Martin, *Sex and the Single Savior: Gender and Sexuality in Biblical Interpretation* [Louisville, Ky.: Westminster John Knox Press, 2006], 1). As much as this may be a literally accurate and necessary corrective for

biblical fundamentalism's claims to inerrancy, those who have found themselves in affective entanglements with religious and nonreligious texts, works of fiction and nonfiction alike, know that although texts may not literally speak or "mean," they most certainly hold great affective intensities.

5. See Édouard Glissant, *Caribbean Discourse* (Charlottesville: University of Virginia Press, 1989) and Gayl Jones, *Liberating Voices: Oral Tradition in African American Literature* (Cambridge, Mass.: Harvard University Press, 1991).

6. See Patrick Taylor, "Sheba's Song: The Bible, the *Kebra Nagast*, and the Rastafarians," in *Nation Dance: Religion, Identity, and Cultural Difference in the Caribbean*, ed. Patrick Taylor (Bloomington: Indiana University Press, 2001), 74. Taylor states unequivocally, "The Bible is a Caribbean text; in general, people in the Anglophone Caribbean know their Bible better than North Americans" (74). In "Sheba's Song," in fact, Taylor understands the weaving together of the Bible and the *Kebra Nagast* by the Rastafari in the creation and construction of their own counternarratives and identity to be exemplary of Caribbean creolization. Also see Rex Nettleford, "Discourse on Rastafarian Reality," in *Chanting Down Babylon: The Rastafari Reader*, ed. Nathaniel Samuel Murrell, William David Spencer, and Adrian Anthony Mc-Farlane (Philadelphia: Temple University Press, 1998), 311–25; and Nathaniel Samuel Murrell and Lewin Williams, "The Black Biblical Hermeneutics of Rastafari," in *Chanting Down Babylon*, 326–48.

7. The present essay is but one expression of my profound respect, devotion, and indebtedness to the Rastafari movement and the goodly folk—Jamaican and non-Jamaican alike—who introduced and encouraged me in study and in practice to pursue a Rastafarian biblical hermeneutics. I also acknowledge the complexities and complications that appear to inhere in this entanglement, since I myself am neither Jamaican nor Black. I cannot assuage any of my readers' discomfort but can certainly assure them that this project is more than a hermeneutical endeavor, much more than an exegetical experimentation. I am wholeheartedly committed to this work as a vehicle of spiritual, philosophical, professional, social, and personal transformation.

8. Murrell and Williams, "Black Biblical Hermeneutics of Rastafari," 343.

9. Glissant, *Caribbean Discourse*, 146–47. Murrell and Williams expound on the Rastafarians' challenge of the predetermined (Eurocentric) biblical interpretations inherited by many Jamaicans: "The Rastafarians' own ethnic experience, historical and cultural background, and social and economic reality are not divorced from their reading of and meditation on the Bible. The questions, issues, and challenges that surface from their social existence, which are of a most comprehensive nature, are lived through and in relation to the Scriptures. Reading the Bible from where they are, seeing what is redeemable there for their own reality, they detect convergence, correspondence, and continuities between the story of the people in the Bible and their own story in Jamaica" ("Black Biblical Hermeneutics of Rastafari," 343). These are the resonances the Rastafari capitalize on as they "cite up" the Bible.

10. Taylor, "Sheba's Song," 71.

11. Glissant, *Caribbean Discourse*, 108–9. Glissant writes that Reggae "in the realm of the 'audio-visual' corresponds to 'poetry.'" Rastafari is both a creolized (Caribbean) discourse and a poetics of relation. Bronwen Low and Mela Starker write that Glissant's oraliture "is writing infused with the characteristics of oral expression and tradition. . . . Within this vision the oral and the written enrich, contest, subvert and repeat the other—always in relationship" ("Translanguaging in the Multilingual Montreal Hip-Hop Community: Everyday Poetics as Counter to the Myths of the Monolingual Classroom," in *Heteroglossia as Practice and Pedagogy*, ed. Adrianne Blackledge and Angela Cleese [London: Springer, 2014], 114). Also see Nettleford, "Discourse on Rastafarian Reality," 312.

12. See my explanation of Glissant's comparison of archipelagic and continental thinking. Also see note 23.

13. Glissant, *Caribbean Discourse*, 108. Reggae, Glissant writes, is "a necessary barbarian invasion [of] . . . the intellectual dream of the learned." He likens it to the drum-poetry of Derek Walcott as Caribbean discourse, which, as Glissant writes, "finds its expression as much in the explosion of the original cry, as in the patience of the landscape when it is recognized, as in the imposition of lived rhythms" (108).

14. As the Rastafari have reminded us through Reggae since the '70s, rhythm can be rambunctious, raucous, and rebellious, but it can also be rigid, apathetic, and unforgiving.

15. A *"levier de conscience"* in Glissant's *L'intention Poetique* (Paris: Éditions du Seuil, 1969), 216. A materialization of this distinctively Caribbean orality-musicality and the rhythm of the islands, Reggae was created by the Rastafari in relation to their landscape, history, culture, and community.

16. Bruno Latour, *Politics of Nature: How to Bring the Sciences into Democracy* (Cambridge, Mass.: Harvard University Press, 2004), 205: "If the opposite of being a body is dead [and] there is no life apart from the body . . . [then] to have a body is to learn to be affected, meaning 'effectuated,' moved, put into motion by other entities, humans or nonhumans. If you are not engaged in this learning, you become insensitive, dumb, you drop dead." Seigworth and Gregg write: "The body becomes less about its nature as bounded substance or eternal essence and more about the body [quoting Latour] 'as an interface that becomes more and more describable when it learns to be affected by many more elements'" ("An Inventory of Shimmers," 11).

17. Resonance as it appears across discourses and disciplines, in art (music), science (physics), and philosophy—and in each of its affective trajectories. Rather than rehearsing the traditional bifurcated mapping of affect, I will simply appeal to this common thread in its multiple (and multiplying) discourses. (Resonance has significance regardless of the affective family tree from which you've fallen . . . and no matter how far.)

18. Silvan Tomkins, *Affect Imagery Consciousness:* vol. 1, *The Positive Affects* (New York: Springer, 1962), 296.

19. In addition, the affects provide urgency or motivation to less powerful drives, intensifying positive and negative experiences. Both Sedgwick and Berlant pick up the notion of resonance in their own work; see Eve Kosofsky Sedgwick, *Touching*

Feeling: Affect, Pedagogy, and Performativity (Durham, N.C.: Duke University Press, 2003), 21–23, 83–85, 170–171, and Lauren Berlant, *Cruel Optimism* (Durham, N.C.: Duke University Press, 2011), 4–7.

20. Gilles Deleuze and Félix Guattari, *What Is Philosophy?* (New York: Columbia University Press, 1996). Deleuze and Guattari juxtapose the notions of concept (an abstract idea) and proposition (an assertion of judgment or opinion that may be deemed true or false): "The concept is act of thought, it is thought operating at infinite (although greater or lesser) speed" (21).

21. Deleuze and Guattari, *What Is Philosophy?* 22. As skeptical of totalizing transcendence as Glissant, Deleuze and Guattari conceptualize resonance in terms of a nondiscursive consistency between concepts. Concepts, in distinction from propositions (and prospects), "have only consistency or intensive ordinates outside of any coordinates, [and] freely enter into relationships of nondiscursive resonance—either because the components of one become concepts with other heterogeneous components or because there is no difference of scale between them at any level. . . . There is no reason why concepts should cohere" (*What Is Philosophy?* 22).

22. *Archipelogic* is a neologism I created, which signifies (and is, therefore, synonymous with) the oralitural archipelagic thinking (and epistemologies) Glissant identifies as emerging within the Caribbean islands through Creolité. It thinks, writes, and creatively expresses the creolized creativity of a poetics of Relation (i.e., the *archipelogos*).

23. Glissant, *Caribbean Discourse*, 139. Comparing the Caribbean Sea with the Mediterranean, Glissant describes the latter as "an inner sea surrounded by lands, a sea that concentrates . . . [and, therefore,] imposes the thought of the One)," while "the Caribbean is, in contrast, a sea that explodes the scattered lands into an arc. A sea that diffracts" (33). Glissant observes, "The reality of archipelagos in the Caribbean or the Pacific provides a natural illustration of the thought of Relation" (34). Expounding on archipelagic thinking in Manthia Diawara's documentary on Glissant, the poet reiterates, "A tiny island cannot be closed upon itself. It needs the openness of the surrounding sea, which ties it to other places." Édouard Glissant, *One World in Relation*, dir. Manthia Diawara, TWN (2011). Diawara followed Glissant in a transatlantic journey from Southampton (U.K.) to Brooklyn (New York) on the Queen Mary II and then on to Martinique. *One World in Relation* documents the journey as Glissant reflects and offers his poetic ruminations on Relation and the tout-monde. For more on Glissant's ruminations regarding "the world becoming archipelago," see Édouard Glissant, "The Unforeseeable Diversity of the World," in *Beyond Dichotomies: Histories, Identities, Cultures, and the Challenge of Globalization*, ed. M. Elisabeth Mudimbe Boyi (Albany: State University of New York Press, 2002), 290; and idem, *Traité du Tout-Monde* (Paris: Gallimard, 1997), 194.

24. Deleuze and Guattari, *What Is Philosophy?* 22.

25. Ibid., 23.

26. Particularly in the unconscious reception of movement.

27. Deleuze and Guattari, *What Is Philosophy?* 23.

28. *Merriam-Webster's Dictionary*. The ways in which the Rastafari and Reggae are *resistant*—particularly to dominant culture and its discursive modalities and paradigms—is prolific and well established. The notion of *resonance*, however, offers us a new way to think of and with the Rastafari, politically, philosophically, and relationally. In fact, I would contend that thinking musicality with/in the Reggae rhythms of the Rastafari requires rumination on resonance—an affective term, which signifies *the quality in a sound* (especially a musical tone) *of being deep, full, and reverberating* due to its intensification, reinforcement, or prolongation by reflection from a surface *or* by the synchronous, or sympathetic, vibration of a neighboring body or bodies. Resonance is, then, the reflection of bodies with a lasting effect and, I would argue, a continuing *affect*—both its literal and figurative connotations convey this point. Equally as important to affect theorists such as Berlant, Ahmed, Cvetkovich, and even Sedgwick are questions of why persons are drawn to or repelled by certain music, images, objects, and/or affects.

29. Seigworth and Gregg, "Inventory of Shimmers," 1.

30. Eric Shouse, "Feeling, Emotion, Affect," *M/C Journal* 8 (December 2005): journal. mediaculture.org.au/0512/03.php. According to Shouse, music provides perhaps the clearest example of how the intensity of the impingement of sensations on the body can "mean" more to people than meaning itself. "While it would be wrong to say that meanings do not matter, it would be just as foolish to ignore the role of biology as we try to grasp the cultural effects of music." Appealing to the role of biology on the cultural effects of music, Shouse argues that in many cases "the pleasure that individuals derive from music has less to do with the communication of meaning, and far more to do with the way that a particular piece of music 'moves' them" (13).

31. *Irie* is patois for "all right." It signifies pleasure (i.e., nice, good, pleasing) and is also a greeting.

32. What I also consider is its *aura*. Aura has elsewhere been identified as "essence." I, however, find this attempt to associate affect with origin or static identity far too constricting, not to mention inaccurate. That is, an inimitable atmosphere or quality encompasses and emanates from Reggae and resonates around the world. Rather than examining *who* resonates with or is resistant to Reggae's vibe or *why*, I would like to instead consider *how* this vibe—the resonance of the Rastafari— might matter/materialize otherwise for and in biblical studies now.

33. As human animals, we are often but not always drawn to that with which we resonate—the people, the places, the music, and the stories with which we identify. Although the rhythm of Reggae has an often-inexplicable draw for some, it indubitably repels others. "I see ya, I hear ya, I get ya." I-an-I will never forget those words, spoken to me by Althea Spencer-Miller when I was on the cusp of quitting—questioning myself and resisting my career path. What did she do (with her words) that day? She related to me; more than that . . . she *resonated with* me.

34. Shouse, "Feeling, Emotion, Affect," 13. Quoting Jeremy Gilbert, Shouse asserts, "Music has *physical effects* which can be identified, described and discussed but

which are not the same thing as it having *meanings*, and any attempt to understand how music works in culture must . . . be able to say something about those effects without trying to collapse them into meanings." See Jeremy Gilbert, "Signifying Nothing: 'Culture,' 'Discourse' and the Sociality of Affect," *Culture Machine* 6 (2004): culturemachine.net/index.php/cm/article/view/8/7.

35. Eugenie Brinkema, *The Forms of the Affects* (Durham, N.C.: Duke University Press), 31. It is, unsurprisingly, her ironic antidote, her argument for the resurrection of formalism as vaccine (and lever) for virility, that most *moves* me.

36. Ibid., xv. Brinkema writes: "The one way out for affect is via a way into its specificities. That approach will be called—unsurprisingly, for historically it was always the way to unlock potentialities—close reading. There is a perversity to this: if affect theory is what is utterly fashionable, it is answered here with the corrective of the utterly unfashionable, with what is, let us say, an *unzeitgemässe* call for the sustained interpretations of texts. This book's insistence on the formal dimension of affect allows not only for specificity but for the wild and many fecundities of specificity: difference, change, the particular, the contingent (and) the essential, the definite, the distinct, all dense details, and—again, to return to the spirit of Deleuze—the minor, inconsequential, secret, atomic. Treating affect in such a way deforms any coherence to 'affect' in the singular, general, universal and transforms it into something not given in advance, not apprehendable except through the thickets of formalist analysis" (xv).

37. If affect is en vogue, then I suppose we might just save each other.

38. Which is not of original or organic singularity but systemically enforced segregation.

39. See Numbers 6:1–21 for the entire list.

40. Leading scholars of the Hebrew Bible, such as James Crenshaw, Cheryl Exum, Claudia Camp, Carole Fontaine, Susan Niditch, Edith Davidson, and Gregory Mobley, consider Samson's story to be a comedic and even carnivalesque-grotesque folktale.

41. See Glissant, *Caribbean Discourse*, 107. Take, for instance, the paradigmatic Reggae beat, One Drop: defined as much by the space between the beat as the beat itself, the space creates relationship between beats, *coaxing the rhythm forward*, and—in the words of Glissant—"creat[ing] a new economy of expressive forms."

42. Not to mention why it matters that we continue to do so.

43. See Gilles Deleuze, *Spinoza: Practical Philosophy* (San Francisco: City Lights Publishers, 2001), 122. In her volume on Deleuze, Claire Colebrook describes the affect of fear in this way, employing the poetry of Emily Dickinson to illustrate her claim. Claire Colebrook, *Gilles Deleuze* (London: Routledge, 2002), 22. See also Rebecca Coleman, "Affect," in *Gender: Sources, Perspectives, and Methodologies*, ed. Renée C. Hoogland (Macmillan Interdisciplinary Handbooks; Farmington Hills, Mich.: Macmillan Reference USA, 2016), 21; idem, "'Be(come) Yourself Only Better': Self-Transformation and the Materialisation of Images," in *Deleuze and the Body*, ed. Laura Guillaume and Joe Hughes (Edinburgh: Edinburgh University Press, 2011), 144–64. Also see Rebecca Coleman, *Transfiguring Images: Screens, Affect, Futures*

(London: Routledge, 2012); and Henri Lefebvre, *Rhythmanalysis: Space, Time, and Everyday Life* (New York: Bloomsbury Academic, 2013).

44. Ludwig Koehler, Walter Baumgartner, Johann Jakob Stamm, and M. E. J. Richardson, *The Hebrew and Aramaic Lexicon of the Old Testament* (Leiden: Brill, 2001), 952–53. Henceforth, *HALOT*.

45. *HALOT* 952. *Pa'am* translated as "time" is essentially a shorthand version and a literal and literary translation. Its other denotations—"foot, anvil, occurrence," or *event*—are not without import, and I explore them in my dissertation, "Re-membering the Bible Other-Wise: An Archipelogical Hermeneutic of Bibliorality, Wisdom as Rhizome of Relation, and Other Poetic, Archipelagic Assemblages" (Drew University, 2017).

46. Judges 15:3; 16:15; 16:18; 16:20a; 16:20b; 16:28.

47. See Gilles Deleuze and Félix Guattari, *A Thousand Plateaus* (London: University of Minnesota Press, 1987), 312–16, and Félix Guattari, *Chaosmosis: An Ethico-Aesthetic Paradigm* (Bloomington: Indiana University Press, 1995), 15. Also see Stewart, "Worlding Refrains," 342. Stewart writes, "a bloom space is pulled into being by the tracks of refrains that etch out a way of living in the face of everything. These refrains stretch across everything, linking things, sensing them out—a worlding. Every refrain has its gradients, valences, moods, sensations, tempos, elements, and life spans." The notion of refrain with which she is working is a Guattarian conceptualization on which Lone Bertelsen and Andrew Murphie expound in their essay "An Ethics of Everyday Infinities and Powers: Félix Guattari on Affect and the Refrain," in *The Affect Theory Reader*, ed. Gregg and Seigworth, 138–60. For Bertelsen and Murphie, as for Guattari before them, the refrain, as a repetition, was constitutive and something akin to Stewart's notion of worlding. Refrains, they write (appealing to Guattari), "structure the affective into 'existential Territories.'" Bertelsen and Murphie continue, quoting Brian Massumi (in his introduction to Deleuze and Guattari, *Thousand Plateaus*, xv), "If affects are intensities, then refrains are affects 'cycled back'" (139).

48. See Seigworth and Gregg, "Inventory of Shimmers," 3.

49. The irony here is, of course, that each of the italicized words could be represented by *pa'am* in biblical Hebrew.

50. Cf. Deleuze and Guattari, *Thousand Plateaus*, 151: "Mistress . . . [you] may tie me down on the table, ropes drawn tight, for ten to fifteen minutes, time enough to prepare the instruments." Enter the Philistines. . . .

51. See Susan Ackerman, "What If Judges Had Been Written by a Philistine?" *Biblical Interpretation* 8, no. 1 (2000): 39.

52. The sexual innuendo here is thick. Psychologist Joan Gould is not the only scholar outside biblical studies who has drawn connections between Delilah, Judith, and Lorena Bobbitt. Gould, like so many others, identifies this as a metaphorical castration which reflects man's age-old fear of the woman's power to annihilate him by draining his "sexual juices." See Joan Gould, *Spinning Straw into Gold: What Fairytales Reveal about the Transformations in a Woman's Life* (New York: Random House, 2005), 93.

53. Cf. Gilles Deleuze, *Francis Bacon: The Logic of Sensation* (Minneapolis: University of Minnesota Press, 2005), 21. The sensation produced in his encounter with these active forces is not enough to liberate him.

54. All, indeed, is not lost for in 16:21b the storyteller reveals that Samson's hair begins to *grow*.

55. I am sure that when performed this scene invited and involved raucous laughter and building excitement in anticipation of retaliation.

56. Samson's first words to the *na'ar* leading him by the hand are literally, "Let me go and let me *feel* the *amudim*" (16:26). While it seems to echo the request/command for release of the Hebrew people in Exodus 9:1, the roots are not the same.

57. Cf. Deleuze and Guattari, *Thousand Plateaus*, 400. Interestingly, the reader is left to assume that Jah responds for while Samson is certainly infused with the strength to pull down the pillars, there is no explicit acknowledgment of Jah's involvement nor even a textual reference to Jah by means of the divine signifier. Further on Deleuzoguattarian discharges of emotion, see Stephen Moore's "The Messiah Who Screamed," in his *Gospel Jesuses and Other Nonhumans: Biblical Criticism Post-poststructuralism* (Atlanta: SBL Press, 2017), 48–49.

58. The word here for remember (*zakar*) is incidentally the same word as for "male" in Genesis 1:27, which I believe holds a degree of significance for the re-membering of Samson as Israel. Interestingly, Samson cries out to YHWH but appeals to *Elohim* for vengeance.

59. There is also an oblique reference here to the infamous retributive injunction of Hammurabi's Code, "An eye for an eye" (cf. Exodus 21:24).

60. Taylor, "Sheba's Song," 75. In his conclusion to "Sheba's Song," Taylor identifies the I-an-I "logic of Rastafari discourse" as reflected in other discourses—particularly Buber's "I-Thou" and Kierkegaard's "God-relationship." While he gives a nod to poststructuralism, he only refers to Derrida to acknowledge that I-an-I is a supplement to "a European Judeo-Christian tradition told in accordance with the doctrine of 'the One'" (ibid.). Taylor does not, however, explicitly identify the resonances of I-an-I and deconstruction and poststructuralist discourse writ large, nor does he acknowledge the complexities and/or possibilities resident within this relationship.

61. Also see Adriane Anthony McFarlane, "The Epistemological Significance of 'I-an-I' as a Response to Quashie and Anancyism in Jamaican Culture," in *Chanting Down Babylon*, ed. Murrell et al., 107–21. McFarlane points out that "the zealous Rastas see no difference between being, knowing, and doing. This ontology underpins Rasta theory of knowledge and sense of responsibility. For one to know, one must be; and for one to do anything (efficaciously), one must know" (117).

62. See Nettleford, "Discourse on Rastafarian Reality," 311–25. Nettleford proclaims, "The Rastafarians have tuned into a major strategy of demarginalization: religion. Having one's own God in one's own image was a grand flowering in Rastafari of what had earlier begun in Myal and developed in Zion revivalism and Pocomania, with the hijacking of the oppressor's God in a move that served to discommode the oppressor. The slave forebears of Rastafarians understood fully that there are

areas of inviolability beyond the reach of oppressors, and that these are what guarantee survival and beyond. Such exercise of the creative imagination and intellect remains, then, the most powerful weapon against all acts of inhumanity; and the Rastafarians have drawn on the tradition, which was nurtured since the eighteenth century, to cope with and defy the harshness of twentieth-century indulgences. Wresting the Christian message from the Messenger as a strategy of demarginalization helped bring slaves and the free peasantry nearer a perceived mainstream as 'children of God.' Rastafari were to extend this by proclaiming themselves as 'pieces of God.' The divinity of all black people—in fact, of all human beings—here becomes the basis for the equality, liberty, dignity, mutual respect, and equity in terms of access to economic resources, and all the values claimed by civil or democratic society but yet to be achieved in . . . Babylon" (315). The contingency of identity (Rastafarian cultural and communal construction and co-constitution) is but one reason why the Rastafari re-membering of Samson must also be read in conversation with the experience of other (interpretive) bodies, including those of "Israel," within the Persian province of Yehud.

63. Édouard Glissant, *Poetics of Relation* (Ann Arbor: University of Michigan Press, 1997), 33. "The Caribbean, as far as I am concerned, may be held up as one of the places in the world where Relation presents itself most visibly, one of the explosive regions where it seems to be gathering strength" (ibid.).

64. Deleuze, *Francis Bacon*, 39.

65. The Rastafari themselves do not employ the word *understanding* to represent cognitive resonance, nor any other terminology within the English vernacular which incorporates a word that signifies oppression or subordination of any sort (e.g., *under* is replaced by *over*). Not only that, but the Rastafari consider true understanding to lead to overstanding in the face of the violent hegemony of Babylon. "Oppression" itself is represented in Rastafari dialect (*patois*) by the word "downpression," signifying resistance and making manifest the intention and result of such activity.

66. Deleuze, *Francis Bacon*, 40.

67. Judges 16:30, my translation.

68. Seigworth and Gregg, "Inventory of Shimmers," 3.

69. *HALOT* 692–93. Aptly, *natah*, the verb used here, has a vast and varied semantic range, signifying either/or, both/and, push/pull.

70. Deleuze, *Francis Bacon*, 40. Deleuze writes, "The organism is not life, it is what imprisons life. The body is completely living, and yet nonorganic. Likewise sensation, when it acquires a body through organism, takes on an excessive and spasmodic appearance, exceeding the bounds of organic activity. It is immediately conveyed in the flesh through the nervous wave or vital emotion" (ibid.)—a statement that describes Samson's spasmodic flesh throughout the story.

71. Following the beat, reading with rhythm, leads us to re-member Samson's final act, where his massacre-suicide effects *resistance* to imperial domination and difference constructed according to Western hierarchical dualisms, always already invigorated by the *resonance* of *I-an-I* theo-logics. It is uncertain just how the Rastafari reconcile Samson's status/subjectivity as a disabled, blind, bound, and enslaved body in their

renderings and re-memberings of him. Although I believe there is great political potential within the symbol of Samson's disabled (disfigured, disdained, yet not disqualified) body, in my admittedly limited research I have not yet found this body as accessible to, or appealing for, Rastafari re-membering Samson.

72. Édouard Glissant, "The Unforeseeable Diversity of the World," in *Beyond Dichotomies: Histories, Identities, Cultures, and the Challenge of Globalization*, ed. Elisabeth Mudimbe-Boyi (Albany: State University of New York Press, 2002), 290. Glissant is expounding on our "worldness" as that which we all have in common according to creolization (i.e., "the meeting, interface, shock, harmonies, and disharmonies between cultures of the world, in the realized totality of the earth world" or what Glissant has elsewhere deemed the *tout-monde*). He proceeds to further elucidate creolization, which "has the following characteristics: the lightning speed of interaction among its elements; the 'awareness of awareness' thus provoked in us; the reevaluation of the various elements brought into contact (for creolization has no presupposed scale of values); and unforeseeable results. Creolization is not a simple crossbreeding that would produce easily anticipated syntheses" (ibid.). (It is neither *méstissage* nor hybridity.) And Glissant's ultimate proposition is: "Today the whole world is becoming an archipelago and becoming creolized" (ibid). Also see Glissant, *Traité du Tout-Monde*, 194.

73. And, just like Samson, the Bible is a corpus that just won't die (no matter how much we wish it would)!

74. Now, there are at least three resonances—what Greg Seigworth and Melissa Gregg might deem affective bloom spaces—in effect in my interpretation of Samson's folktale (which, through an oral-literate hermeneutics, I consider an ambient affective assemblage). These are: (1) the resonance between Africana/Orality Theory (I mean no disrespect in this conflation, but following the work of African scholars such as Chinua Achebe, Solomon Iyasere, and Isodore Okpwewho in particular, I consider Diasporic Africana Critical Theory to be at the forefront of the complex discourse that is Orality Theory) and Affect Theory (most prolific in the work of Deleuze and Guattari), which I consider to be present in Édouard Glissant's poetics; (2) the irie vibes of the Rastafari, Reggae, and the Bible; and (3) the dynamic relationship emerging amid these diverse bodies and inaugurating new possibilities for avant-garde biblical interpretation, which hinges on the distinctively Caribbean musicality of the Reggae Riddims of the Rastafari.

75. Seigworth and Gregg, "Inventory of Shimmers," 3.

76. Very much alive to us because alive in and through us today.

❧ The "Unspeakable Teachings" of *The Secret Gospel of Mark*: Feelings and Fantasies in the Making of Christian Histories

ALEXIS G. WALLER

A certain woman whose brother had died . . . prostrated herself before Jesus and says to him, "Son of David, have mercy on me." But the disciples rebuked her. And Jesus, being angered, went off with her into the garden where the tomb was, and straightway a great cry was heard from the tomb. And going near, Jesus rolled away the stone from the door of the tomb. And straightway, going in where the youth was, he stretched forth his hand and raised him, seizing his hand. But the youth, looking upon him, loved him and began to beseech him that he might be with him. And going out of the tomb they came into the house of the youth, for he was rich. And after six days Jesus told him what to do and in the evening the youth comes to him, wearing a linen cloth over his naked body. And he remained with him that night, for Jesus taught him the mystery of the kingdom of God. And thence, arising, he returned to the other side of the Jordan.

—The Secret Gospel of Mark

Reading historically may mean reading against what is conventionally referred to as history.

—CARLA FRECCERO, *Queer/Early/Modern*

The reception history of *The Secret Gospel of Mark* is, among those who know anything about it, famously controversial. Thick with mystery and rumor, rife with volatile accusations, betrayals, and defensiveness, it is an affective history par excellence.[1] The short text at its center has been variously described as evidence of the earliest surviving version of the Gospel of Mark, a second-century forgery pieced together from other gospel narratives, a modern hoax, an "ironic gay joke," and even "the most grandiose and reticulated 'Fuck You' ever perpetrated in the long and vituperative history of scholarship."[2] No clear consensus has been reached on the gospel's status as forged or authentic, although impassioned arguments have been mounted from both sides. Whether the manuscript was forged or not, however, it has become an object of longing and repulsion, a marker and maker of alternative narratives—be they ancient and "authentically historical," or modern fictions—of early Christian traditions, as well as an incitement to emotionally charged debates about methods and ethics in reconstructing the past. As such in what follows, I read *Secret Mark* and its reception history alongside some queer historiographical projects that take interest in the social, affective dimensions at work in notions of the "historical" in order to reconsider how we might handle (our feelings about) the early Christian past.

LOST QUEER THINGS

> The drama of existence is a central, compelling narrative or mystery inhering in queer archives, a drama borne out by countless scholars' efforts to find lost queer things.
>
> DANIEL MARSHALL, KEVIN P. MURPHY, AND ZEB TORTORICI,
> "Queering Archives: Historical Unravelings"

The Secret Gospel of Mark was found—or forged—by Morton Smith, a Columbia professor of ancient history, while he was cataloguing manuscripts at the Mar Saba monastery library outside of Jerusalem in 1958. The gospel fragment is quoted in a letter that claims to have been composed by the second-century church father, Clement of Alexandria. Copied onto the blank endpapers of a sixteenth-century volume of Ignatius of Antioch's letters, Clement's letter is addressed to a certain Theodore, who evidently has heard some gossip about this gospel's "unspeakable teachings" (*tas arrētous didaskalias*). Clement assures Theodore that the gospel says nothing regarding what he seems to have asked about: absolutely not, there is no mention of a "naked man with a naked man" (*to de gymnos gymnō*).[3] To prove that Jesus and the young man who loved him kept their clothes on during their late night rituals, Clement quotes the relevant passage, which is now our only extant copy of this gospel fragment.[4] He explains how Mark came to write a version of the gospel which was kept secret because it contained advanced teachings that would be misunderstood should it get into the wrong hands. Evidently, it *had* gotten into the wrong hands: Clement's letter suggests that a sect of early Christians had been reading it as evidence of a "libertine" gospel in which Jesus practiced some kind of homoerotic baptismal sex magic. Or so Smith would suggest.[5] Smith's presentation of *Secret Mark* at the 1960 national meeting of the Society of Biblical Literature caused a big stir among biblical scholars. It also made the front page of the *New York Times*.[6] In 1973, Smith published two books on *Secret Mark*, one scholarly and one for popular audiences, that would instigate passionate disputes in Christian historiography that continue today.[7]

Dispute over the authenticity of the gospel was exacerbated by Morton Smith's provocative interpretations of the text but also by the absence of the physical manuscript. Smith photographed the handwritten text in 1948 and left the physical copy at Mar Saba when he returned to New York. In 1975, biblical scholar Quentin Quesnell published the first proposal that Clement's letter might be a modern forgery.[8] His suggestion took hold of the scholarly imagination, and, with almost no one else besides Smith having laid eyes on the physical manuscript, the "folklore of forgery took on a life of its own."[9] A year after Quesnell's indictment, three scholars went in search of the manuscript. As one of them, Guy Stroumsa, remembered it, he "had been intrigued by Morton Smith's sensational description of his find, and we wanted to see the text with our own eyes."[10] They drove down from Jerusalem, found the Voss edition of Ignatius in the tower library and saw the hand-copied letter of Clement. Sometime afterward, however, the end pages on which the text had been inscribed were removed from the book and have not been relocated since. Without a wider audience to confirm its continued existence or more thoroughly investigate its provenance, *Secret Mark*'s past has hovered somewhere between fantasy and history for decades. Some have lamented this "stalemate in the academy," fearing that, "unless the academy can reach a closer agreement on *Secret Mark*'s past, the secret gospel has no real future."[11]

If "authentic," *Secret Mark* has important implications for the textual history of the canonical New Testament and the diversity of earliest Christian traditions. If "historical," it would invite reimagining Christian origins (and, *perhaps*, the sex life of the historical Jesus, or, at least, the erotic fantasy life of later early Christians).[12] Neither those committed to salvaging *Secret Mark* as a piece of "real history" nor those who believe it to be a fake will drop their claims because the stakes feel too high: For the one side, giving up *Secret Mark* as a forgery means the loss of potential evidence for the real Christian past, and for the other side, using it constructively means inserting a homoerotically inflected piece of fiction into the realm of proper history. Both possibilities seem too much for either side to bear. Feelings can be far more intractable than facts, it seems, and indeed, feelings can be too intimately bound up with *what gets construed as fact* to distinguish between the two.

In its queer archival dimensions, *Secret Mark's* reception speaks to the ways historical evidence acts as a cover—and a medium—for the transmission of affective and theological investments and anxieties regarding what we can actually know about "what really happened" in the past, as well as to the constitutive role (homo)sexuality plays in the fraught debate about authenticity.[13]

This scrap of text provides a particularly dense site for reflecting on the felt investments that variously saturate the rhetoric of forgery and authenticity, mark the boundaries of what counts as evidence, and circumscribe or fuel the fantasy life of Christian history.

THE QUESTION OF EVIDENCE

> What might its general value be, assuming we could agree that it has a real past?
>
> CHARLES W. HEDRICK, "The Secret Gospel of Mark"

In his review of Smith's work on the Mar Saba find, Quentin Quesnell drew attention to Smith's comment about looking "forward to the scholarly discussion that will follow the publication of the text. What will others see in it? And what evidence will they be able to find to support their insights?"[14] Quesnell proposed that, "since surely many others besides Smith must be equally fascinated with the question of how scholarly conclusions relate to evidence, is it impossible that one of them found himself moved to concoct some 'evidence' in order to set up a controlled experiment?"[15] This suggestion—that a forger might be testing the discipline's historicist standards by producing a forgery, by constructing problematic evidence to see if it could pass for real history—lived on in various forms throughout the debates. Even though Quesnell was urging skepticism, and perhaps insinuating foul play, his fantasy of this evidence experiment, as well as Smith's curiosity about what others would see in it, both resonate with the kinds of open questions that ground queer historiographical endeavors: What personal desires or anxieties influence what scholars, or any readers, see in any given piece of evidence? How does any piece of evidence come to prove a particular past? Queer archives, after all, invite us to consider the affective stakes of what kinds of objects are privileged as "evidence," under what conditions, and for whom.[16]

Queer archival projects, on the one hand, construct or collect evidence that might be foundational for alternative narratives of desire, expressions of gender, or queer community, and, on the other, are positioned to question what kinds of erotic trajectories and normative identities traditional historical archives are invested in constructing or protecting.[17] While acknowledging that traditional historical methods often intend to safeguard the past, to prevent violence that can be done by willful denial of inconvenient or offensive facts or by uncritical, too-imaginative identification and appropriation, queer historiography nonetheless questions what values "objectivity," "authenticity," and "proof" code and enforce, whose desires they subsume and authorize. And so the queer archival turn often takes an explicit interest in the role of desire in finding or making histories—desire registered by historians and institutions for particular versions of the past, as well as instantiations of desire "from the past" as they were recorded and retrieved.

Ann Cvetkovich offers the image of the archive of feelings to describe such unconventional assemblages and the ways they often intimately associate things that in "properly historical" contexts might not be allowed or expected to touch; they value and convey histories of what might have been but can't now be easily told, or they contain histories that could never have been but which their creators long to have known.[18] Cvetkovich proposes the fetish as one model of the archive of feelings, in which "objects derive their significance from the feelings attached to them; not because of their intrinsic meaning or referentiality."[19] Such "archives," be they physical or metaphorical, act as a repository or expression of the kinds of "queer histories . . . made of affective relations" that, for instance, Carolyn Dinshaw has mapped.[20]

Cvetkovich argues explicitly for "the importance of fantasy as a way of creating history from absences," homing in on the kinds of archives that can instantiate (histories of) queer lives and desires from the most ephemeral traces that so often are all that are left to mark the presence and erasures of queer pasts.[21] Queers often know that there is rarely a "historical" place to which one can (re)turn or authoritatively cite, and yet the longing persists, and so we resort to making creative inferences from hints, suggestions, and strange absences—to inventing things that can attest to a *felt reality*. Kathryn Bond Stockton captures this in her description of how "certain queer comedians, who grew up in the sixties before there were any gays on TV, wryly explain that they 'found themselves' as children in TV personas . . . : Ernie, the odd boy on *My Three Sons*; Robin of *Batman*; *The Beverly Hillbillies*' Miss Jane Hathaway; or Josephine the Plumber (in ads for bathroom cleaners)."[22] It's in these sites of fictional or fantasized queerness that queers might feel we have good reason to stake our own varied sorts of "historical" claims.

Such archives, then, "are composed of material practices that challenge traditional conceptions of history and understand the quest for history as a psychic need rather than a science."[23] Cvetkovich cites as one example Cheryl Dunye's 1996 film *The Watermelon Woman*, about a queer black woman (named Cheryl and played by Dunye herself) who is obsessed with finding evidence of a 1930s African American lesbian actress named Fae Richards. Dunye marshals forms of documentary and oral history to tell her story. The film features a fake archive— doctored photographs, antique film clips, and forged letters created for the film by artist Zoe Leonard, but it speaks to "real" history (the real dyke heroines of early Hollywood, the Josephine Bakers, Clara Bows, Marlene Dietrichs, Dorothy Arzners) and to the role of contemporary longings to find queer lost things. *The Watermelon Woman*'s overlapping personal and "historical" narratives provide spaces of meditation on what drives someone to seek intimacy or kinship with figures from the past, how historical obsessions and personal relationships spill over into each other, and how the past, through fantasy and historical fact, obliquely informs and is informed by felt relations in and across the present.

Such queer archives of feelings resonate with the ways disavowed desires and aversions (and their often theological implications) get displaced onto historical events or ancient texts in New Testament historiography.[24] Because the theological has so often been sublimated through the historical in biblical studies, the affective stakes of historicity are heightened, as the reception of *Secret Mark* hotly displays. The collection of scholarly, popular, and personal material that accumulated over the course of *Secret Mark*'s twentieth-century reception functions, then, as a queer affective archive at the very heart of New Testament historiography. It is an "archive" bound together in great part by its obsession with—or by its being unwillingly haunted by—the pressing "question of evidence," as Quesnell emphasized, but the range of "evidence" that shows up in what I'm calling the archive of *Secret Mark*'s reception history is inconsistent with the dispassionate standards of traditional historicism that most of Smith's interlocutors lay claim to or strain to defend. Their use of evidence underscores the affective dimensions that also drive historicist approaches to the past.

QUEER FANTASIES IN THE CHRISTIAN ARCHIVE; OR, AUTHENTICITY AFFECTS

The whole morbid concatenation of fancies does credit to Smith's ability to enter into the spirit of the Carpocratians. . . .

PATRICK SKEHAN, Review of *Clement of Alexandria and a Secret Gospel of Mark*

Smith had in mind a life of Jesus in the grand tradition of nineteenth-century narrative, only a Jesus in the image of Smith's own fantasy of conspiracy and fraud: . . . charlatan, magician, homosexual.

JACOB NEUSNER, *Are There Really Tannaitic Parallels to the Gospels?*

Secret Mark's "archive" includes traditional forms of evidence like handwriting analysis and ancient comparanda, as well as the kinds of biblical scholarly fictions that read as "historical," like form and source critical analyses, and so on.[25] It also includes presentations and personal interactions at academic conferences recorded in published volumes, scholarly articles, and popular media (e.g., a 1973 review titled "Jesus Christ . . . Supergay?" in the *Advocate*, and a 1980s television reenactment of Smith introducing audiences to the manuscript that had long before disappeared[26]) and, more recently, filtered through the blogosphere, leaving traces along the way of the institutional, theological, and emotional stakes of this historical conundrum.[27] These various sources provide the records of vicious public spats, dreams, rumors, and other realia and phenomena that (strangely, for a field as historically-critically invested as New Testament studies) were used as evidence, like pulp fiction, private correspondence, and personal anecdotes about Smith's character. Meaningful silences, unspoken knowledge, code words, and rumors are marshaled as evidence against the authenticity of the ancient text by proving Smith's inappropriate desire for a certain kind of past.

To start, I'd like to draw attention to a piece of "minor" history in the archive. Shortly after the publication of Quesnell's pivotal article, the Center for Hermeneutical Studies in Hellenistic and Modern Culture held a conference at the Graduate Theological Union and the University of California in Berkeley. It was organized by Reginald H. Fuller, who presented a survey of possible readings of *Secret Mark* titled "Longer Mark: Forgery, Interpolation, or Old Tradition?"[28] The agenda for this conference, with its focus on *Secret Mark*, was inspired by a dream Fuller had. Fuller is quoted in the conference minutes: "I'd like to begin by sharing a dream. In the dream, Professor Smith met the man responsible for the Piltdown skull. Then Professor Smith broke down and admitted that he himself had written the supposed letter from Clement. As a result of that dream, I naturally seized upon the whole question of criteria for detecting a forgery, as Professor Murgia did. That is points 1 and 2 on the list."[29] Yes, naturally. Fuller's dream, ephemeral though it may have been, had the rather real and (thanks to publication of the papers) lasting effect of adding evidence to the critique of Smith's discovery and interpretations.

Elsewhere in this archive, Robert Price tells a freely associative personal anecdote of his own to refute Smith's narrative of discovery, taking fiction as a kind of reliable evidence:

> If Secret Mark is Morton Smith's own creation, where might he have derived the idea for it? This question brings me at last to a chance discovery of my own, the event that caused me to reassess the whole question after I thought Professor Hedrick had laid it to rest. Two years ago, I was in Detroit on a speaking tour and chanced to be poring over the shelves of a large but lackluster second-hand bookstore. My eye fell upon the title of one worn-looking volume, *The Mystery of Mar Saba*. Thinking instantly of Morton Smith's fateful visit there, I picked up the book with mild curiosity, thinking, "What if it turns out to be one of those 'lost Gospel' novels?" Son of a gun, it did![30]

From this chance encounter with a work of evangelical spy fiction in a Detroit bookstore, Price wonders if "Morton Smith might easily have become familiar with this popular novel, and I cannot help wondering if it gave him the idea for a hoax of his own, meant to undermine the Christian faith that he found to be oppressive."[31] Elsewhere, Price indicts Smith for giving too much authority to the imaginative dimensions of religious history:

> In 1985 I asked Morton Smith how he responded to charges of forgery, recently renewed in Per Beskow's excellent book *Strange Tales about Jesus: A Survey of Unfamiliar Gospels*. He told me the now-familiar story of the custodians of the manuscript secreting it away out of embarrassment at the notoriety that Smith's book *Secret Gospel* had brought them, henceforth wanting to suppress the evidence. He asked, furthermore, what business Beskow had in condemning all the more-recent New Age Gospels as spurious: if they embodied someone's faith, weren't they authentic Gospels, no matter who wrote them or when? Later I wondered if his words did not apply equally, even especially, to his own Secret Mark![32]

Of course, he concludes, "Short of yet another manuscript discovery, this time perhaps a confession among Smith's own papers, we will never know."[33]

Another piece of "evidence" that simultaneously acknowledges and eludes the contested question of authenticity is a 1984 Channel 4 (U.K.) television special beautifully titled *Jesus: The Evidence*. It features Morton Smith in his late sixties, performing an encounter with *Secret Mark*, visually suggesting the presence of the manuscript in the monastery library.[34] Smith is seated at a desk in a library, or a film studio set up to look like a library. He's holding a facsimile copy of the Voss volume of Ignatius's letters opened to the pages inscribed with the (by then) lost manuscript. "The evidence turned out to show that the evidence was, pretty certainly, authentic. I had to be so careful because the text implied that Jesus himself practiced some sort of secret nocturnal initiation. This is what Clement quotes of the secret gospel." The screen freezes, with the facsimile of the text in the center of the frame and the words of the gospel fragment are heard in voiceover: "But the youth, looking upon him, loved him, and began to beseech him that he might be with him. . . . The youth comes to him wearing a linen cloth over his naked body, and he remained with him that night, for Jesus taught him the mystery of God." The camera cuts back to Smith, who explains that Clement follows the gospel excerpt with a "reassurance that there is nothing in this text . . . to justify the rumors Theodore has obviously heard to the effect that during the ritual Jesus and the initiate were naked together." The episode attempts to visualize evidence that may or may not have ever actually existed to render alternative versions of early Christianity to a popular audience—constructing a historical fantasy (and perhaps an erotic fantasy) for an audience in the act of reimagining Christian origins.[35]

This collection of materials is not some sort of *Secret Mark* sideshow, I argue, but, like so many compelling queer archives, it underscores the contingency of any history and the difference various kinds of desires can make in determining how the past must have been and what kind of future it can have.

Some rendered this desire theological: "Make no mistake," wrote New Testament scholar Walter Wink in his 1974 review, "Smith's is a theological and not just an historical program. He is engaged in a systematic effort to undermine the very ground on which Christian faith rests. His tools are the familiar ones: historical revision and psychological reduction. It is this project, and not his textual discovery, which gives his book the character of a challenge and confrontation."[36] Wink was not distressed by questions of the document's authenticity, but by what Smith made of it. Other critics who were concerned about its authenticity, however, alarmed by what they considered Smith's elision of fiction and fact, denounced his historical work as irresponsible fantasy or needy psychological compensation. Smith's former student Jacob Neusner accused Smith of disgracing the quest for the historical Jesus, arguing that the "'historical' results [that Smith arrived at]—Jesus was 'really' a homosexual magician—depended upon a selective believing in whatever Smith thought was historical."[37] After their public falling out at the 1984 Society of Biblical Literature meeting, Neusner would become one of his most vehement critics, declaring Smith "a charlatan and a fraud, and his discovery a hoax," and in 1993, two years after Smith's death, he published a bitter book-long refutation of Smith's scholarship, spanning from Smith's dissertation to his 1978 *Jesus the Magician*.[38] Smith, said Neusner, "chose to believe everything bad he could about Jesus, perhaps making up what he could not read into the sources."[39] Guy Stroumsa published the private correspondence of Smith and Gershom Scholem, in great part in order to prove Smith's innocence; these letters, Stroumsa hoped, would offer access to Smith's "state of mind" as he worked through the early stages of interpreting the text and communicated with his admired mentor.[40] In spite of Stroumsa's intentions, some of Smith's critics instead turned to those letters for evidence of Smith's burgeoning dislike and eventual break with the church, his youthful fascination with Alistair Crowley, and other seeds of dissent that would lead him to write Jesus into history as a magician conducting (erotic?) baptismal initiations. These came to be read as further clues to why Smith might have wanted to find a piece of evidence exactly like *The Secret Gospel of Mark* fragment.[41] They suggested that Smith was an angry gay man, a lapsed Christian who was looking for a way to undermine Christianity, or whose desire to make a place for homosexuality at the heart of Christianity was so strong that it pushed him to fabricate the evidence.[42]

As biblical scholar Anitra Bingham Kolenkow noticed early in these conversations, Smith was not the only one to exert a strongly felt, theologically motivated agenda in contemporary retellings of early Christian history. In her contribution to the 1975 Eighteenth Colloquy at Berkeley (a conference prompted, as mentioned above, by Fuller's dream), Kolenkow addresses connections between scholars' ideological or theological agendas and how they narrate trajectories between early and late sources. In doing so, she names the elephant in the room—anxiety on the part of biblical scholars about the proximity of homosexuality to any historical or canonical Jesus: "One may also note the furor raised over Morton Smith's charge that Jesus was a homosexual. . . . We know that the Gospel of John long has been known as possibly containing both gnostic and homosexual motifs. . . . What difference does it make to us if Jesus is not separated from a homosexual situation?"[43] She leaves the question open, but many readers already had firm answers to that question.

It often seems that the heightened emotional response to *Secret Mark* has to do with the fear that Smith has slipped some queer fiction into the annals of "real history." Since Smith's interest, however marginal, in the sex life of the historical Jesus, was what seems to have hit such a nerve across the field, those who argue for *Secret Mark*'s authenticity have instead emphasized readings of the gospel that look past the homoerotic implications.[44] Smith's find was authentic but he was wrong to read homoeroticism between the lines, they suggest.[45] In this line of thinking, which is prominent in defenses of *Secret Mark*, the text's "queerness" is what makes it (necessary to call it) a forgery. Either because its particular representation of homoeroticism makes it anachronistic (as some have tried to argue), or because of a more theologically pressing need to distance a text that could so easily be read as involving Jesus and homoeroticism from authentic Christian history or the canonical New Testament.[46]

Hedrick urges the field to see that the value of *Secret Mark*'s contribution to our reconstructions of the past is too great to relegate it to the status of a forgery. He points out how often those who have fought most vehemently for its status as a forgery are also most upset about Smith's interpretation of Jesus' potentially homoerotic relationships with his disciples.[47] Hedrick argues, however, that without this "gay Jesus" narrative getting in the way, we could use this document for what's really important: "Homosexual acts by Jesus should be a non-issue for a historian. . . . The historian's questions are different: for example, did Jesus baptize or not?"[48] Hedrick's well-meaning attempt to pull *Secret Mark* out of the morass of hysterical scholarship has the disciplining effect of discrediting historians for whom "homosexual acts by Jesus" might be an object of interest or desire, thus preventing them from participating in the making or authorizing of history.

But there are other difficulties in naming the ways homophobia is entwined with claims for forgery in the effort to protect the early Christian past from any contact with (a potentially historically viable) homosexual Jesus. In an anecdote that gently reflects both the intimacy that is one of the pleasures of the small world of biblical scholarship, and the discomfort about homosexuality being named, much less authenticated through association with the early Christian historical imaginary, Helmut Koester recollects:

> I first met Morton Smith in 1960 at a conference at which he presented *Secret Mark* for the first time. After that meeting I sought him out, asked for a copy of the transcribed text and began discussing the matter with him. I especially criticized him for suggesting that the initiation rite in the Secret Gospel indicated some homosexual ritual. He was quite open to my criticism, and we became friends. In 1963, when I was a visiting professor at the University of Heidelberg, Morton had a sabbatical, which he spent searching for magical texts in European museums. He then asked me if he could bring me his manuscript, the first draft of what a decade later was to be published by Harvard University Press under the title *Clement of Alexandria and a Secret Gospel of Mark*. We met several hours a day for a whole week, discussing details of the interpretation of *Secret Mark*.[49]

I can't help but wonder, reading suggestively into the affective world of Koester's narrative, if Smith's openness to criticism of his interest in a homosexual Christian past—his willingness to set it aside—opened the way for his friendship with Koester and to Koester's desire to use *Secret Mark* in his reconstructions of canonical New Testament textual traditions. Of course, Bart Ehrman would critique my insinuations of a homophobic structuring of such academic relationships. Ehrman would call for hard evidence, and he would find it elusive:

> As I have intimated, Hedrick suggests that the widespread vitriol found its root in a homophobia in the academy. I too do not know if this is true, but I certainly would like to see some evidence of it, if this in fact is what he wants to claim. For it is a rather serious charge—raised precisely by Hedrick's stated reluctance to raise it!—and not one that we should allow into general discourse without some supporting argument.[50]

However, just as José Muñoz has reminded us how "queerness is rarely complemented by evidence, or at least by traditional understandings of the term," securing proof of homophobia here would challenge conceptions of evidence, calling on a kind of suspect, affective knowledge.[51] The exaggerated responses to Smith's so-called "homosexual" designs on the Christian past might be felt, however, as speaking *symptomatically* to a kind of panic reverberating across the field. They point not only to anxiety about some scholarship touching the historical Jesus in inappropriate ways but also to the anxiety New Testament scholars generally feel about their own desires to make contact with the past. People on both sides of the argument seem to hold out hope that stabilizing the reputation of *Secret Mark* as definitively forged or authentic will shut down uncomfortable uncertainties and, perhaps, alleviate anxiety about their own theological, imaginative, perverse, relations with the past.

As squeamish or dismissive as much of the scholarship may be about this, and as much as the gospel's defenders might like to purge everything related to sexuality from the conversation, Smith's perhaps minor historical Jesus interpretation sheds light on exclusions and repressions in the study of the New Testament and Christian beginnings. As Hedrick has put it: "It is understandable that some people might feel it would be better had the document never been discovered."[52]

As with any new discovery, questions about evidence and criteria for making interpretive choices come to the fore, but in his responses to the criticism Smith pressed consciously against the normative assumptions in the field about the kinds of interpretive moves canonical boundaries protect against, just as others were beginning to accuse Smith of inappropriately having his way with canonical Mark or the historical Jesus. He was, in a sense, reminding his colleagues of the kind of fictions most New Testament scholars prefer to treat as facts.[53] Smith asserted that "*all* accounts of [Jesus'] teaching and practice are conjectural, and I claim to my conjectures only that they fit the reports as well as any and better than most. Of course nothing can be *proved* about this subject."[54] Many of his interlocutors would disagree with him on one or both points, and, as Ehrman puts it, Smith's interpretations "left most scholars breathless and many incensed."[55] But the fact that *Secret Mark* and Smith's conjectures generated so much energy and became the object of so many scholarly—and for a time popular—cathexes, is exactly what I want to take up as evidence of how feelings fuel certain kinds of factualizing work. Disputes over the text's authenticity and Smith's (pure or impure) desires continue to be intimately tied to certain readers' anxieties about the particular kind of historical Jesus that Smith saw behind it, and, relatedly, to the "personal" reasons that might have motivated Smith in particular to find that version of Jesus in history.[56]

This debate about *Secret Mark* makes explicit some of the ways evidence is saturated with ambivalent but intense affective investments. Although he doesn't question how the loaded notion of authenticity is a placeholder for a host of other values and agendas, Bart Ehrman frames the problem well:

If authentic, this letter would raise significant questions for the study of the New Testament and the history of early Christianity. It would make us rethink our interpretations of the earliest surviving accounts of Jesus. It would drive us to reconsider our reconstruction of the historical Jesus. It would be one of the most significant discoveries of the twentieth century. If it were authentic.[57]

He does not think Clement's letter or the gospel fragment is authentic, and, so—rest assured—they do not have what it takes to push us to do this rethinking of early Christianity, our reconstructions of the historical Jesus, or the theological implications that these revisions could have. Or do they? Ehrman puts his finger on the animating forces for the affective intensity saturating (primarily North American) New Testament scholarship generated by this proposed insertion of *Secret Mark* into canonical gospel literature and early Christian history.

The *Secret Mark* controversy pushes the desired or claimed objectivity, or affective neutrality, of historicism as the authorizing ground of New Testament scholarship to its limits—over its limits, even, spilling into the murky territory where desire and the writing of history intermingle in the messiest, most perverse ways. Authenticity is the bulwark: If this document *in fact* had a "real past," *then* we would be forced to let our interpretive imaginations run loose a little, *then* we would have to deal with perhaps uncomfortable revisions of certain social, theological, and political investments generated by or transformed into a canonical version of the Christian past.

Those who condemn Smith for forging *Secret Mark* implicitly suggest that his desire (for a queer historical Jesus) was so inappropriately strong that he went so far as to manufacture an object *"from the past"* that he could put his hands on. Those who argued against forgery, however, nonetheless admit that, implicitly, Smith's desire for a particular (queer) Christian past was so strong that it blinded him to more appropriate (heteronormatively comfortable) interpretations of the text.

Secret Mark provokes a set of imaginative possibilities that might seem dangerous perhaps because it makes explicit the ways "psychic needs" do shape history. In 1973, the *Advocate* published an article about Smith's recently published *Secret Gospel of Mark*, which points to another alternative gay life this secret gospel could lead. It begins: "Was Jesus gay? . . . Few have been convinced, though some serious scholars have conceded that some of the reported incidents in Christ's life could be interpreted as supporting the notion that He occasionally showed homosexual feelings."[58] Perhaps, at a certain level, readers of the *Advocate* would not disagree with Peter Jeffery's (albeit disparaging) assessment: "Like the pseudonymous authors of so much of the New Testament, he might tell himself, he would only be bringing new clarity to the true teaching that had always been there."[59] And if so, what might it change? Whose fantasies would be honored, and whose would be crushed?[60] Like Carolyn Dinshaw's reading of Boswell's "fan mail" after the publication of *Christianity, Social Tolerance, and Homosexuality*, one is put in mind of the hunger felt by people who read Boswell's history—and even of those who had only heard about the book—to find a place of origin, including at the (imagined) origins of Christianity.[61]

In his analysis of the anxious and theologically driven backlash to Smith's publications, Shawn Eyer concludes with a plea for a more "objective" approach, which can ultimately better reveal the historical truths to which the evidence points:

> *Secret Mark*'s plight constitutes a warning to all scholars as to the dangers of allowing sentiments of faith to cloud or prevent critical examination of evidence. . . . After twenty years of confusion, it must be time to set aside emotionalism and approach both this fragment and Morton Smith's assessment of the role of magic in early Christianity with objective and critical eyes.[62]

But the thrust of the argument I'd like to make here is different. None of us is immune from such investments (driven by "sentiments" of faith, or any other sentiment). Histories constructed from any early Christian text will always be fraught, although they may appear less histrionic. It is the disavowal of theologically and emotionally inflected claims that obscures important historiographical questions about the slippery, unpredictable nature of evidence itself and about narratives that would try to shore up the foundational place of evidence in traditional historicism.

Attachments, anxieties, rumors, and fantasies circulate around the almost inseparable assemblage of the text of *Secret Mark and* the person who found (or forged) the text and presented it to his colleagues and the public *and* the histories generated to explain where the text comes from. The text cannot be peeled apart from its reception (to the chagrin of those who would like to restore it to a clean historical slate). As such, the various emotional responses— to *Secret Mark*, to Smith and his interpretations of the secret gospel, to the fact of the controversy itself—function *as sites of evidence*, rather than as barriers or blinders that blur and overwrite more concrete, verifiable evidence or otherwise block the possibility of objective interpretation.

The anxieties that this affective dimension of evidence speaks to are not just about the place of *The Secret Gospel of Mark* but also about the often unnamed but still forceful affective stakes of any historical conjecture, particularly those about the historical "archive" from which we generate narratives of early Christianity. Without questioning what's at stake in any given notion of historicity, we can never look "objectively" at the evidence with which we make sense of the early Christian past. Not that I hope to disenchant our historical investments, our various assumptions about how, quite magically, sometimes quite erotically, the past touches and transforms our various presents. Our reasons for loving, hating, and remembering various versions of the past can never be completely transparent to us—nor are they ever completely "ours" alone (which is part of both the eros and the magic of historical imagination). And so, I insist that the *Secret Mark* controversy's "archive" of evidence lends itself more to "fantasmatic historiography" than to traditional historicist reading practices, speaking to the rather queer and unpredictable effects of the biblical past's ongoing affective life, as well as the longings that lie at the heart of any reconstruction of the past.[63]

NOTES

1. In *Getting Medieval*, Carolyn Dinshaw offers "affective history as an enabling concept with which readers could work in order to respond to their own situations—their places in space and time—and their needs and desires for a past" (Dinshaw, "Got Medieval?" *Journal of the History of Sexuality* 10, no. 2 [April 2001]: 203; *Getting Medieval: Sexualities and Communities, Pre- and Postmodern* [Durham, N.C.: Duke University Press, 1999]). In making "affect central to the project of queer history writing," Dinshaw hoped to "further the aim (shared by me and other restive historians of sexuality) of transforming history writing altogether. It would *queer* historiography" ("Got Medieval?" 203). I draw on her articulation, as well as the historiographical possibilities Ann Cvetkovich gestures toward in her work on affective archives, in order to reimagine some alternative historical significances of *Secret Mark* and its reception and the ways affect saturates evidence in historical-critical biblical studies. See Ann Cvetkovich, *An Archive of Feelings: Trauma, Sexuality, and Lesbian Public Cultures* (Durham, N.C.: Duke University Press, 2003).
2. Peter Jeffery, *The Secret Gospel of Mark Unveiled: Imagined Rituals of Sex, Death, and Madness in a Biblical Forgery* (New Haven, Conn.: Yale University Press, 2007), 242. Jeffery's entire book amounts to an elaboration of what kind of "Fuck You" the *Secret Mark* "forgery" could have been for Smith. *Secret Mark* was, however, also employed in various scholarly accounts of Christian origins, some of which interpreted the gospel as evidence of an early stage of the Markan textual traditions that may have predated canonical Mark, perhaps drawn from a source shared by canonical Mark and John (thus making sense of the resonance with John's raising of Lazarus in 11:1–44). Morton Smith had asserted the possibility that this "secret gospel" material was "probably in the earliest form of Mark," and, "if so, the canonical text of Mark would have been produced by abbreviation" (*The Secret Gospel: The Discovery and Interpretation of the Secret Gospel According to Mark* [New York: Harper and Row, 1973], 61). Ten years after Smith's publication of *Secret Mark*, Helmut Koester advanced a theory of the priority of a longer form of proto-Markan material, out of which both the "secret gospel" would be constructed and canonical Mark would be abbre-

viated, in "History and Development of Mark's Gospel (From Mark to *Secret Mark* and 'Canonical' Mark)," in *Colloquy on New Testament Studies: A Time for Reappraisal and Fresh Approaches*, ed. Bruce Corley (Macon, Ga.: Mercer University Press, 1983), 35–57. John Dominic Crossan followed Koester but argued that *Secret Mark* was it-self the earliest version of the gospel (instead of Koester's proto-Mark), from which canonical Mark would stem (as a deliberate revision of the Carpocratian version) (*Four Other Gospels: Shadows on the Contours of Canon* [Minneapolis: Winston Press, 1985], 91–121). Raymond Brown and Robert Grant argued that the canonical mate-rial existed first and *Secret Mark* was formed out of a pastiche of gospel traditions: R. E. Brown, "The Relation of 'The Secret Gospel of Mark' to the Fourth Gospel," *Catholic Biblical Quarterly* 36, no. 4 (1974): 466–85; R. M. Grant, "Morton Smith's Two Books," *Anglican Theological Review* 56, no. 1 (1974): 58–64. Characterizing it as a modern hoax, Philip Jenkins and Robert M. Price both imagined ways in which Smith could have been inspired to invent his discovery narrative and the text itself by reading pulp fiction, in particular an evangelical Christian mystery novel, *The Mystery of Mar Saba*, by James Hogg Hunter (New York: Evangelical, 1940), which dramatizes the discovery of an ancient Christian textual fragment discovered in the Mar Saba monastery that scandalizes the church but is then revealed to be a hoax. See Philip Jenkins, *Hidden Gospels: How the Search for Jesus Lost Its Way* (New York: Oxford University Press, 2001), 102; Robert M. Price, "Second Thoughts on the Secret Gospel," *Bulletin for Biblical Research* 14, no. 1 (2004): 131. Donald Harman Akenson described *Secret Mark* and its "discovery" as an "ironic gay joke . . . [and an] amusing bit of post-modern scholarly theatre" (*Saint Saul: A Skeleton Key to the Historical Jesus* [Oxford: Oxford University Press, 2000], 87–88).

3. Clement's letter begins mid-conversation with Theodore: "You did well in silenc-ing the unspeakable teachings of the Carpocratians," he says, warning that these Carpocratians, who evidently made claims about the text in question, "wander from the narrow road of the commandments into a boundless abyss of carnal and bodily sins" (I.2–4). Theodore seems to have been wondering if the Carpocratians did in fact find something about a "naked man with a naked man" (III.13) in this "di-vinely inspired Gospel according to Mark" (I.12). Clement responds unequivocally: "I shall not hesitate to answer the questions you have asked, refuting the falsifica-tions by the very words of the Gospel," and he assures Theodore that no "naked man with naked man" is mentioned. He gives some context first: after Mark wrote down the public gospel, as it were (saving the Lord's "secret" or "mystic" teachings for the spiritually advanced community), the gospel writer came to Alexandria, bringing his own notes and Peter's, and he added to "the former book" the suitably spiritually advanced additions (I.18–21). Carpocrates evidently got his hands on this mystic book and started teaching his "blasphemous" and "carnal" readings of it. In offering the "correct" reading of one of these secret passages, Clement provides us with a partial text of this "secret gospel."

4. If, indeed, "extant" is the appropriate term here, since we now have only photo-graphs of the text. As I recount below, sometime after several scholars visited the Mar Saba monastery library in 1975 and had color photographs of the manuscript

taken, the pages on which Clement's letter was inscribed were cut from the volume containing them and disappeared altogether. No one currently knows where the manuscript is held, if it (still) exists at all.

5. See Smith, *Secret Gospel*, especially chapters 12 and 13 (97–139), and *Clement of Alexandria*, chapter 4 (195–278). Smith speculates on what other "unknown ceremonies" may have occurred during the nighttime baptism in *The Secret Gospel of Mark,* in which "the disciple was possessed by Jesus' spirit and so united with Jesus. . . . Freedom from law may have resulted in completion of the spiritual union by physical union. This certainly occurred in many forms of gnostic Christianity; how early it began there is no telling" (*Secret Gospel*, 113–14).

6. Sanka Knox, "A New Gospel Ascribed to Mark: Copy of Greek Letter Says Saint Kept 'Mysteries' Out," *New York Times*, December 30, 1960, 1. The next day Knox reported on the dispute, not about the authenticity of the Clementine attribution, but about whether or not Clement was correct in attributing the secret material to the author of canonical Mark (Knox cites Pierson Parker's critique of Smith's SBL presentation), in "Expert Disputes 'Secret Gospel': Theologian Says Style of Excerpts Does Not Show They Were by Mark," *New York Times*, December 31, 1960, 7. Early on the debate in response to Smith's publications was taken up in other exchanges for a public audience outside of biblical scholarship: see W. H. C. Frend, "A New Jesus?" *New York Review of Books* 20 (August 9, 1973): 34–35; Pierson Parker, "An Early Christian Cover-up?" *New York Times Book Review*, July 22, 1973, 5. The Jesuit New Testament scholar Joseph A. Fitzmyer flagrantly criticized Smith's *Secret Gospel* in an article titled, "How to Exploit a Secret Gospel," published in a national Catholic weekly, *America* 128 (June 23, 1973): 570–72, and Smith shot back his response in "Mark's 'Secret Gospel'?" in the same magazine (*America* 129 [August 4, 1973]: 64–65). Fitzmyer then suggested that Smith had delayed his academic treatment of the gospel until the popular version could also be released, in order to boost sales (Fitzmyer, "Reply to Morton Smith," *America* 129 [August 4, 1973]: 65).

7. Representative voices from those ongoing discussions can be found in *Ancient Gospel or Modern Forgery? The Secret Gospel of Mark in Debate: Proceedings from the 2011 York University Christian Apocrypha Symposium,* ed. Tony Burke (Eugene, Ore.: Cascade Books, 2013). Conversation continued at the 2015 York University symposium. In 2015, yet another book on the controversy and document was published: Robert Conner's *The "Secret" Gospel of Mark: Morton Smith, Clement of Alexandria and Four Decades of Academic Burlesque* (Oxford: Mandrake, 2015). The *Biblical Archaeology Review* (November/December 2009) also featured *Secret Mark* in a series of articles discussing the forgery claims, and presenting the results of a new handwriting analysis, suggesting an authentic text, commissioned by the *BAR*.

8. Quentin Quesnell, "The Mar Saba Clementine: A Question of Evidence," *Catholic Biblical Quarterly* 37, no. 1 (1975): 48–67.

9. Scott G. Brown, *Mark's Other Gospel: Rethinking Morton Smith's Controversial Discovery*, Studies in Christianity and Judaism 15 (Waterloo, Ont.: Wilfrid Laurier University Press, 2005), 12.

10. Guy Stroumsa, "Comments on Charles Hedrick's Article: A Testimony," *Journal of Early Christian Studies* 11, no. 2 (2003): 146. Stroumsa, David Flusser, and Shlomo Pines drove down to the Mar Saba Monastery from Jerusalem. Concerned about its safe-keeping, they had the volume transferred to the Jerusalem patriarchate's library. Color photographs were also taken around this time. Stroumsa explains that, although they had hoped to do an ink analysis, they were told at the National and University Library "that only at the police headquarters were people equipped with the necessary knowledge and tools for such an analysis. . . . We gave up, I went back to Harvard, and when I came back to Jerusalem to teach, more than two years later, I had other commitments. It was only recently, more than a quarter-century later, in talking to American colleagues, that I realized that I am the 'last living Western scholar' to have seen the Clement manuscript, and that I had a duty to testify in front of a skeptical scholarly world" ("Comments," 148). Bruce Chilton interprets the subsequent events: "After Stroumsa's intervention photographs in color were arranged by Kallistos Dourvas. The Greek Patriarchate has, since Stroumsa's visit, cut the page from the volume, and keeps it separately. The inability to examine the manuscript and test its ink is a problem, since otherwise it is impossible to confirm Smith's contention that the writing was done during the eighteenth century." See Bruce Chilton, "Provenience," in *Ancient Gospel or Modern Forgery?* ed. Burke, 73. See also Charles W. Hedrick with Nicolaos Olympiou, "Secret Mark: New Photographs, New Witnesses," *The Fourth R* (September–October 2000): 13–15.

11. Charles Hedrick, "The Secret Gospel of Mark: Stalemate in the Academy," *Journal of Early Christian Studies* 11, no. 2 (2003): 141.

12. I understand "authenticity" and "historicity" to be rhetorical constructions with powerful effects, funded by and productive of powerful affects, and I take *Secret Mark*'s reception history as a kind of parable for examining such effects and affects.

13. As those who work with queer archives and as *Secret Mark*'s reception demonstrate equally well, sexuality is intimately entangled with constructions of objectivity and investments in the authority of (certain versions of) the historical past. In the field of New Testament Studies specifically, we might compare the explosive dispute and invective around the role of gender or sexual orientation in discussions of *Secret Mark* or the *Gospel of Jesus' Wife*, the latter a papyrus fragment made public by Karen King in 2012. This Coptic text, which King proposed derives from a late-second-century original, includes the truncated sentence, "Jesus said to them, 'My wife. . . .'" Tony Burke notices the similarities between the responses to Morton Smith and to Karen King in an online interview for *Talk Gnosis after Dark*, Episode 49, March 25, 2015, "Secret Gospels, Gay Jesus, Jesus' Wife, & Pinocchio" (http://gnosticwisdom.net/secret-gospels-gay-jesus-jesus-wife-pinocchio/). This topic was also touched on at the 2015 York University symposium, recorded in notes on the panel on *Secret Mark* by James McGrath: "Carrier Schroeder noted that people do make jokes about Smith and homosexuality, and that Carlson's phrase 'lifelong bachelor' is a code for that, and that so too gender issues and sexism were there from the beginning in

discussions of the Gospel of Jesus' Wife" (September 25, 2015: http://www.patheos
.com/blogs/exploringourmatrix/2015/09/ycas2015-fourth-panel.html).

14. Smith, *Secret Gospel*, 25, quoted in Quesnell, "Mar Saba Clementine," 57.

15. Quesnell, "Mar Saba Clementine," 58.

16. José Esteban Muñoz probes the conflicted relationship between "queerness" and
    "evidence": "Evidence of queerness has been used to penalize and discipline queer
    desires, connections, and acts," to shape when, where and how one might express
    or discover queer sexualities, performances, lineages in the past, and how one might
    engage them in the present. "When the historian of queer experience attempts to
    document a queer past, there is often a gatekeeper, representing a straight present,
    who will labor to invalidate the historical fact of queer lives—present, past, and
    future" (José Esteban Muñoz, *Cruising Utopia: The Then and There of Queer Futurity*
    [New York: New York University Press, 2009], 65). Queering the hierarchical rela-
    tionship between, on the one hand, institutional archives, what they collect, how
    they preserve it, and, on the other, repeated gestures and performances, spreading
    rumors, the shoebox or scrapbook in the closet containing zines, pornography,
    love letters, and so on, is partly an act of redefining what a historical document is,
    but it's also a mode of being curious about the structures that determine what his-
    tory is most reliably preserved and to what ends.

17. It is not only the *queer* archival turn that attends to questions of desire in the ar-
    chives, of course. Antoinette Burton sets as a central motivating question in *Ar-
    chive Stories,* an edited collection of personal accounts that purport to offer "self-
    conscious ethnographies" of archival research: How much is desire "a crucial
    constituent of the archive experience?" (introduction to *Archive Stories: Facts, Fic-
    tions, and the Writing of History*, ed. Antoinette Burton [Durham, N.C.: Duke Uni-
    versity Press, 2005], 11). *Archive Stories* brings together narratives of the impact of
    researchers' race, gender, and personal histories on access to and relationship with
    collections of historical materials. Burton uses the concept of "archive" to refer to
    "traces of the past collected intentionally or haphazardly as 'evidence'" (6). "His-
    tory is not merely a project of fact-retrieval . . . but also a set of complex processes
    of selection, interpretation, and even creative invention—processes set in motion
    by, among other things, one's personal encounter with the archive, the history of
    the archive itself, and the pressure of the contemporary moment on one's reading
    of what is to be found there" (8). Such archives include but are not limited to "of-
    ficial spaces or state repositories": "From the Rosetta stone to medieval tapestry
    to Victorian house museums to African body tattoos, scholars have been 'read-
    ing' historical evidence off of any number of different archival incarnations for
    centuries" (3).

18. Cvetkovich proposes the archive of feelings as a way to approach "cultural texts as
    repositories of feelings and emotions, which are encoded not only in the content of
    the texts themselves but in the practices that surround their production and recep-
    tion" (*Archive of Feelings*, 7). To address and reimagine the kinds of objects, however
    substantial or ephemeral, that speak our various histories as an archive of feelings
    is to consider not simply the documentation but also the affective life that went

into the making, collecting, and preserving of those "documents," and to account for one's own and others' desires in entering a relationship with those archives. Cvetkovich both examines literal (physical) and metaphorical archives, and she also organizes her own work as a response to the challenge of historicizing queer and lesbian public cultures, and other trauma cultures, *as* an archive of feelings (7). Christian history, like other historical endeavors defined by contemporary identity politics, could be read as one vast, messy, traumatic archive of feelings, as in Maia Kotrosits's larger project in *Rethinking Early Christian Identity*, and her application of Cvetkovich's queer approach to trauma in readings of early Christian texts in particular (*Rethinking Early Christian Identity: Affect, Violence and Belonging* [Minneapolis: Fortress Press, 2015], esp. 141–44, 178–84). The archive of feelings becomes one way of accounting for histories of trauma, particularly intimate traumas, histories marked paradoxically by disassociation and forgetting (Cvetkovich, *Archive of Feelings*, 7).

19. Ann Cvetkovich, "Photographing Objects: Art as Queer Archival Practice," in *Lost and Found: Queerying the Archive,* ed. Mathias Danbolt, Jane Rowley, and Louise Wolthers (Copenhagen: Nikolaj Copenhagen Contemporary Art Center, 2009), 54.

20. Dinshaw aims to render such histories "by making entities past and present touch," to touch across time through calculated juxtapositions (*Getting Medieval*, 12). For examples of queer archives engaged in such affective historiographical experiments apart from those described in Cvetkovich's *An Archive of Feelings*, see Danbolt, Rowley, and Wolthers, eds., *Lost and Found*, an exhibition catalogue and collection of essays. Alison Bechdel's graphic memoir *Fun Home: A Family Tragicomic* (Boston: Houghton Mifflin, 2006) serves as such an archive, confirming for Cvetkovich the (historical, social, political, affective) importance of "queer perspectives" on traumatic experience that is hard to speak, hard to archive, particularly trauma that challenges "the relation between the catastrophic and the everyday and that makes public space for lives whose very ordinariness makes them historically meaningful" ("Drawing the Archive in Alison Bechdel's *Fun Home*," *Women's Studies Quarterly* 36, nos. 1–2 [2008]: 111).

21. Cvetkovich, *Archive of Feelings*, 271. Cvetkovich developed her notion of the archive of feelings in order to capture the hard-to-speak, hard-to-historicize evidence of trauma that so often plays a formative role in the construction of queer communities (7–12). She thus reads "cultural texts as repositories of feelings and emotions, which are encoded not only in the content of the texts themselves but in the practices that surround their production and reception" (7). Queer archival projects do the double work of constructing or reconstituting evidence that might be foundational for alternative narratives of sexual desires, expressions of gender, traumatic experience, or queer community, and, by contrast, of questioning what kinds of erotic trajectories and normative identities traditional historical archives are invested in constructing or protecting. In this sense, queer archives invite us to pause and consider the affective (messier, more fractured and contradictory than ideological) stakes of "evidence." These include questioning the affective as well as

social and political stakes of what kinds of objects are privileged as evidence under what conditions and for whom, and what kinds of objects get forgotten, written off, suppressed under different circumstances, and taking seriously the felt dimensions of the preservation or loss of such objects.

22. Kathryn Bond Stockton, *The Queer Child, or Growing Sideways in the Twentieth Century* (Durham, N.C.: Duke University Press, 2009), 1. Writing about the challenge of historicizing queerness in childhood, Stockton says: "Even if we meet [these queer, strange children] in our lives and reading (inside an Anglo-American context), they are not in History, as we are going to see. They are not a matter of historians' writings or of the general public's belief. The silences surrounding the queerness of children happen to be broken—loquaciously broken and broken almost only—by fictional forms. Fictions literally offer the forms that certain broodings on children might take" (2).

23. Cvetkovich, *Archive of Feelings*, 268.

24. In their analysis of the "invention" of biblical scholarship, Stephen Moore and Yvonne Sherwood point to its self-conscious split from the theological and the moral: "Questions of historical possibility were easier to deal with than questions of moral possibility. Even the 'Deists' seemed to recoil from the audacity of charging the biblical god of immorality and declaring Holy Writ antecedently unfit, impossible, or incredible on moral grounds. It is hardly surprising, therefore, that the more orthodox form of emergent biblical criticism entailed taking up the programmatic question 'Could it have happened?' in its historical sense while closing the question down in its moral or philosophical sense. . . . Thus the category of the historical in biblical scholarship became a surrogate not only for the ethical but also for the theological, and did not disturb either category directly. . . . The historical now served as a place marker for the theological, but also, paradoxically, as a license to do biblical scholarship in a thoroughly de-theologized mode . . . one that shattered every biblical-scholarly mold that has been handed down since antiquity" (Stephen Moore and Yvonne Sherwood, *The Invention of the Biblical Scholar* [Minneapolis: Fortress Press, 2011], 58–59). Maia Kotrosits analyzes the affective dimensions of this sublimation of the theological and the ethical through the historical in New Testament studies, theorizing some of the effects of New Testament studies' investment in "a kind of apparently *un-affected* practice and self-presentation," even as the stakes for contemporary Christian identities and relations with nation and empire press forcefully on such historical endeavors (*Rethinking Early Christian Identity*, 6).

25. Neusner in *Are There Really Tannaitic Parallels to the Gospels? A Refutation of Morton Smith* (South Florida Studies in the History of Judaism 80 [Atlanta: Scholar's Press, 1993], 21) manages to both gesture toward this long New Testament legacy of fantasy (that some would say saturates all historical Jesus enterprises: the search for a Jesus in "our" own image) and condemn Smith's embeddedness in its traditions as especially egregious. One could point to a long history of fantasy that saturates early Christian history-writing, filling in gaps in imaginative ways. I'm thinking about the hunt for the ever-receding original text, the highly imaginative,

and contested, principles for determining earlier and later textual variants, and the kinds of stories spun to explain the logic of the canons of textual criticism (e.g., shorter or harder readings are more likely to be original because we imagine the ancient scribe wouldn't have added to the original, or would have simplified a prior difficult reading); or when biblical scholars posit—and even reconstruct and produce critical editions of—the Q source, a hypothetical sayings gospel constructed to explain the connections between the gospels of Matthew and Luke); or even the nineteenth-century construction of Gnosticism as a historical entity and an elaborate syncretistic religion to make sense of certain bodies of texts (see Michael Williams, *Rethinking "Gnosticism": An Argument for Dismantling a Dubious Category* [Princeton, N.J.: Princeton University Press, 1996], and Karen King, *What Is Gnosticism?* [Cambridge, Mass.: Belknap Press of Harvard University Press, 2003]).

26. Rob Cole, "Jesus Christ . . . Super Gay?" *The Advocate* 115 (July 4, 1973): 1, 10. *Jesus: The Evidence* was a 1984 Channel 4 (U.K.) television special that featured a segment on *Secret Mark*, which I discuss further below.

27. In the back and forth between supporters and detractors of Smith and *Secret Mark*, a stream of monographs and articles on *Secret Mark* ensued. Some ignored the question of forgery, focusing instead on what the gospel meant in relation to the canonical gospels or the historical Jesus (e.g., Crossan, *Four Other Gospels* and "Thoughts on Two Extracanonical Gospels," *Semeia* 49 [1990]: 155–68; James D. G. Dunn, *Christianity in the Making*, vol. 1: *Jesus Remembered* [Grand Rapids, Mich.: Eerdmans, 2003], 169–70; Koester, "History and Development of Mark's Gospel"). Others continued to argue for its "true" or "false" past. A selected list of titles after Neusner's *Are There Really Tannaitic Parallels to The Gospels?* includes Neusner, "Who Needs 'the Historical Jesus'? Two Elegant Works Rehabilitate a Field Disgraced by Fraud," in his *Ancient Judaism: Debates and Disputes: Third Series,* South Florida Studies in the History of Judaism 83 (Atlanta: Scholars Press, 1993), 171–84; Raymond E. Brown, "The *Gospel of Peter* and Canonical Gospel Priority," *New Testament Studies* 33, no. 3 (1987): 321–43, in which Brown registers his theological objection to *Secret Mark*; Charles Hedrick and Nikolaos Olympiou's publication of the color photographs (taken in 1977) of the manuscript in "*Secret Mark*: New Photographs, New Witnesses," *The Fourth R* 13, no. 5 (2000): 3–16; Bart D. Ehrman, "The Forgery of an Ancient Discovery? Morton Smith and the Secret Gospel of Mark," in his *Lost Christianities: The Battles for Scripture and the Faiths We Never Knew* (New York Oxford University Press, 2003), 67–89; Craig Evans, *Jesus and His Contemporaries: Comparative Studies* (Leiden: E. J. Brill, 1995), 32–33; Hedrick, "The Secret Gospel of Mark"; Akenson, *Saint Saul* (84–91); Brown, *Mark's Other Gospel*; and Jeffery, *Secret Gospel of Mark Unveiled*, while Jeff Jay renewed the argument for the authenticity of Clement's letter specifically, "A New Look at the Epistolary Framework of the Secret Gospel of Mark," *Journal of Early Christian Studies* 16, no. 4 (2008): 573–97. Subsequently, in the spring of 2011, Tony Burke organized the York University Christian Apocrypha Symposium to focus on *Secret Mark* (which grew out of a 2008 SBL Annual Meeting's *Secret Mark* session) in hopes of bridging the divide and putting forward the best arguments about authenticity and forgery in, as one of the

contributors stated, a more affectively neutral environment. Paul Foster's foreword to the volume of essays collected from the conference emphasizes the affective dimensions of this jostling over evidence and asserts that this book will provide reprieve from the emotional intensity of the debate: "Amid such strident assertions and counter-claims, one may turn to this collection of essays to find a relative sense of scholarly tranquility, as scholars wrestle robustly but respectfully with one another's views" (*Ancient Gospel or Modern Forgery?* xiii). These conversations were picked up again at the York University symposium of 2015: See James McGrath's account of the panel on forgery and *Secret Mark* at the symposium: http://www .patheos.com/blogs/exploringourmatrix/2015/09/ycas2015-fourth-panel.html.

28. Reginald Fuller, "Longer Mark: Forgery, Interpolation, or Old Tradition?" in *Longer Mark: Forgery, Interpolation, or Old Tradition?* ed. Wilhelm H. Wuellner, Protocol of the Eighteenth Colloquy: December 7, 1975 (Berkeley, Calif.: Center for Hermeneutical Studies in Hellenistic and Modern Culture, 1976), 1–11.

29. "Minutes of the Colloquy of 7 December 1975," in *Longer Mark,* ed. Wuellner, 56.

30. Robert M. Price, "Second Thoughts on the Secret Gospel," *Bulletin for Biblical Research* 14, no. 1 (2004): 131. Price opens this essay by drawing a rather freely associative parallel to Irving Wallace's novel, *The Word,* which tells the story of scholar who pulls off a hoax, and this narrative seems to remind Price of Smith (127).

31. Price, "Second Thoughts on the Secret Gospel," 132. Cf. Scott Brown on how unlikely it would have been that Smith would have picked up a work of evangelical pulp fiction as well on how different Smith's and *The Mystery of Mar Saba*'s stories actually are (*Mark's Other Gospel,* 57–59).

32. Price, "Second Thoughts on the Secret Gospel," 130.

33. Ibid., 132.

34. I was first alerted to this TV special by Mark Goodacre, who writes about it in a 2009 blog entry, "Morton Smith, Mar Saba and *Jesus: The Evidence.*" The description of the show is filtered through Goodacre's memory: "I am pretty sure that I am able to provide the date and the occasion. I am lucky to have a good memory, and I can recall seeing Morton Smith on the Channel 4 (U.K.) documentary *Jesus: The Evidence,* talking about Secret Mark, in 1984. According to the BFI, the three-part series was broadcast in April 1984. My memory is enhanced not only by the fact that at the time my parents had recently purchased a Betamax video recorder, which I used to tape the series, but also by the fact that I had my first appearance on TV criticizing the series that same month, on the show *Right to Reply* (I was a precocious teenager, I am afraid!)." http://ntweblog.blogspot.com/2009/11/morton -smith-mar-saba-and-jesus.html.

35. This episode might be read in light of what Carla Freccero calls "fantasmatic historiography," where fantasy is treated as an epistemologically valuable means of accessing or making sense of the past. Championing the use of psychoanalysis alongside queer theory to intervene in productions of empirical history and attend to the play of affect in constructions of the past, Freccero argues that allowing "fantasy and ideology an acknowledged place in the production of 'fantasmatic' historiography [functions] as a way to get at how subjects live, not only their histories,

but history itself, to the extent that history is lived through fantasy in the form of ideology" ("Queer Times," in *After Sex? On Writing Since Queer Theory*, ed. Janet Halley and Andrew Parker [Durham, N.C.: Duke University Press, 2011], 20).

36. Walter Wink, "Jesus as Magician," *Union Theological Seminary Quarterly Review* 30, no. 1 (1974): 11.

37. Neusner, *Are There Really Tannaitic Parallels to the Gospels?* 28. Scott Brown narrates some of the likely backstory to make sense of the intensity of Neusner's critique of his former teacher, especially since he had supported Smith's work up until the early 1980s. See Brown, *Mark's Other Gospel*, 39–48. He relies in part on information recounted by Shaye J. D. Cohen, who was also a student of Smith's; see Cohen, Review of *Are There Tannaitic Parallels to the Gospels? Journal of the American Oriental Society* 116, no. 1 (1996): 86.

38. Jacob Neusner and Noam M. M. Neusner, *The Price of Excellence: Universities in Conflict during the Cold War Era* (New York: Continuum, 1995), 78; Neusner, *Are There Really Tannaitic Parallels to the Gospels?* Cohen's review of the latter refers to this book as "Neusner's obituary for Smith, bringing closure to an intense but troubled relationship" (Review of *Are There Really Tannaitic Parallels to the Gospels?* 85). For an early account of the public confrontation that may have led to Neusner's attacks on Smith's work, see Hershel Shanks, "Annual Meetings Offer Intellectual Bazaar and Moments of High Drama," *Biblical Archaeology Review* 11, no. 2 (1985): 16. Shanks recounts how, at a session honoring Neusner, Smith stood up and announced: "Since I have often and deservedly recommended Professor Neusner's earlier historical works, so that his reputation reflects to some extent my sponsorship, I now find it my duty to warn you that his translation of the Palestinian Talmud contains many serious mistakes. It cannot be safely used, and had better not be used at all." He went on to enumerate the errors, explaining he had brought copies of the review to prove it. Shanks continues: "Smith then descended from the dais, ripped open the cardboard boxes in his shopping bag and, with reviews in hand, began marching up the aisle like a staff sergeant, distributing the reviews to a stunned audience. Professor Davies asked Smith if he would wait until the end of the session to distribute the reviews. Smith replied that he would not and continued to pass out the reviews. Neusner made a brief, humorous reply, and "the session was ended without further discussion. But the talk in the halls went on into the night."

39. Jacob Neusner, *Rabbinic Literature and the New Testament: What We Cannot Show, We Do Not Know* (Valley Forge, Pa.: Trinity Press International, 1994), 5. Neusner elaborated the Gay Gospel Hypothesis in his *Are There Really Tannaitic Parallels to the Gospels?* 27–31, which he also published as "Who Needs 'the Historical Jesus'?"

40. "While no definitive proof will ever satisfy Smith's debunkers, his correspondence with Scholem sheds some new light on Smith's Mar Saba discovery and on his state of mind afterwards, while he was working on the presentation of his discovery to the scholarly world. The correspondence should provide sufficient evidence of his intellectual honesty to anyone armed with common sense and lacking malice" (Guy Stroumsa, *Morton Smith and Gershom Scholem, Correspondence 1945–1982* [Leiden: Brill, 2008], xv).

41. In one of his early letters to Scholem, Smith writes with enthusiasm about having read *White Stains* and a biography of Alistair Crowley: "Reacting to his upbringing he developed hatred towards Christianity and already at the age of twenty he published his first book: *White Stains*, based on Krafft-Ebing's *Psychopathia Sexualis*. *White Stains* was published in 1896, and from then until 1906 Crowley lived as a litterateur, off his parents' money. Then he became interested in magic. . . . Why am I interested in a fool like him? I cannot say. I just am. He has a certain 'Keckheit, Kühnheit und Grandiosität' (as Goethe said about Byron) which I find lacking in your usual research student and your average Anglican minister" (Stroumsa, *Morton Smith and Gershom Scholem*, 10–11). Why was Smith so captivated with Crowley's un-Anglican "cheekiness, boldness and grandiosity"? Smith writes this from Philadelphia, where he was living at home with his father and had just begun serving as vicar at St. Ambrose's Mission in Philadelphia (ibid., 9).

42. Peter Jeffery especially harps on this: "I believe we have to conclude that he had a larger goal than simply authenticating and interpreting an interesting text he had found. In time I think it will be clear that the historic Christian opposition to homosexuality was a subject of great personal importance to Smith, well beyond the investment that any scholar would have in seeing his research findings widely accepted. The shape of Smith's obsession will gradually emerge as we consider what else he had to say on the subject of sex" (*Secret Gospel of Mark Unveiled*, 121). Jeffery rails against Smith's work, his emotionalism, his representation of events. Jeffery particularly faults Smith for being angry with the church, with "Christianity," for conflating Roman Catholicism and Anglicanism, even for feeling hurt and overpowered by "the church"—suggesting Smith was wrong about (what Jeffery understands to be) his sense of woundedness at the hands of Christianity and that Smith misrepresented the church's teachings on homosexuality, making them worse than they actually, doctrinally, were (154–56).

43. Anitra Bingham Kolenkow, Response to Fuller's "Longer Mark," *Protocol of the Eighteenth Colloquy*, ed. Wuellner, 33.

44. Scott Brown has critiqued the propensity of scholars "to project onto Smith's entire interpretive work an imaginary emphasis on Jesus being a homosexual," and Hedrick has portrayed Smith's interest in Jesus' homosexuality as marginal (Scott Brown, "The Question of Motive in the Case against Morton Smith," *Journal of Biblical Literature* 125, no. 2 [2006]: 355; Hedrick, "Secret Gospel of Mark," 135–36). Although I agree with Hedrick, Brown, and others that Smith had different interests than writing gay Christian history, I do share Bart Ehrman's opinion (if not his affective orientation) that the possibility of Jesus' homoerotic teaching was at some level very important to Smith and to his interpretation of *Secret Mark*: "One point that Hedrick does want to make explicit is that since the homoerotic interpretation of Clement's first citation of *Secret Mark* is not a central component of Smith's reconstruction it should not have played so large a role in the debate over the letter. In my opinion this is a misconstrual of the situation. For much of Smith's entire work on the Secret Gospel does indeed move towards the homoerotic aspects of the historical 'facts' he has uncovered about Jesus, his explication of which, coming

at the end of his long story of discovery, is the denouement of the entire argument. The letters to and from Scholem, so usefully cited for us now for the first time by Stroumsa, show that it was precisely the libertine character of the material that struck Smith at the outset. And reading the popular account, *The Secret Gospel*, leaves no doubt that the statements that raised the hackles of some of Smith's reviewers were not simply passing remarks open to some kind of homoerotic (or homophobic) misreading. Smith is much more explicit than that" ("Response to Charles Hedrick's Stalemate," *Journal of Early Christian Studies* 11, no. 2 [2003]: 156–57). Ehrman also humorously plays up what he considers to be "possibly the most telling footnote of the book," in which "Smith makes a suggestion about what these 'unknown ceremonies' may have entailed: 'Manipulation too was probably involved; the stories of Jesus' miracles give a very large place to the use of his hands.' Indeed" (157).

45. Tony Burke and Charles Hedrick suggest that if more of their conservative interlocutors could just separate Smith's homosexual innuendos from the text itself, they wouldn't need to argue for its inauthenticity. Burke has explicitly said he thinks this is what's going on with *Secret Mark* (and in a different way with *The Gospel of Jesus' Wife*). See Burke, "Secret Gospels, Gay Jesus, Jesus' Wife, & Pinocchio."

46. Hershel Shanks critiques this reading, noting the arguments that Stephen Carlson and Peter Jeffery make about the role of homosexuality in discerning the forgery: "The attitudes toward homosexuality reflected in the Clement letter are those of the 1950s, not the attitudes toward homosexuality in ancient times, they say. As Carlson puts it: 'Secret Mark exude[s] the sexual mores of the 1950s.' I am by no means an expert on homosexuality, but I do know that there is great disparity among scholars as to what ancient homosexuality was. I recently read a review of a new book titled *The Greeks and Greek Love*, which the reviewer describes as 'a counterblast to Kenneth Dover's classic *Greek Homosexuality* (1978).' Clearly scholars vehemently disagree about the nature of ancient homosexuality, as I suspect they do about modern homosexuality. This is hardly enough to establish that the document has been forged" (Shanks, "'Secret Mark': A Modern Forgery? Restoring a Dead Scholar's Reputation," *Biblical Archaeology Review* [November/December 2009]: 59–61, 90–92; Stephen Carlson, *Gospel Hoax: Morton Smith's Invention of Secret Mark* [Waco, Texas: Baylor University Press, 2005], xvii).

47. Hedrick: "This initiation, Smith notes (but only in passing, I might add), may have included a physical union between Jesus and the initiate. At least, a physical encounter could not be excluded, Smith avers. Smith never develops this concept any further in the book, but it is the one line in the book that most disturbed reviewers. Smith argues that the Christian church in the second and third centuries covered up this baptismal founding rite of Christianity, a rite initiated by Jesus himself" ("Secret Gospel of Mark," 135).

48. Ibid., 142.

49. Helmut Koester, "Was Morton Smith a Great Thespian and I a Complete Fool?" *Biblical Archaeology Review* (November/December 2009): 58.

50. Ehrman, "Response to Charles Hedrick's Stalemate," 156. Ehrman is responding to Hedrick's statement: "I have been asked in public gatherings, after presenting papers on Secret Mark, whether the negative reaction in the academy was due to homophobia. I cannot answer that question—I seriously doubt that anyone can. But the question is natural enough, in light of the strong response to Smith's one line about homosexuality in both his books. On the other hand, homophobia may well have contributed to the disappearance of Clement's letter. A homophobe who was also deeply religious would, not surprisingly, be greatly upset at the disrespect Smith's suggestion accords Jesus. In addition, the 'endorsement' of homosexuality by Jesus, which Smith's suggestion implies, creates a practical problem for religious institutions rejecting homosexuality as a sin, but promoting communal monasteries and convents. It is understandable that some people might feel it would be better had the document never been discovered" (Hedrick, "Secret Gospel of Mark," 136).

51. Muñoz, *Cruising Utopia*, 65. "Queer evidence," as José Esteban Muñoz imagines it, would have to be "an evidence that has been queered in relation to the laws of what counts as proof." There's a built-in paradox here, an essential paradox that "queer evidence" has to harbor to be both "queer" and "evident" (ibid.).

52. Hedrick, "Secret Gospel of Mark," 136.

53. For instance, Smith's brief reply to the dream of Reginald Fuller concerning him (see 10–11 above) renders his biting humor, frustration, and confidence about his interpretation of the text. He criticizes Fuller's position, particularly questioning the applicability of the categories proposed by Fuller's title: "Forgery, interpolation, and old tradition" are all "modern categories" that distort any ancient material to which we apply them, and Smith questions whether or not his interlocutors would comfortably apply such categories to canonical material: "Is John 21 a 'forgery'? Or is the sermon on the mount in Matthew and Luke, an 'interpolation'? Or is Matthew's form of it 'old tradition'? . . . We should waste no time trying to classify it in modern categories, but should ask how these new pieces fit into and help us reconstruct our mostly missing mosaic of the first century of Christianity" (Smith, Response to Fuller, *Protocol of the Eighteenth Colloquy*, ed. Wuellner, 15). John 21 is commonly regarded by scholars as a "second ending" added to the gospel, while Jesus' Sermon on the Mount in Matthew 5–7 is commonly regarded as the evangelist's own composition assembled from his sources.

54. In Smith's letter to Scholem on July 12, 1974, Smith continues provocatively: "For practical purposes the Gospels are our sole substantial evidence. And they are two generations later than the events and contradict both themselves and each other. Therefore every school of criticism concerned about consistency begins by forming arbitrarily its own concept of what Jesus 'must' have been—a pious '*am ha'aretz*,' a Hillelite rabbi, an eschatological preacher, a prophet like Elijah, etc. etc.—and then declares authentic the material that supports its predetermined conclusion, forces as much neutral material as possible into the picture, and brands the rest 'secondary.' The strength of my position, I think, is that, into this arbitrary

guessing game, I have introduced the common-sense observations that (a) *it is more likely than not* that a man's teachings are reflected by the practices of his disciples. . . . Now I have made my case, the next moves are up to my opponents. Let *them* explain: *If Jesus did* not *practice magic*, how does it happen that the central ritual of the *earliest* known Christianity is a rite of erotic magic (the eucharist)?" ("Morton Smith and Gershom Scholem," 160–61).

55. Ehrman, "Forgery of an Ancient Discovery?" 80.

56. Scott Brown tries to come up with a "more plausible" motive than gay revenge, imagining that if Smith forged it, it might more reasonably have been his blind ambition, his hunger for the kind of fame that comes from finding foundational pieces of (Christian) history: "the fame and prestige that comes from being the discoverer of an important historical document. . . . Hardly any other motive for forgery could account for the monumental effort Smith put into preparing his analysis of the gospel fragments and the letter. So there is at least one plausible motive, which has often been passed over in favour of less plausible ones (such as that Smith wanted to discredit Christianity by showing that Jesus was gay)" (*Mark's Other Gospel*, 49).

57. Ehrman, "Forgery of an Ancient Discovery?" 70.

58. Cole, "Jesus Christ . . . Super Gay?" 1.

59. Jeffery, *Secret Gospel of Mark Unveiled*, 224.

60. The two-page article is one element of a multifaceted archive of feelings held together in this issue of the *Advocate*: On the front page, a long section of the fragment of *Secret Mark* is reprinted, telling the story to a readership who would be inclined to get the sexual innuendo of the narrative about the young man who loved Jesus and stayed the night with him. A cartoon illustration of the young man presenting himself to Jesus, scantily draped with a cloth, graces the cover below the headline. The article continues on most of page 10, accompanied by two advertisements that are particularly poignant, given the era. One ad, for New York City's Church of the Beloved Disciple has as its tagline: "Gay People of New York, This is YOUR Church." Directly below, another ad for an insurance company features a black and white photograph of a beautiful nearly nude man sprawled with abandon on a sandy beach, reminiscent of a gracefully muscular Michelangelo *pieta*. The caption below the photograph reads: "RELAX . . . take the risk out of your life. Insure with us. Call for auto, health, fire, disability, life and retirement incomes to fit your needs. We have it all. Let us help you avoid discrimination."

61. Dinshaw, *Getting Medieval*, 22–34. "For some the very existence of *Christianity, Social Tolerance, and Homosexuality*, a chunky university press history book—read or unread—whose author taught at Yale, was enough to strengthen claims to cultural legitimacy. (The footnotes became something of a 'fetish,' as one correspondent put it, standing in for or at least signifying such legitimacy)" (ibid., 25). This *Advocate* article might also put one in mind of ways in which Boswell's historical study filtered into a cartoon from the gay magazine *Christopher Street*, making "a point about the way this gay history book fostered a separate gay culture: it featured two

guys at a bar, one saying to the other: 'How about coming back to my place for a little Christianity, Social Tolerance and Homosexuality?'" (28).

62. Shawn Eyer, "The Strange Case of the Secret Gospel According to Mark: How Morton Smith's Discovery of a Lost Letter of Clement of Alexandria Scandalized Biblical Scholarship," *Alexandria: The Journal of the Western Cosmological Traditions* 3 (1995): 103–29.

63. For Carla Freccero such an approach is indebted to a psychoanalytic logic: "Psychoanalysis, as an analytic, is also a historical method, albeit one denigrated by disciplinarily historicist practices. On the one hand, it argues for an eccentric relation between events and their effects; on the other it often challenges the empiricism of what qualifies as an event itself. Psychoanalysis affords the possibility of producing a fantasmatic historiography" (*Queer/Early/Modern*, 4). Freccero's indebtedness to Michel de Certeau is strong here: In her articulation of queer time, Freccero draws, for instance, on Certeau's "Psychoanalysis and Its History," which compares the "different strategies of time [put to use by historiography and psychoanalysis] to confront analogous problems: understanding the relationship of continuities and differences between the past and the present, making the present capable of explaining the past, and transforming temporality into narrative. . . . By bringing elements of psychoanalysis into historiography in order to write the history of discourses on the other (heterologies)—by tracking, in part, the unconscious of the discourse of scientific knowledge—Certeau's writing practice seeks to enable" recognition of the irrational and the affective at work in the production of history (Freccero, "Toward a Psychoanalytics of Historiography: Michel de Certeau's Early Modern Encounters," *South Atlantic Quarterly* 100, no. 2 [2001]: 366; Michel de Certeau, *Heterologies: Discourse on the Other*, trans. Brian Massumi [Minneapolis: University of Minnesota Press, 1986], 3–16).

❧ Gender:
A Public Feeling?

MAX THORNTON

There are two ways for a person's gender to be legally and socially recognized in the United States. One is to have the gender declared by a medical professional, at birth or even before, based on visual examination of the newborn or fetal genitalia. The other is to have one's self-declared gender affirmed by a different medical professional, based on a psychological exam. It is rarely noted that these two forms of gender assignment—both sanctioned by the medical establishment, both necessary for full participation in the highly gendered legal and social realms—are mutually contradictory. In *Testo Junkie* Paul Preciado points out that the assignment of a gender to a newborn or fetus "depend[s] on a model of visual recognition" and "an optical ontology: the real is what you can see." Conversely, transgender people are required to aver "a true 'psychological sex' distinct from the one that has been assigned at birth," which "belongs to the model of radical invisibility, or the nonrepresentable . . . an immaterial ontology."[1] How can this be? How can the medical and legal requirements for gender assignment rely on two mutually exclusive ontologies?

In fact, the contradictory nature of medical gender assignment is only one example of the many complex, inconsistent, and incoherent ways gender is understood in U.S. society. Our social, legal, and medical attitudes toward gender rely on a constellation of incomplete, inadequate, and often contradictory understandings of gender, and the results are constraining and damaging to everyone, especially those who are nonnormatively gendered. In this essay, I try to sketch a theoretical framework for understanding gender as an affective assemblage. My goal is to offer an account of gender that is expansive enough to encompass a multiplicity of gendered experiences, and at the same time robust enough to point toward ways of materially improving life for nonnormatively gendered people. Using conceptual resources from phenomenology, new materialisms, and affect theory, I examine the limit case of nontransitioning transgender people in online communities. I trace their use of the internet as a technology of gender, understanding their gendered experiences as an enfleshed assemblage, one which is no less "real" than more traditional experiences of gender. Finally, I turn to the Christian ecclesiological notion of the church as the corporate body of Christ, where the affective assemblage model might offer a way to address conflicts about gender and sexuality within the Anglican Communion.

A PUBLIC FEELING? WHAT GENDER IS NOT

My title riffs on Ann Cvetkovich's *Depression: A Public Feeling* in order to signal some affinities between our projects. Her account of depression resonates in many ways with my account of gender. Being transgender, like having depression, is something that is generally viewed in the West as a pathology, with a biological cause and a clinical-medical treatment; but this view flattens a complex reality that also has political and spiritual dimensions, and might more accurately be termed "an interdisciplinary phenomenon . . . where doctors, journalists, patients, and self-help experts weigh in through a variety of genres and media."[2] Of course, medical treatment is hugely important for many people, and one of the most crucial aspects of transgender activism in the United States right now is the movement fighting for trans people's hormones and surgeries to be covered by medical insurance. However, complete medicalization ignores some essential aspects of both gender and mental health (not least the complex political nature of the medical system itself). Like Cvetkovich, I am indebted to the decades-long feminist lineage of the slogan "the personal is political" for help interrogating the partitioning of public and private that is enforced by simple pathologization. Cvetkovich suggests that depression is to some degree a rational response to the political climate, that it "can be seen as a category that manages and medicalizes the affects associated with . . . corporate culture and the market economy."[3]

Gender might similarly be seen as a category for managing affects associated with late capitalism's sociopolitical order, a way of naming and thus making legible certain clusters of feelings and tendencies and behaviors. To name depression as a public feeling challenges both the medical assumption that depression is an apolitical interior state resulting from neurochemical imbalance and the political assumption that the public sphere is the realm of rational action and emotionless debate. The project begun in the very term "public feelings" is "to find new ways of articulating the relation between the macro and the micro."[4] What this means for both gender and depression is that embodied personal experience and broad systems of political power are intimately related. To explain this intimate relation, Cvetkovich's "archive of feelings" is a useful tool for understanding the complex and ambivalent resources many trans people use to construct a narrative of gendered selfhood.

The archive of feelings involves "cultural texts as repositories of feelings and emotions, which are encoded not only in the content of the texts themselves but in the practices that surround their production and reception."[5] In a trans context, the archive encompasses the many and mixed messages about gender each of us has received throughout our lives and the varying ways we have responded. The cultural texts of gender range from the respective contents of the "boys" and "girls" clothing displays at Target; to the animated TV shows that convinced one child I know to discount the evidence of her own father's face in favor of insisting that "boys do not have eyelashes"; to the coming-out memoir that transforms a young teen's life; to the seemingly endless slew of bathroom bills denying trans people the right to exist in public. These texts are ingested, internalized, and transformed in different and unpredictable ways by each person who is exposed to them, as an archive of feeling that is forever being edited into a self. Messages about gender, whether parental, pop cultural, or public policy, are felt in the body, an inextricable interleaving of the external and the internal, dismantling the artificial separation of personal and political, of body and mind.

A whole range of dualisms dog the discourse around gender, most of them centering on an artificial and unsustainable separation of internal and external. The popular oversimplification "sex is between your legs, gender is between your ears" maintains this mind-body divide, so that its ostensible inclusiveness sloganeers medical transition out of existence—if what's between your legs and what's between your ears have no relation to one another, why would anyone need surgery? Other oversimplified dualisms are prevalent even within trans communities. For example, trans discourse often distinguishes gender identity (self-identification as male, female, neither, both, or other) from gender presentation (perceptible cues such as clothing, hairstyle, and mannerisms that invite others to read the presenter's gender in a certain way). This distinction is a valuable tool for interrogating the broad but erroneous cultural assumption that gender identity and gender presentation always align; however, emphasizing a radical gulf between the two risks totally individualizing gender and abstracting it from its social and material contexts—and gender's contexts matter if only because some gendered embodiments face more material oppressions than others. Visible gender transgressors face disproportionate levels of economic precarity and interpersonal violence, vulnerabilities that are multiplied by race, as attested by the horrific numbers of trans women of color murdered each year. In a similarly untenable dualistic move, some trans people theorize a distinction between social dysphoria and physical dysphoria, where social dysphoria refers to discomfort with gendered modes of address and pronouns, whereas physical dysphoria denotes specifically bodily unease. Again, these are to some extent separate issues, but because pronouns and genitalia are both implicated in this thing we call gender, they bleed over and interact.

It is, apparently, very hard to talk about gender without succumbing to oversimplification and dualism—either completely collapsing or completely bifurcating things that are more justly held in a complicated tension. Rather than reducing gender to any spuriously simplistic definition, we are better off understanding gender as an assemblage. In its technical usage by Deleuze and Guattari, assemblage (*agencement* in the original French) means both the act of assembling and the resulting assembly. None of the elements of the assemblage—material and discursive, organism and technology and environment—is given greater ontological status than the others, and each assemblage is in a constant state of becoming and unbecoming. In Jasbir Puar's words, "The Deleuzian assemblage, as a series of dispersed but mutually implicated networks, draws together enunciation and dissolution, causality and effect."[6] Puar's work adds an important political edge to assemblage by bringing it into contact with the feminist of color theory of intersectionality. My approach to assemblage is indebted to her accounts of the politics of queer and terrorist bodies. The assemblage accounts for the multiplicity of factors that are implicated in the matter of gender, and it allows us to uplift certain aspects of the gendered assemblage for analysis at certain times while still recognizing that all aspects are inextricably entangled with all other aspects.

GENDER AS AFFECTIVE ASSEMBLAGE: AN OVERVIEW

Often, theorizing about trans people takes one or another experience of gendered embodiment as a given, assuming that the body as such—as a discrete entity with clear boundaries, inhabited and inhabiting the world—simply and straightforwardly *is*, prior to or outside of any social meanings inscribed thereon. Many writers treat so-called biological sex as the natural unmarked state of the body, a body which is assumed to come clearly pre-gendered. In reality, however, the concept of biological sex does not name what preexists, but imposes the gender binary on the many possible variations among the organs and genetic material that make up the gendered body. Anne Fausto-Sterling identifies at least five different types of sex that the newborn infant possesses: chromosomal sex, gonadal sex, hormonal sex, internal reproductive sex, and genital sex.[7] These sexes can assemble in configurations that defy the framework of two discrete genders. The very idea of a given, naturalized biological sex serves to occlude the ideological nature of birth-assigned gender. Assigning a sex to a fetus or infant is a social and biomedical intervention with political consequences, not the value-neutral uncovering of an empirical reality. I refer to what is commonly called biological sex as birth-assigned gender in order to emphasize that there is nothing given or natural about it.

For some trans writers, the bodily experience that is taken as given is that of dysphoria—the misalignment of gendered body image with birth-assigned gender. In *Second Skins*, Jay Prosser argues that the transsexual body image is "unimpeachably real," a material fact that "gives the lie to social construction."[8] Your gendered body image is the relation between your mental map of your (gendered) body and the embodied knowledge of your (gendered) body—in a word, what it feels like to be your gender. For Prosser, this feeling is not influenced by social or political factors, but it is the innate material reality underlying what he considers to be the mere surface play of queer theorizing about gender. Prosser's attempt to moor transgender experience in material reality is understandable in light of trans people's political vulnerability: If the symptom of transsexuality preexists its naming, if it is simply there in the body waiting to be discovered, then trans people are "born this way" and can no more be denied hormones than astigmatic people can be denied eyeglasses. However, this is basically the old sex-gender dualism rehashed, with transsexual body image playing the role of material substrate and every other factor reduced to the "lie" of empty surface; ultimately, Prosser reinscribes the very mind-body dualism that he seeks to overcome.

Like Prosser, I am committed to the primacy of people's self-avowed genders over the other elements of their gendered assemblage; however, I do not believe that doubling down on bornthiswayism is the best method for affirming this. It is too pat, leaving the givenness of gendered bodily experiences uninterrogated as a kind of material core unaffected by any archive of feelings. For Prosser, trans people's genders are so intensely personal that they cannot also be public feelings; for my model of gender as affective assemblage, genders are intensely personal even as—even perhaps because—they are public feelings. This complicated relation of personal and public can be clarified through closer attention to the workings of agency in the assemblage, using body phenomenology influenced by Merleau-Ponty and Karen Barad's concept of agential realism. Agential realism enriches the account of distributed agencies implicit in the Deleuzian assemblage, while body phenomenology provides the ethical impetus to prioritize each individual's gender self-identification.

Karen Barad's concept of agential realism, as laid out in *Meeting the Universe Halfway*, is "an epistemological-ontological-ethical framework that provides an understanding of the role of human *and* nonhuman, material *and* discursive, and natural *and* cultural factors in scientific and other social-material practices."[9] Agential realism is a way of describing processes in the world, seeing them as performative (their being occurs through their doing), posthumanist (displacing the centrality of the human), and intra-active (involving "the mutual constitution of entangled agencies")[10]—all of which apply to gender when understood as an affective assemblage. Gender is performative in that its being occurs through its doing; it does not exist in some prediscursive realm of Aristotelian essence, nor in some inanely simplistic teleology that reduces a complex trait like gender to a deterministic "trans gene." Gender is posthumanist in its displacing of the human subject, whose agency recedes from the popular illusion of mastery and total free choice to being one agency among many, including those of nonhuman and nonorganic factors. Gender entails the intra-actions of agencies that are already always in complex relation with one another: chromosomes, hormones, genitalia, gonads, body schema, social ideas of gender, gendered sense of self, gender presentation, how others treat you, and so on. As an example, consider the hormone injection. Agents involved in this gender technology include the trans person who receives the injection, the endocrinologist who oversees it, in some circumstances the mental health professional and parent or guardian who approved it, the pharmaceutical company that manufactures and sells it, the hormones themselves intra-acting with the endocrine system, causing the body to suspend certain operations and begin others. Additionally, the person injected with hormones must negotiate associated archives of feeling, assimilating and rejecting them in various degrees at various levels of conscious decision making: every tired joke about testosterone; the timeline of expected results in the informed consent literature; other trans people's testimony. Hormone replacement therapy is an assemblage of performative, posthumanist, intra-active agencies spanning human and nonhuman, material and discursive, natural and cultural, personal and public. What could be more personal than the medical substance injected into your body? What could be more public than changing the very face you present to the world?

Moreover, agential realism attends to the local and the specific. The body and its gender are always situated in time and place and social context, so that factors of race, class, ability, environment, and so on are all intra-actively entangled in gendered bodily experiences. For example, the structures of racism in the United States will make a black transgender man's experience of masculinity very different from a white transgender man's experience. Indeed, Lucas Cassidy Crawford invokes the distinctions between rural and urban transgender experiences in order to argue that "choosing where to live and how to live with/in its spaces are technologies of the (undoing of the) subject, equally as much as those surgical and hormonal technologies we recognize more easily as body/gender modification."[11] In the Deleuzian assemblage, organism and technology and environment are inseparable from their relations with each other. The location of the trans person is not only a constitutive element of their experience of gender; it has agency in the constitution of this gender. This agency operates in more obvious ways, such as whether or not a given location has access to an endocrinologist and a surgeon, and in less obvious ways, such as the very archive of feelings to which the person has access. Crawford's account of transgender subjectivity and spatiality finds resonances between the Deleuzian concept of deterritorialization and the experiences of transgender people, seeing both as implicated in the unsettling of a narrowly individualistic subjectivity. Deterritorialization is the process by which assemblages are made less homogeneous and more unstable, a process that is ever in push-and-pull relation with reterritorialization. Deterritorializing gender complicates and unsettles it, for example, redefining the assemblage "woman" to include people who had been excluded from it under a previously held definition or challenging the pervasive metaphors of movement inherent in gender "transition" to include people whose trans experiences do not involve movement either literal or metaphorical. In his interrogation of the use of movement as both metaphor and literal expectation for trans lives, Crawford challenges the locus of agency and complicates the factors constituting gender: a good example of how to address gender as an affective assemblage.

However, this agential realist account of gender risks underemphasizing a robust ethical commitment to honoring the other's lived experience; body phenomenology can provide that emphasis. Body phenomenology follows Merleau-Ponty in asking, "Why there are two views of me and my body: my body for me and my body for others, and how these two systems can exist together."[12] For a transgender person, these questions are painfully pointed: From the moment we are assigned a birth gender, "my body for others" has been given primacy. Gender transition can be conceptualized as a phenomenological undertaking, an attempt to facilitate the coexistence of "my body for me" and "my body for others." As such, the ethics of transgender phenomenology demand a generosity toward self-definition. In the interviews with transgender men that Henry Rubin recounts in "Phenomenology as a Method in Trans Studies," he found that trans men, "like most other people, tend to essentialize and ahistoricize their identities."[13] Although an agential realist perspective disagrees with this (nonlocal, nonspecific) conception of identities, a phenomenology of bodily experience allows us to hold open a space for self-understandings with which we disagree. Transgender phenomenology refuses to hold trans people to a higher standard of gendered self-awareness, as some critics do (for example, Bernice Hausman considers trans people to be "dupes of gender" in a way that non-trans people, in her view, are not).[14] Incoherent and restrictive ideas about gender are naturalized and enforced every day, and nonnormatively gendered people suffer most under disciplinary regimes of gender. Rather than criticizing them for essentializing and ahistoricizing their identities, the ethical path is to affirm their self-identification, even when this may differ from an agential realist description of gender. If another trans person understands his gender as located in "brain sex," I can respect the phenomenological embodiment whereby he experiences this and give primacy to his self-understanding, even as I recognize distributed agencies at work in the assemblage of his gender.

Gender as affective assemblage is a Deleuzian, agential realist, body phenomenological understanding of the embodied public feeling we call gender. It accounts for the material and discursive entanglements of organism and technology and environment in a way that emphasizes becoming and relation rather than being and essence. It describes gender as performative, posthumanist, and intra-active. It is ethically committed to self-description as primary, recognizing that public feelings are both intensely personal and enmeshed in political systems. Our gendered archives of feeling are overlapping and non-identical, as perhaps are the genders we experience and draw out of them. Understanding gender as an affective assemblage permits us to recognize that different factors of gender matter differently to different people, and to understand how the determinants of an individual's gender might shift over time. This understanding requires us to give primacy to self-definition in a way that honors the other's radical difference from myself while still accounting for the body's situation among flows of power. This model provides a way to remain philosophically committed to the lived experiences of transgender individuals, listening to their voices and needs, without sacrificing a thick description of the complexities and ambiguities of gender.

GENDER AS AFFECTIVE ASSEMBLAGE: A CASE STUDY

It would not be difficult to apply the model of gender as affective assemblage to a conventionally legible example of a transgender person, whose transition encompasses obvious technologies such as clothes, a legal name change, hormones, and surgeries. However, my illustration is a more unusual example, a limit case who is rarely if ever accounted for in theories of gender: a non-transitioning person who identifies herself as transgender online. I choose this partly because I think the test of any solid theoretical framework is its applicability to limit cases, and partly because this example offers rich possibilities for understanding the complexities of gender. My example is a hypothetical composite of people I know, people I have read about, and my own experiences—hypothetical to avoid further exploiting a community with a decades-long history of being the objects of voyeuristic academics who did little to alleviate their material difficulties, composite to demonstrate multiple aspects that would not all be present for any single individual.

The trans person in this example understands herself to be transgender. Her gendered body image is that of a woman, but she was assigned male at birth. She is not currently taking steps to transition in life, for whatever reason: Perhaps her parents disapprove and force her to continue living as a boy;

perhaps she goes to a small conservative school and fears the consequences of living openly; perhaps she currently lacks the resources to describe or inhabit her gender, knowing only what it is not. This non-transitioning trans person uses social media to find community and to have gendered experiences. She swaps tips with others for managing dysphoria; she follows transition blogs and admires others' selfies to feed her hope of one day getting there herself; she talks with friends who only know her as her female self; she vents her frustrations to those in a similar situation. She is doing the affective labor of gender, internalizing and digesting the gendered archive of feelings to produce her own gendered self-understanding; and although her gender might be imperceptible to those around her, it is no less real.

Rather than recapitulate the mind-body dualism that views online experiences as purely virtual, discursive, or disembodied, I want to take seriously the internet as a locus of gendered experience—as affective, fleshly assemblage. The internet is affective because it is a social, interactive world where your sense of self is influenced by how others treat you. Most trans people who came of age in the internet era can probably describe how much it meant the first time someone online addressed them as a person of their true gender. The internet is fleshly because the flows of social and discursive affect are felt bodily, as anyone who has received a horrible death or rape threat online can attest. The instantaneous communication facilitated by the internet feels immediate, even as it is highly mediated: an assemblage that enfolds organism and technology. Moreover, as Mayra Rivera points out in *Poetics of the Flesh*, many of us now incorporate our web-enabled devices into our body image, perhaps feeling the phantom buzz of a notification in a pocket that does not even contain a device. The internet is part of our fleshly assemblage when we carry it with us wherever we go. So many intra-acting elements are implicated, from the touch of fingers on the keyboard to the programmers who wrote the code for your software to the corporations that sold you the hardware to the wires and satellites that transmit electronic signals to the exploited children abroad who mined the components of your device. All these social and political worlds are enmeshed here, focused in the figure of a transgender person using the internet as an affective technology of the flesh.

The material of trans communities online is the archive of feelings for the participant, a chance to interrogate and explore affects and bodily sensations that are otherwise unnamable. Growing up in a world in which transsexuality is represented only as otherness and deviance, in popular media texts such as *Myra Breckenridge* or *The Silence of the Lambs*, the trans person might never find gendered self-actualization on the basis of such an archive. The alternative archive of online trans communities might offer an initial affective resonance, a spark of recognition that ultimately deterritorializes the narrowly circumscribed subjectivity of the unquestioned birth-assigned gender. Online communities, and all the elements implicated therein, become agents in the lived gender of the participant.

The trans person who lives her gender online is not faking or practicing or playing, though these are all things that can be done online, and may in fact look identical. Gender as affective assemblage clarifies the difference: To pass or play or do drag as a gender that is not your own is to enact a public gender that is an element of an assemblage, but it is not itself a public *feeling*. Drag is a degree of public participation in a certain gendered experience, but it maintains a certain detachment and irony. A trans person's gender is not detached, but fully embodied, publicly felt. (Of course, some trans people have a pretransition history with drag, or with otherwise being publicly identified as the gender they did not yet inhabit. In these cases, the drag experiences have been absorbed as an archive of feeling contributing to the current constitution of the gender assemblage.) Rather than faking or lying, the trans person online is participating in complex networks of agents that are embroiled in power structures that reflect and reiterate those found offline. Recognition, harassment, affirmation, solidarity, helpful tips, misinformation: All of these are bestowed on the trans person online by networks of distributed agencies, and all are experienced affectively in the flesh. By requiring us to begin by affirming her gendered self-identification, and to think through a multiplicity of elements (material, discursive, personal, public), the model of gender as affective assemblage allows us to understand how these online experiences are real, embodied factors in the trans person's gender, participating in her public feeling.

GENDER AND THE BODY OF CHRIST

For a theologian working in the Christian tradition, this talk of bodily assemblages can't help but evoke that great assembly (or assemblage?) of bodies, the *ekklesia*: the church. The church is an assembly of bodies, but it is also a bodily assemblage. "We are one body because we share one bread and one cup": The church is the body of Christ, both mystically and also quite literally, as sinews and flesh and brick and stone and bread and wine in the world. Without the physical body that is the church, Christianity is a purely spiritualized affair, and then how can it hope to affect or be affected by the world? The church is Christ's body, an affective assemblage of flesh in the world, a reality at once visible and invisible. The church, and the God whose body it is, inhabit its members' innermost beings, while also and at the same time being external to them: Christ in the church, and the Creator in Christ, until interior and exterior are all so dizzyingly entwined that they were clearly never separated to begin with.

My own beloved assemblage, the Anglican Communion, is currently at war with itself over issues of gender and sexuality.[15] The situation cannot be understood without attending to a whole complex archive of affects and effects in the world, not least the history of colonialism without which the Anglican Communion would not exist.[16] Transgender assemblages offer a helpful frame of self-understanding for a church that is tearing itself apart, a model to live with difference and complexity and even contradiction while honoring the otherness of gendered and theological multiplicities. The non-transitioning trans person online, described in the preceding section, parallels in many ways the situation of Christians in the church. Just as the non-transitioning trans woman straddles the disjunction of gender, with the reality of her female gender in constant tension with the artificial maleness she was assigned at birth, so too the Christian inhabits the "already" of life in Christ and the "not yet" of a world awaiting the redemption to come. Much like the internet, the church is a virtual space that is no less real or material for being virtual. It is a territory of distributed agencies, where individuals with differing and sometimes clashing agendas unite under the Headship of Christ. It is a communal endeavor, knitting together an enormous archive of feelings over its many centuries of existence. Church, like gender, is a public feeling.

Of course, for as much as Anglicans valorize maintaining unity amid difference, this is never straightforward to put into practice. Resolving theological conflict, or at minimum finding a way to coexist despite it, demands good faith all around. All parties need to approach with the ethics of body phenomenology in mind, recognizing the depth and intensity of others' self-avowed feelings, and all parties need to be open to the possibility of deterritorialization, the potential for encounters that restructure the assemblage. Only then can participants lay bare the structures of their own archives of feeling and begin the hard work of co-constructing future assemblages. Like a trans person combing through her life history to assess her damage and make a coherent gender narrative for herself, the Anglican Communion needs to take a long hard look at its own history and address its most uncomfortable moments: What are its worst sins concerning colonialism, slavery, exploitation? How did these sins make it what it is today? And how are their effects still felt? Like a trans person figuring out whether and how to transition, the church needs to take seriously various what-if scenarios: Where might we go from here? What are we afraid of? What could happen, and how would it make us feel? Like a trans person living her gender online, we will have to lean into the discomfort to understand ourselves: Which parts of our archive do we want to embrace, and which parts reject? Who do we want to be?

Adding nuance to oversimplifications, recognizing the existence of dispersed agencies, and approaching phenomenological differences with humility and grace are all essential to the ongoing life of any assemblage. Trans writer Ryka Aoki may or may not be consciously echoing Paul's words in 1 Corinthians 12 when she describes her vision for queer community: "The heart isn't busy breathing, the heart's pumping blood. The kidneys aren't thinking, that's what the brain does. The brain isn't processing air, that's what the lungs do. If we'd just respect each other and trust that we're all doing our job, and are happy doing our job—our passion—I'd be for that."[17] In Paul's version, "The eye cannot say to the hand, 'I have no need of you,' nor again the head to the feet, 'I have no need of you. . . .' If one member suffers, all suffer together with it; if one member is honored, all rejoice together with it" (1 Corinthians 12:21, 26, NRSV).

To suffer together and rejoice together, the church must dare to take seriously its own claim to be Christ's body. Christ's body is an assemblage of its members' bodies, in all their messy, fleshly fragility and complexity. Queer and trans bodies are already part of Christ's body, and these bodies make a difference, theologically and materially. We are not on the outside waiting to be let in—we are already part of the church's archive of feeling, and we must be addressed. The church as a whole needs to honor our self-recognition and be open to its own deterritorialization. Then we can begin the collaborative venture of reevaluating our public feelings; then perhaps the church could be a place that facilitates gendered exploration and discovery: a queer community of mutual respect and trust, of communal suffering and rejoicing.

NOTES

1. Paul Preciado, *Testo Junkie: Sex, Drugs, and Biopolitics in the Pharmacopornographic Era* (New York: Feminist Press at the City University of New York, 2013), 102.
2. Ann Cvetkovich, *Depression: A Public Feeling* (Durham, N.C.: Duke University Press, 2012), 91.
3. Ibid., 12.
4. Ibid.
5. Ann Cvetkovich, *An Archive of Feelings: Trauma, Sexuality, and Lesbian Public Cultures* (Durham, N.C.: Duke University Press, 2003), 7.
6. Jasbir Puar, "Queer Times, Queer Assemblages," *Social Text* 23, no. 3–4 (2005): 127.
7. Anne Fausto-Sterling, *Sex/Gender: Biology in a Social World* (New York: Routledge, 2012), 5.
8. Jay Prosser, *Second Skins: The Body Narratives of Transsexuality* (New York: Columbia University Press, 1998), 7.
9. Karen Barad, *Meeting the Universe Halfway: Quantum Physics and the Entanglement of Matter and Meaning* (Durham, N.C.: Duke University Press, 2007), 26.
10. Ibid., 33.
11. Lucas Cassidy Crawford, "Transgender without Organs? Mobilizing a Geo-Affective Theory of Gender Modification," *Women's Studies Quarterly* 36, no. 3 (2008): 137.

12. Maurice Merleau-Ponty, *Phenomenology of Perception*, trans. Colin Smith (London: Routledge, 1962), 121n17.

13. Henry Rubin, "Phenomenology as Method in Trans Studies," *GLQ: A Journal of Lesbian and Gay Studies* 4, no. 2 (1998): 267.

14. Bernice Hausman, *Changing Sex: Transsexualism, Technology, and the Idea of Gender* (Durham, N.C.: Duke University Press, 1995), 140.

15. For an overview, see Jane Shaw, "Conflicts within the Anglican Communion," in *The Oxford Handbook of Theology, Sexuality, and Gender*, ed. Adrian Thatcher (Oxford: Oxford University Press, 2015), 340–56.

16. The missionary spread of Anglicanism occurred within, and often was used to justify, the geopolitical colonialism of the British Empire. Victorian British sexual and gender norms, enforced by missionaries and other colonizers, remain deeply embedded in many Anglican communities of the Global South. See Kwok Pui-lan, "The Legacy of Cultural Hegemony in the Anglican Church," in *Beyond Colonial Anglicanism: The Anglican Communion in the Twenty-First Century*, ed. Ian T. Douglas and Kwok Pui-lan (New York: Church Publishing, 2001), 47–70.

17. Quoted in *Queer and Trans Artists of Color: Stories of Some of Our Lives*, ed. Nia King, Jessica Glennon-Zukoff, and Terra Mikalson (CreateSpace Independent Publishing Platform, 2014), 4.

❧ Writing Affect and Theology in Indigenous Futures

MATHEW ARTHUR

THIS TEXT'S TERRITORY

I think, read, and write from a seaport city whose colonial name has re-inscribed (with scars) the coastlines, cedar backwoods, and laminous outcrops that make up the stolen territories of the Musqueam, Squamish, and Tsleil-Waututh peoples. Where I am from, it is protocol to acknowledge territory.[1] Borders are alien to the Coast Salish and, when paths cross, the porosity of territory is worked out in responsibilities to webs of relation that include spirit-beings, ancestors, and human and nonhuman kin. Where I live, ter-ritory is a verb and, when used by Indigenous peoples, colonially imposed words like "sovereignty" or "self-determination" resist the "map-drawing ex-ercise" of marking exclusions.[2] Instead, Indigenous sovereignties coalesce into forms of governance—intellectual and political—in both the retelling of ever-evolving millennia-old stories that string together and enact responsibilities in lived relationships to the material and immaterial constituents of place and in the storied and storying performance of ceremonies that provoke human participation in the renewal of land in Earth-processes. Mistakenly gathered up in the word "animism," Indigenous sovereignties are based in ongoing self-determinations where "self" always already includes the co-makings of human and nonhuman persons and "determination" is a process of afford-ing consent and continuity to all life and nonlife in a place.[3] To participate in territorial protocols as a trespasser on Coast Salish territories, I open my work to a crowd of obligations: responsibilities to Indigenous peoples and their languages, stories, and systems of governance, to land-based technical-ceremonial practices, and to the spirited plants, animals, waters, landforms, and other geologic and meteorologic entities co-present on Indigenous lands. Here, Indigenous intellectual and political sovereignties are markedly nons-overeign and do not suppose the authority to claim a material or conceptual territory—but propose, instead, that the material and immaterial entities that make up a territory are kin, that the beings and knowings co-constitutive of territory are entangled and themselves co-constituting, and that the governance of difference between heterogeneous beings and their varied knowings is not founded on abstract rights that rely on the enclosures of mainstream Western philosophy and science—like "subject" or "species"—but is carried out in kinship responsibilities to the spirited inhabitants of place, including living and nonliving nonhumans.[4]

In part, I inherited Western intellectual and political sovereignties in the form of normative stories (theologies, philosophies, and natural and social scientific theories) and the living-out of such stories in practices that maintain the imperial-colonial authority to say what counts as being or knowing in the ongoingness of working out a common world. I am not implying that theology or theory are synonyms of sovereignty, but rather that Western-monotheist concepts and their afterlives in what gets called "secular" have historically organized and continue to legitimate the connection between humans (only some of them) and both material and conceptual territories as the common denominator of land and collective life in the still-ongoing projects of colonialism that are constantly at work maintaining Western ontologies, epistemologies, axiologies, and methods at the expense of Indigenous sovereignty.[5] I am suggesting that theologies (and atheologies) are reality-patterning stories that are performed in and by institutional practices and the practices of everyday life that make up a common world and, as such, are integral to the inscription of authority in a place as enactments of material and conceptual borders.[6] What I am trying to describe, in centering on storying-as-practice, is the hunch that even nonsovereignties—here, I am thinking of process and vitalist thought—enact a kind of authority in their methodological allegiance to Western writing conventions and language registers, citational practices, and conceptual objects when they gain traction in a place by outperforming other nonsovereignties. So I start with two appraisals of territory—one, anthropocentric and abstractive, the other situated in local webs of human-nonhuman kinship—and the idea that sovereignty as an ontological, epistemological, and ethical engagement (political across all three registers) is staked out in stories. Of course, there are more than two ways to think non/sovereignty, and process thought has much to offer here, but I am drawn to what is being done when Indigenous territory-as-relation is translated as "sovereignty" and to what is disclosed in the reworlding potential of restorying a word. To say words or stories make and remake non/sovereignties is to set Indigenous story, non-Indigenous theory, and the -logia of theology on level ground and to put pressure on the ways in which their heterogeneous histories, sensibilities, warrants, meanings, and modes of encounter are performed and thus grounded in (even as they tendril-out beyond) a place.[7]

From the place where I am, standing on Indigenous territory as a non-Indigenous theologian witness to the ongoing violence of monotheism's antagonism to the human and nonhuman subjects of Indigenous sovereignty (and Christian theology's persuasive role in fueling doctrines of discovery, manifest destinies, missionary endeavors, and Indian residential or boarding schools),[8] I want to unravel the ways in which Indigenous sovereignty has been storied as primitive or fictional when encountered as animism. Moreover, I want to position the undoing of Western-colonial intellectual and political sovereignties as a central task of doing theology on Indigenous territory. I have a hunch that while the terms of thinking, theory-, and theology-making are often recalibrated in sovereignty-disrupting moves, a shift in accountabilities does not necessarily follow. Of the many tacks and tactics of sovereign power from the governance of land, life, nonlife, and death (geopolitics, biopolitics, geontopolitics, and necropolitics) to the governmentality of cognition or genetics (neuropolitics and genopolitics), I am most interested in the ways in which Western metaphysics—as implicated in histories of theological thought or in their overturning—govern the overlapping territories of ontology and epistemology in having already set the terms of what entities can be actualized (spirited nonhuman people are out, for example) and the bodies of knowledge on which their articulations depend.[9] Even as the analytics listed off above offer useful renderings of power and potentials for its reconfiguration, in my reckoning both the conditions of being able to say what makes up land, life, nonlife, or death and the easy givenness of cognition or genetics as workable conceptual categories are useful only insofar as they are already patterned by histories of the imperial-colonial regulation of knowledge in relationship to land as constitutive of sovereignty. In saying this, I expect pushback—to be told I am working from an outdated metaphysic or have misread what enclosures are in play. I hear the rejoinder: But we have multiplicity; we have the event; we have what is ever-surging-over into the still-coming. I am not mistaking what is generative in recent unfoldings of theory or theology, but asking whether—as storying practices—Western metaphysics make-capable encounters with non-Western worlds. That what is able to emerge in theory-making recurses back to what has already cohered in a place is evident in the simple task of reading North American process thought for any reference to millennia's worth of Indigenous relational-creative ontologies and world-sustaining knowledge practices (and the radically different crowd of nonhuman processes/entities such worlds of practice encounter) and finding only appeals to Whitehead, Deleuze, and contemporary Western science.

Which brings me to the organizing theme of this volume—*affect*, the power to affect and be affected—and in the case of my text, renderings of affect that figure subject- or world-making forces as pre-personal or infralinguistic and thereby (like animisms) democratize vitality, make-porous the enclosures of Western sovereignty, and open the realms of culture, politics, and even religion to the nonhuman. Generally, I am referring to a constellation of ways of thinking through/with affect as movement beyond the sedimentations of language that maneuver together (sometimes with friction) to contour theoretical takes like Brian Massumi's animal politics or Donovan Schaefer's animal religion.[10] Although "affect" and "animism" share no urgent etymological roots, around the turn of the eighteenth century they both take shape in words that aim at what is vital. First on the scene is Spinoza's *affectus*, a term that conjures an animate link between ontology and agency premised on God (or nature) as a multimodal single substance of which bodies and their capacities and variform states are an effect.[11] A quarter-century later, animism arrives as *anima*, an invisible force likewise with bodily effects: Georg Ernst Stahl's vital agent that controls physiological processes through motion.[12] Words, of course, shift over time, accumulate or lose specificity, and are transposed into other registers of meaning. In Edward Tylor's nineteenth-century account of the evolution of religion, Stahl's *animismus* is repurposed as "animism" to designate the "idea of pervading life and will in nature far outside modern limits" (both Tylor and the social Darwinism crowd believed animism to be a primitive stage in an evolutionary tack moving from animism, through polytheism, to monotheism, then science).[13] Marking the emergence of social and cultural anthropology and their privileging of an infantilizing mode of encounter— most often called ethnography—as a means to catalogue and make sense of Indigenous life, the word "animism" is implicated in more than a century's worth of storying Indigenous sovereignty as "primitive" as a pretext for dispossession on every front: lands, languages, knowledges, and kin and models of kinship.[14]

Yes, there are better terms for what animism fails to grasp. Describing the entanglements of place and its human and nonhuman constituents as "territory" premised on the dual affirmation that "land is alive and thinking" and human and nonhuman agencies are an extension of living land, Anishinaabe and Mohawk theorist Vanessa Watts describes the imbrications of Indigenous-relational knowledge practices and forms of governance as "place-thought."[15] Or, working between contemporary Western scientific understandings of matter as agential and Indigenous conceptions of matter as spirited and in "constant flux," Niitsitapi theorist and education activist Leroy Little Bear describes the inter-impingements of spirituality, philosophy, and kin-centered politics in Indigenous practice as "native science."[16] But, and crucially, in thinking through and with affect as a way forward for theology, I want to—instead—stick with animism (especially in its resonance with what processual spillings-over theories of affect work at following around) and all its disciplinary and methodological-ethnographic mistakes. This is a bait-and-switch staged so that I might ask: What distinguishes affect from animism as an acceptable means to story a world of relations—and, importantly, what is risked when the power to affect and be affected accumulates in the word "affect" and surfaces in texts through predominantly Western citational architectures, economies of publishing and publicity, and institutional forms.[17] It is not enough, I think, to recalibrate theoretical/theological methods and metaphysics, refocusing on processes, events, or relational atmospheres[18] in order to land on a more generous sense of who or what counts in making a world without a thoroughgoing appraisal of the ways in which these systematics are deemed capable objects of analysis by the institutions of colonial sovereignty—the state, the academy, the seminary—while Indigenous frameworks characterized as animism are most often ignored.[19] I want to stick with animism, then, as a practice of what Donna Haraway calls "staying with the trouble": attending to the messy, sometimes violent, and perhaps irreparable (but not irrecuperable-from) effects of what has already been done without recourse to the excuses of utopias or apocalypses—and doing so as a multispecies practice of keeping on together in a place while working at (and remaining culpable in) projects of always flawed translation across difference.[20] Whereas both might work to story animate worlds that outpace inherited categories like "human" or "subject," the difference between affect and animism is a matter of what trouble one wants to stay with. The loaded question of this text, then, is: What trouble is made absent in putting affect and theology together?

My first hack at an answer is: language. I do not want to overdetermine how "infralinguistic" or "asignifying" are deployed in affect studies—and I recognize that often (and, explicitly, in Brian Massumi's recent work) affect belongs in/to a continuum of capacities that includes language and cognition.[21] Central to my project, though, is the uneasy feeling that, in thinking through and writing about relations in theoretical registers that do not (it is not that they cannot) reflexively account for how words and stories are deployed or taken up as world-making practices, affect sidesteps asymmetries in how (and by whom) theories and worlds are made and fixes citational and theoretical latitudes to canons and conceptual takes such as Western process or vitalist thought. My uneasiness does not amount to a reproach, but it offers a way into feeling through a tension: how to think a nonsovereign subject, human or otherwise—but not so diffuse that what accrues, however temporarily, in or as certain bodies or bodies of knowledge cannot somehow be held to account in the midst of a world that is, yes, still being made but—and here is my point—has already been made by some beings and knowings and not others. Although perhaps not a replay of language imperialism, reading and writing only about what is alongside words and stories (often in English) seems to conveniently forget the join of language death and Indigenous dispossession or the colonial politics of land implicit in negotiating whose version of reality or scheme of beings and knowings participates in worldly goings-on in a place—what Walter Mignolo identifies as a "geopolitics of knowledge" that includes epistemic and ontological violence inscribed in and by language.[22] Language was and is, after all, the weapon of settler nation-building projects and missionary endeavors, intoned to eliminate Indigenous life and expropriate Indigenous lands.[23] Binding land and its human constituents together in a shared territory, language is the glue of sovereignties spoken into existence in the co-presence of nonhuman life and nonlife. "By speaking our languages," says Iñupiaq language educator Tim Aqukkasuk Argetsinger, "we are speaking our connection to our lands."[24] Or, as Little Bear writes of native science, "Our languages allow for talking to trees and rocks." If everything is animate, he reckons, then "all are my relations"—a working definition of Indigenous sovereignty that starts in the world-making power of words.[25] That intellectual and political sovereignties are bound up in language recalls Mel Chen's caution that animacy, to animate with words, is political ("shaped by what or who counts as human"), and it is here—in this register of thinking and theorizing—that I want to hold open a space for affect in theology. Because this is another way of staying with trouble: to recognize, with Chen, that the sorting of nonvehicular languages and their animate and sentient words and worlds into the category of "other" in the animacy hierarchies of linguistics arrives at the tail-end "of a long journey through Aristotelian categorizations, Christian great chains of being, Linnaean typologies," and imperial-colonial projects.[26] If we do not talk to trees and rocks, it is because even our words have been storied with a sovereign subject in mind.

Sovereignty, if I am thinking alongside Chen, is not merely carried out in the intent, content, or form of a story, but in the very power of language to affect what can affect and be affected. More than an affect studies–inflected theology or any theology of affect(s) that would attend to subject- and world-making forces or fugitive embodied states in the temporary bracketing-out of what surfaces from within a wider field of emergence as language—however generative an exercise—the encounter I am staging in this text stays with the trouble of words such as "animism," "affect," and "theology" (in their many accruals, shifts, and stabilizations of meaning) as reality-storying practices that act with and on a world always being made. I am not hung up, for example, on whether affect is a subject- or world-making force, a state that bodies-in-the-making experience, or simply a conceptual web of forces linked to lineages and modes of theory-making—when typed out or spoken, the word "affect" stories the world with these meanings and more. Likewise, whether theology speaks of God as a being, as the force of becoming, or simply as a mode of storying the world's unfolding as linked to histories, sacred texts, and rituals, is not what is at stake—the word "theology" works on the world with meanings-multiple. Although there is no "in general" other than abstractions enacted in practices,[27] I do not want to think from the specificities of versions of affect or theology. Instead, as a situated theory- and theology-making practice, I want to pace affect and theology through what responsibilities arise by way of belonging to a place where Indigenous sovereignty has been storied as animism. To trace what is sovereignty-maintaining or -disrupting in the rangy unfurlings of affect theories or contextual theologies across variously situated and regionally inflected generic and disciplinary zones or authorial and institutional intentions/exertions is not my project. Rather, I want to attend to what "gets done"[28]—what beings and their knowings are enacted—when affect and theology are jointly invoked.

As I venture what is risked when affect and theology are put together in the task of keeping my own theorizations and theologizations grounded in a place, three interrogatives, snarled up together, pattern the short remainder of this text. First, I think through the "who" of theory as a matter of citational practice—but, relationally, as a matter of citational patternings or (admittedly, tangled and ever-changing) pathways that orient how beings and their knowings are storied in theory-making or made-capable of arriving in theory at all. Second, I take up "how" as a question of method, landing on the idea— borrowed from anticolonial science studies—that realities are enacted in practices[29] as a way to think through accountability in making accounts of the relations that make worlds. Third, I put pressure "when" as I wonder which pasts and presents are making worlds in order to submit practices of writing affect and theology to the responsibilities of Indigenous futures in which ancestral and ever-evolving place-based knowledges intimately shape human-nonhuman encounters and the responsibilities such encounters provoke. Along the way, I hope to disrupt the citational and lexical orbit of affect theories and theologies that, however alert to the coloniality of Western knowledge practices, lay claim to material and conceptual territories of animate worlds in ways that curb Indigenous futures. I end this text with a conclusion that is only half worked out, sketching an animist theology that stays with the trouble of how Indigenous sovereignty has been storied, listens carefully to the words of Indigenous thinkers, and remains accountable in reality-storying projects as a decolonizing practice of making room for Indigenous futures. An animist theology brings the subject- and world-making forces of a world unfolding to theology and holds pasts, presents, and futures together in practice—but always in a place. In an always emergent place, what is good can be worked out only in practice, by paying attention to what is being made and made again in relation. And stories are key: In a world where humans have named and narrated almost everything, the power to affect and be affected is primed by words and stories that shape the coming-into-coherence of an encounter.

CITATIONAL PATTERNINGS

"Words become paths." These words, Sara Ahmed's, slow my writing. Set below words arranged into paragraphs, footnotes—too—are busy path-making. Citational patterns, as Ahmed notes, reproduce techniques of selection: making certain bodies (and their appraisals of what a body is and can do) core to a discipline and excluding others.[30] Here Ahmed is tracking what she calls the "performativity of lines of thought." Citational or otherwise, following a path is never disinterested and, as Ahmed discerns, requires capability such that bodies and paths are made-alongside: Subjects reproduce the paths they follow; paths ensure the reproduction of certain kinds of subjects; and paths that are not followed—perhaps their followers have been rendered incapable—disappear.[31] Theology is not always citationally plastic, tending even in its progressive forms toward recuperating an often-closed canon of sacred texts (and their historical or imagined authors) or rephrasing the words of early proponents.[32] In making space for affect in theology, then, this is something to stay with: that the power to affect and be affected is citationally conditioned. The one-liner that opens this section, then, can also be read as giving words to the long arc of theology's history of wrestling the relationship between texts, authorship, and interpretation in ways that have oriented how that which makes a world is made-capable of being encountered—especially when read through feminist science studies' charge that the widespread authority of science to stipulate who counts as a knowledge-making subject is caught up in Christian theology.[33] By way of science studies, it is also worth considering what relationship theology already has to affect when the capacity to affect and be affected is tethered, at least rhetorically, to the explanatory force of scientific authorship. Constantine Papoulias and Felicity Callard point out that affect studies' engagement with neuroscientific texts often crops up in terms of "evidence and verification" with language that offers "legitimation through the experimental method."[34] By now this is a familiar takedown—and Grant Bollmer, too, is wary of affect's sometimes-proximity to neuroscience-as-authorization, suggesting that the ontological terms of affect theory-making "appear to be about biology" rather than situated theorizations of what are otherwise time- and place-bound "conditions of political agency."[35] While Bollmer looks to "pathologies of affect" in bodies that have been rendered incapable (by science) as a corrective to reproducing behind-the-scenes normativities—as if the capacity to be affected somehow accrues in bodies that are already done being made, I am suggesting a path-ology of affect: a theory of how affect-as-theory is arrived at citationally along paths that are made by (and make) some beings and knowings and not others.

Riffing off Ahmed's thinking, I want to briefly work through what it means to arrive at affect as a matter of "path dependence": a "mangled bit of physics jargon" that gets at the no-frills idea that futures hinge on past knowledge practices and the adoption strategies that shoulder how knowledge is taken up.[36] During the 1980s, for example, bureaucratic investments in touch-typing skills produced a "lock in" whereby the Qwerty keyboard layout (often held to be less efficient than, say, Dvorak) became the reigning configuration—not because it was better, simply because it was being used.[37] As my own fingers hit keys, form phrases, and become paths—just by way of writing something out—I am reproducing what has been made standard in Qwerty. Likewise, through repetition (my hitting this key or that), Qwerty is making-standard a typing "me." In this way, path dependence cues the mutuality of practices and subjects-in-the-making without forgetting what is at stake in adoption—an exclusion. All this to say: I want to stay with the idea of a nonsovereign subject as a generative asset of theorizing affect, as a challenge to (some) theological anthropologies, and as a means, in general, to shake up the usual politics of attribution that individualist metaphysics demand—and Qwerty allows me to think the carvings-out of standardization in knowledge practices not as a matter of individual or corporate interest but as a matter of everyday performance. Even in all its ambiguities and transformations, as affect continues to gain purchase across interests and disciplines (yes, even theology), I wonder if—just by doing affect studies—other relational-emergent knowledge practices and their beings and bodies are being repressed and, moreover, if a kind of standard theory-making subject is being made. Either way, Indigenous "animisms" are being made unfit.

That continental (and not, for example, Indigenous) thought is the mainstay of theory in the postcolonial North American academy is no mistake. Arriving along subject- and world-reproducing citational paths, new materialisms, posthumanisms, critical animal studies, and affective and ontological turns are all in on the project of restoring nonhuman bodies to intellectual and political life. Resonant with Indigenous ontologies and knowledge practices, these bodies of work only provisionally cite Indigenous elders, theorists, and activists.[38] Dakota theorist Kim TallBear reminds us that Indigenous peoples, those de-animated and made "animal" by colonial dint, have never forgotten that nonhumans are agential and enmeshed in relations that make and mark human lives. Forces like "stones, thunder, or stars," TallBear says, "are known within our ontologies to be sentient and knowing persons."[39] If we do not want to—again—dispossess Indigenous peoples, we cannot story the ever-shifting relations of an animate and agential world as only/always articulable in (for example) Spinozan, Deleuzian, or Massumian terms of capacity or body our stories with the beings and knowings such capacities produce. The "who" of theory is not simply a matter of reimagining what or whom—stone or thunder—amounts to a subject or making-porous what edges a subject has. To think the openings and limitations of what counts as a subject through the capacity to affect and be affected is also to remain accountable to and for the co-patternings of practices and subjects-in-the-making that are always reproduced at the expense of what is excluded. If we do not know stones as sentient and knowing persons, it is because our citational architectures-in-practice continue to build at the expense of Indigenous theorists, theologians, and the worlds they inhabit. On stolen territory, any theology or theory hatched to story the forces that make subjects and worlds might rest with Red River Métis anthropologist Zoe Todd's sobering charge to include Indigenous interlocutors unambiguously without "filtering ideas through white intermediaries" and to engage contemporary Indigenous scholars as "dynamic philosophers and intellectuals, full stop."[40]

SYNCRETISMS IN PRACTICE

As a trespasser on Indigenous lands, how do I remain accountable in making accounts of the relations that make worlds? A diagram tacked to the wall in front of my desk is where I start: Opaskwayak Cree educator Shawn Wilson's sketch of an Indigenous research paradigm—research as ceremony. Four terms (ontology, epistemology, axiology, and methodology) are arranged in a circle with bidirectional connecting lines to demonstrate that, as ceremony, research is done in a place in real-time receptivity to the relationships in which inquiry arises and to its emergent world-making effects. Because reality is an ever-shifting set of relations, practices of knowing and evaluating as occurring between co-constituting relata are equivalent to ontology. Every set of relations threaded into research (relational accretions we might call, as a shorthand, humans, nonhumans, places, practices, ideas, and words) marks a world-making relationship to be accountable to.[41] I should foreground, though, that in Wilson's take the relationships in which knowledge projects initiate are exactly the place to start with accountability—and, here, I will have to read Todd and Wilson together: To engage Indigenous scholarship as an avowedly global practice is not equivalent to adopting local ceremonies to which one has no relationship. Part of staying with the trouble of animism as the ongoing colonial restorying of Indigenous sovereignty is to challenge Western notions of intellectual and political sovereignty from within one's own communities of practice. I look to science studies. Outlined in an ethnography of cattle farming, Vicky Singleton and John Law's characterization of ritual, like ceremony, forges a vital link between humans, nonhumans, practices, and "macrocosmic fates." Rituals, in Singleton and Law's drift, are repetitions that reproduce heterogeneous patterns of relation. The repetition of certain relations between (again, in shorthand) subjects, objects, spaces, ideas, and words structures what is being done together in practice.[42] And here is where accountability in storying relations comes in—words are rituals. As the repetition of patterned and patterning relationships, language is not a hard line segregating human from nonhuman (Massumi would agree) and, as both Law and Annemarie Mol insist, to locate ontologies-plural in practices (including language) is a necessary philosophical interference deployed to deflate abstraction.[43]

Then there is the problem of English. For Piikani Blackfoot theorist Betty Bastien, English is a language of abstraction—capable only of contextualization within the colonizer's philosophical orientation. Linguicide and forced assimilation, Bastien explains, have impaired Indigenous peoples' experiential relationships with natural phenomena.[44] Looking at the morphological qualities of English, I suspect the rest of us are likewise impaired. We rely on modal or "defective" verbs (void of tense, aspect, or mood) to indicate capacity, consent, and belief. English has few inflectional cases, save for the genitive case and only anthrospecific pronouns. Here is what is happening: To make coherent, we must make order, determine likelihood or permissibility, and indicate gender and ownership. Not least of all, we order and organize individual words. In contrast, consider the meaning-bearing unit of Niitsipowahsin (spoken in the Great Plains). Unlike what we might call a morpheme, *áóhtakoyi* cannot be defined in isolation and carries what Niitsitapi educators Leroy Little Bear and Ryan Heavy Head call a "relationship-dependent-meaning-emerging-trait." Strung together, *áóhtakoistsi* become *aanissin*: a lexical utterance that registers an event with no subject and no noun-verb interaction. "He will run very fast" becomes "expected-very-fast-running." If the event is current, it is rendered "evident-running" and if it has passed, "remembered-running." The *aanissin* is assembled ad hoc to fit an event or memory—it does not hold a fixed meaning or perform an abstraction. Little Bear and Heavy Head suggest that how *aanissin* are built relates to Niitsitapi metaphysics: Events arise from a constant flux, are registered as they appear, and fade into memory.[45] Here, words are always already located in a particular body-being-made in a web of relations. While what counts as "affect" to Niitsitapi dynamism may be pre-personal in its indivisible relationality, the meaning-bearing capacity of matter is profoundly personal: between human and nonhuman persons. It is a stone that first teaches a Niitsitapi woman how to talk to buffalo.[46]

If we cannot learn from stone-teachers or talk to buffalo, perhaps we need to stay longer with language in all its contaminations, makings-pure, and reshapings until our use of the word "person" is bodied with echoes of other earthly collaborators. I want to put pressure, again, on the coloniality of thinking relationality outside of the words-as-rituals that reproduce or re-press patternings of relation and the responsibilities such patternings provoke (this is crucial for theology in its religious-productive mode). In practice, this means that the naming of affect—like the naming of God—be slowed down to make room for other names and conceptual assemblages. Borrowing from science studies, again: John Law and Wen-yuan Lin hold that the use of Western analytical-conceptual language works to replicate and maintain colonial intellectual asymmetries that reinforce disciplinary paths, corrode hybrid or syncretic modes of knowing, and shut out non-Western ideas. While the symmetry at work in science studies methods (treating competing knowledge claims equally and recognizing humans and nonhumans as actants) should dodge the privileging of what is enacted as standard, Law and Lin want to push symmetry further by encouraging the commonplace use of non-English ideas and mapping the analytics and politics of thinking Western and non-Western terms together.[47] Of course, the "use" of non-English ideas risks exoticizing Indigenous knowledges—but there is a lesson here: A syncretic, symmetrical approach to reality-storying practices might include the many other names of affectings and beings-affected as a practice of accountability.

INDIGENOUS FUTURES

To wrestle the citational and conceptual overwritings of theory and theology as they work at storying emergent worlds is really to ask about a future. Which pasts and presents—which relational patternings—are made-capable of being imagined forward? Here is a scene: A tribal figure is posed mid-sway at the bend of a dune. A shock of synthetic hair crowns her head to form a headdress, and her face is masked in a fringe of multicolored broadcloth—salmon, neon yellow, amethyst. She is surrounded by an alien atmosphere of ochre haze falling away into a shimmering vacuum. This is not a future I have learned to imagine. Wearing "futuristic powwow" regalia, the figure is Apsáalooke sculptor Wendy Red Star. The image belongs to a series of digital composites in which Red Star inhabits a succession of otherworldly planetscapes as a means to stir up the strangeness of first contact.[48] With historical knowledge of a spirited force animating human and nonhuman forms of existence, the space nomad of Indigenous speculative fiction, film, and art-making encounters the strange inhabitants of sci-fi futures as kin—impossibilizing the colonial summing-up of new worlds (real or imagined) as empty and ready for inscription. Indigenous futurisms, as Diné theorist Lou Catherine Cornum writes, "enact contact differently."[49] Dispossessed and made diasporic when encountered as an inconvenience of otherwise "empty" landscapes, Indigenous peoples earthwide have already lived through an apocalypse of first contacts. Even dislocated, Indigenous languages and stories are relation-storying practices that braid pasts and presents together with speculative futures—what Cornum calls "bundled" time—to sustain and adapt ancestral place-based knowledges in ceremonial frameworks (like Wilson's Indigenous research paradigm) from which new attunements to the rhythms and demands of Earth's regeneration in a place can be intuited. As Cornum says, "The creation story is a spaceship."[50]

How can we learn to imagine Indigenous futures if our own process and vitalist stories of ongoing creation weave worlds dense with the relational knottings of Western citational-conceptual practice? Here, I want to hold on to Haraway's caution: "It matters what relations relate relations."[51] Anticipating what Haraway calls "situated knowledges" and "the corporeality of theory," Sallie McFague moves that stories are productive of realities—they are never-innocent and always-partial engagements that structure the shape of earthly encounters and thus govern what beings and knowings are maintained in a place.[52] Theory and theology, I think, have always been speculative-productive endeavors that (at their best) make-capable an otherwise by unraveling what has been maintained in repetition. As McFague says, speculative fictions and fabulations are crucial for theology.[53] I agree. This is what Haraway calls "staying with the trouble"—and to McFague's list she would add string figures as another way to think pasts, presents, and futures together—passing shifting patterns back and forth in contingent practices that "conjugate worlds in partial connections."[54] But I am back to where I started. Which trouble to stay with? Which proximities of relational entanglement from which to name what cannot be named? Animism or affect? If I am listening to McFague and Haraway, it is not a question of Deloria Jr. or Deleuze, but rather of how to conjugate both-together from where I am standing—partially, culpably. Maybe I am hoping for a different language, a way to speak with the force of reality that does not make-stillborn other words, worlds, and futures—an animist-affect theology that holds colonial pasts/presents and Indigenous futures in tension. The language I am hoping for is a ritual that patterns relations alongside the many other ebbs and flows of relation that story without words—or with words if "language" can be rent open to include other-than-human meanings. An animist theology makes citational and conceptual restitution for the violence of saying who counts when a world is storied into being—it is a practice that reenacts subjects and worlds with caution. To be an animist theologian is to negotiate what it means to be a subject always being made-as-capable on Anishinaabe, Dakota, Lenape, or Tsleil-Waututh territory. I cannot become Indigenous, but I can do the careful work of passing patterns back and forth. I can remain accountable for the power of storying practices to affect what can affect and be affected. I can learn the proper names of Indigenous sovereignties that have been mistakenly storied as animism or affect: *Aki, Snawayalth,* or *Tmixw.* As Indigenous peoples put their bodies on the line to exercise ancestral responsibilities to beings irreducible to the immanence of continental philosophy and unapprehendable within the logics of Western science, this text is a an attempt to breach the monologic tenor of process and immanence as articulated through the citational and conceptual overwritings of Western thought in order to tend to what is at risk in the encounter of Indigenous and non-Indigenous worlds when—of a world-in-process—I say "affect" or "God," a singular name.

NOTES

1. To start with where I live and work (Vancouver, Canada) as a place in which to ground my theory- and theology-making is not to enlist the local as an uncomplicated set of relations to think from. To acknowledge territory as a non-Indigenous theorist is to trace over and again the ways in which I am always being made and remade as capable of standing here in and through the often global relational patternings at play in pasts and presents of colonial dispossession and displacement. To acknowledge is also to put into practice attenuations of the always re-enabling of a colonial thinking, reading, and writing subject by foregrounding the anticolonial work of Indigenous elders and activists, lifting up urban and diasporic Indigenous insights, and taking notice of regenerative place-based practices that press on in the absence of territorial access. The varied markers of belonging to place (like Anishinaabe, Iñupiaq, or Niitsitapi) that appear alongside the names of Indigenous thinkers in this text are meant to act as placeholders that signal the complexities of indigeneities-multiple and to coax readers to do the work of understanding the worlds held together in these proper names. An early version of this text was presented on the stolen land of the Lenape people who were forcibly relocated to Indian Territory in the 1860s under the Indian Removal Act. Anticolonial relations, too, make capable the work of this text—and my thinking and writing has taken shape through conversations with Phanuel Antwi, Keisha Charnley, Kerrie Charnley, Reuben Jentink, Sallie McFague, Greg Seigworth, and Donovan Schaefer.
2. Brian Thom, "The Paradox of Boundaries in Coast Salish Territories," *Cultural Geographies* 16, no. 2 (2009): 179–206; "Shared Territories/Overlap Resolution," presentation, All-Chiefs Assembly on Proposed Recognition Legislation, First Nations Summit, Chief Joe Mathias Centre, North Vancouver, Canada (2008).
3. Saying "Indigenous sovereignties" risks bulldozing difference—but something of a common thread runs through what is called "sovereignty" in critical Indigenous scholarship. Richard Atleo's sketch of Nuu-chah-nulth governance assembles around three constitutional principles: recognition, consent, and continuity. Although sovereignties necessarily vary between peoples and places, Atleo's rubric gets at the place-based logic of Indigenous governance in general: recognition of both process and individuation as constitutive of reality in a place, diplomacies and protocols for consensual interactions with nonhumans, and the earthly continuity

of all life and nonlife as a measure of what works in a place. Atleo (Umeek), *Principles of Tsawalk: An Indigenous Approach to Global Crisis* (Vancouver: University of British Columbia Press, 2014). On the entanglement of stories, governance, and the nonhuman in Indigenous thought, see Daniel Heath Justice, "'Go Away, Water!' Kinship Criticism and the Decolonization Imperative," in *Learn, Teach, Challenge: Approaching Indigenous Literatures*, ed. Linda Morra and Deanna Reder (Waterloo, Ont.: Wilfrid Laurier University Press, 2016), 349–71.

4. There are examples of territorial dispute, yes, and even violence. I am not glossing over historical frictions (some of which are colonial fictions). Instead, I aim to foreground the intent of Indigenous sovereignty as I understand it through the words of Indigenous scholars and knowledge-keepers. See, for example, Jeff Corntassel, "Re-envisioning Resurgence: Indigenous Pathways to Decolonization and Sustainable Self-Determination," *Decolonization: Indigeneity, Education & Society* 1, no. 1 (2012): 86–101.

5. Science studies/STS have crafted many names for the social, political, economic, ideological, and analytical-conceptual operations that get called "monotheism": "monotheistic technology" (Whitney Bauman), "Christian realism" (Donna Haraway), "one-world world" (John Law), "monotheist heritage of monorealism" (Annemarie Mol), and "logic of the One" (Laurel Schneider), to name a few. Whitney Bauman, "Technology and the Polytheistic Mind: From Global to Planetary Theologies," *Dialog* 50, no. 4 (2011): 344–53; Donna Haraway, *Modest_Witness@Second _Millenium.FemaleMan Meets_OncoMouse™: Feminism and Technoscience* (New York: Routledge, 1997), especially 10, 179; John Law, "What's Wrong with a One-World World?" *Distinktion: Scandinavian Journal of Social Theory* 16, no. 1 (2015): 126–39; Annemarie Mol, "A Reader's Guide to the 'Ontological Turn' (Part 4)," *Somatosphere* (2014), http://somatosphere.net/2014/03/a-readers-guide-to-the-ontological-turn-part-4.html; Laurel Schneider, *Beyond Monotheism: A Theology of Multiplicity* (New York: Routledge, 2008), 74–90.

6. The performativity of practices (including storying practices) is central to feminist material semiotics. Haraway, *Modest_Witness*; Law, "What's Wrong with a One-World World?" and "Actor Network Theory and Material Semiotics," in *The New Blackwell Companion to Social Theory*, ed. Bryan S. Turner (Chichester, U.K.: Wiley-Blackwell, 2009), 141–58.

7. On Indigenous story as theory, see Atleo, *Principles of Tsawalk*, 141–54. On stories and nation-building, see Sara Ahmed, *Strange Encounters: Embodied Others in Postcoloniality* (New York: Routledge, 2000), 98.

8. See George Tinker, *Missionary Conquest: The Gospel and Native American Cultural Genocide* (Minneapolis: Fortress Press, 1993).

9. See note 5 above. William Connolly, *Neuropolitics: Thinking, Culture, Speed* (Minneapolis: University of Minnesota Press, 2002); Michel Foucault, *The Birth of Biopolitics: Lectures at the College de France, 1978–1979*, trans. Michel Senellart (New York: Palgrave Macmillan, 2011); James Fowler and Christopher Dawes, "In Defense of Genopolitics," *American Political Science Review* 107, no. 2 (2013): 362–74; Achille Mbembe, "Necropolitics," trans. Libby Meintjes, *Public Culture* 15, no. 1

(2003): 11–40; Elizabeth Povinelli, Mat Coleman, and Katherine Yusoff, "An Interview with Elizabeth Povinelli: Geontopower, Biopolitics and the Anthropocene," *Theory, Culture and Society* 34, nos. 2–3 (2017): 169–85.

10. Brian Massumi, *What Animals Teach Us about Politics* (Durham, N.C.: Duke University Press, 2014); Donovan Schaefer, *Religious Affects: Animality, Evolution, and Power* (Durham, N.C.: Duke University Press, 2015).

11. Baruch Spinoza, *Ethics*, preface; part I, proposition 25, corollary; part III, definition 3; part IV, proposition 4, proof.

12. Ku-Ming (Kevin) Chang, "Stahl, Georg Ernst," in *The Complete Dictionary of Scientific Biography*, vol. 24 (Detroit: Charles Scribner's Sons, 2008), 504–8; Georg Ernst Stahl, *Theoria medica vera: Physiologiam & pathologiam, tanquam doctrinae medicae partes vere contemplativas, e naturae & artis veris fundamentis, intaminata ratione, & inconcussa expientia sistens* (Halae: Literis Orphanotrophei, 1708), 40–52.

13. Tylor's non-Darwinian stage theory of social evolution has trajectories in common with social Darwinism in formulations like magic, religion, science (or savage, barbarian, civilized). Edward Tylor, *Primitive Culture: Researches into the Development of Mythology, Philosophy, Religion, Language, Art, and Custom*, vol. 1 (New York: Brentano's, 1924), 260. See also Lewis Henry Morgan and Geographical and Geological Survey of the Rocky Mountain Region, *Houses and House-Life of the American Aborigines* (Chicago: University of Chicago Press, 1965); Herbert Spencer, *Progress: Its Law and Cause; with Other Disquisitions . . .* (New York: J. Fitzgerald, 1881).

14. In a now-famous 1984 land title case, for example, the Gitksan and Wet'suwet'en nations' claim to tenure was deemed unreliable, recalling Tylor in the judge's claim that the plaintiffs' form of social organization occupied a "much lower, even primitive order." Allan McEachern, "Reasons for Judgment: Delgamuukw v. B.C." (Smithers, B.C.: Supreme Court of British Columbia, 1991), 31. Also Julie Cruikshank's summary of *Delgamuukw v. British Columbia*, "Invention of Anthropology in British Columbia's Supreme Court: Oral Tradition as Evidence in *Delgamuukw* v. B.C.," *BC Studies*, no. 95 (1992): 25–42.

15. Vanessa Watts, "Indigenous Place-Thought and Agency amongst Humans and Non Humans (First Woman and Sky Woman Go On a European World Tour!)," *Decolonization: Indigeneity, Education & Society* 2, no. 1 (2013): 20–34.

16. Leroy Little Bear, "Native Science and Western Science: Possibilities for a Powerful Collaboration," The Simon Ortiz and Labriola Centre Lecture on Indigenous Land, Culture, and Community, Arizona State University, Tempe (2011).

17. Andrew Murphie rightly nuances the harder edges of my argument in pointing out that process/affect thought is itself marginalized in the academy and, moreover, that those thinking with affect tend toward open access or other knowledge-democratizing projects. Murphie, Facebook comment, Capacious/WTF Affect group, November 13, 2017.

18. Here, I am thinking of theologies of becoming that rely on Whitehead, weak theologies of "the event" that rely on Derrida, and an eventual affect theology that will likely trail a Western citational genealogy to include Deleuze. For example,

John Caputo, *The Weakness of God: A Theology of the Event* (Bloomington: Indiana University Press, 2006); and Catherine Keller, *Cloud of the Impossible: Negative Theology and Planetary Entanglement* (New York: Columbia University Press, 2015).

19. With the exception of a "new animism," which crests in citational relay around a closed-loop of non-Indigenous interlocutors: Eduardo Viveiros de Castro, Philippe Descola, Tim Ingold, Bruno Latour, and Marilyn Strathern. See Darryl Wilkinson, "Is There Such a Thing as Animism?" *Journal of the American Academy of Religion*, 85 no. 2 (2017): 289–311.

20. Donna Haraway, *Staying with the Trouble: Making Kin in the Chthulucene* (Durham, N.C.: Duke University Press, 2016).

21. Brian Massumi, *Politics of Affect* (Cambridge, U.K.: Polity, 2015) and "The Autonomy of Affect," *Cultural Critique*, no. 31 (1995): 83–109.

22. Walter Mignolo, "The Geopolitics of Knowledge and the Colonial Difference," *South Atlantic Quarterly* 101, no. 1 (2002): 66–67.

23. See Malathi Michelle Iyengar, "Not Mere Abstractions: Language Policies and Language Ideologies in U.S. Settler Colonialism," *Decolonization: Indigeneity, Education & Society* 3, no. 2 (2014): 40, 53.

24. Tim Aqukkasuk Argetsinger, "Language and Sovereignty: Speaking Indigenous Sovereignty into Existence," *Alaska Indigenous*, https://alaskaindigenous.wordpress.com/langauge-and-sovereignty-walking-the-talk-of-indigenous-sovereignty.

25. Little Bear, "Native Science and Western Science."

26. Mel Chen, *Animacies: Biopolitics, Racial Mattering, and Queer Affect* (Durham, N.C.: Duke University, 2012), 29–30, 233.

27. John Law, "Collateral Realities," in *The Politics of Knowledge*, ed. Patrick Baert and Fernando Dominguez Rubio (London: Routledge, 2012), 156–78.

28. Ibid.

29. On the performativity of method, see John Law, "Making a Mess with Method," in *The Sage Handbook of Social Science Methodology*, ed. William Outhwaite and Stephen Turner (London: Sage, 2007), 595–606.

30. Sara Ahmed, "Creating Feminist Paths," *feministkilljoys*, 2013, http://feministkilljoys.com/creating-feminist-paths; and "Making Feminist Points," *feministkilljoys*, 2013, http://feministkilljoys.com/making-feminist-points.

31. Sara Ahmed, *Queer Phenomenology: Orientations, Objects, Others* (Durham, N.C.: Duke University Press, 2007), 16–17.

32. This is a tension for me: that crucial process-constructive works like Catherine Keller's *Cloud of the Impossible* gain theological traction, in part, from engagements with medieval theologians (like Nicholas of Cusa), contemporary Western thinkers (like Whitehead or Deleuze), and Western science (usually physics).

33. What Donna Haraway calls a "god trick." Donna Haraway, "Situated Knowledges: The Science Question in Feminism and the Privilege of Partial Perspective," *Feminist Studies* 14, no. 3 (1988): 575–99.

34. Constantina Papoulias and Felicity Callard, "Biology's Gift: Interrogating the Turn to Affect," *Body & Society* 16, no. 1 (2010): 37.

35. Grant Bollmer, "Pathologies of Affect," *Cultural Studies* 28, no. 2 (2014): 298–326.

36. Cosma Shalizi, "QWERTY, Lock-In and Path Dependence," 2001, http://bactra .org/notebooks/qwerty.html.

37. Paul David, "Clio and the Economics of QWERTY," *American Economic Review* 75, no. 2, Papers and Proceedings of the Ninety-Seventh Annual Meeting of the American Economic Association (1985): 332–37.

38. See Zoe Todd, "An Indigenous Feminist's Take on the Ontological Turn: 'Ontology' Is Just Another Word for Colonialism," *Journal of Historical Sociology* 29, no. 1 (2016): 7; and Kim TallBear, "Why Interspecies Thinking Needs Indigenous Standpoints," Theorizing the Contemporary, *Cultural Anthropology* (April 24, 2011), https://culanth.org/fieldsights/260-why-interspecies-thinking-needs-indigenous -standpoints.

39. Kim TallBear, "An Indigenous Reflection on Working beyond the Human/Nothuman," Dossier: Theorizing Queer Inhumanisms, *GLQ: A Journal of Lesbian and Gay Studies* 21, no. 2–3 (2015): 234.

40. Todd, "An Indigenous Feminist's Take on the Ontological Turn," 7.

41. Shawn Wilson, *Research Is Ceremony: Indigenous Research Methods* (Black Point, N.S.: Fernwood, 2008), esp. 69–79.

42. Vicky Singleton and John Law, "Devices as Rituals: Notes on Enacting Resistance," *Journal of Cultural Economy* 6, no. 3 (2013): 262, 265, 267.

43. See Annemarie Mol's prepublication comments on Steve Woolgar and Javier Lezaun, "The Wrong Bin Bag: A Turn to Ontology in Science and Technology Studies?" *Social Studies of Science* 43, no. 3 (2013): 321–40; https://www.sbs.ox.ac.uk/ sites/default/files/Research_Areas/Science_And_Technology/Docs/Annemarie Mol2.pdf; and John Law, "STS as Method," in *Handbook of Science and Technology Studies*, ed. Ulrike Felt, Clark Miller, Laurel Smith-Doerr, and Rayvon Fouche (Cambridge, Mass., and London: Society for Social Studies of Science and MIT Press, 2016), 31–57.

44. Betty Bastien, *Blackfoot Ways of Knowing: The Worldview of the Siksikaitsitapi* (Calgary: University of Calgary Press, 2005), 128.

45. Leroy Little Bear and Ryan Heavy Head, "A Conceptual Anatomy of the Blackfoot Word," *ReVision* 26, part 3 (2004): 31–38.

46. Ryan Heavy Head, *Feeding Sublimity: Embodiment in Blackfoot Experience* (Lethbridge, A.B.: University of Lethbridge, Department of Anthropology, 2005), 96.

47. John Law and Wen-yuan Lin, "Provincialising STS: Postcoloniality, Symmetry and Method," working paper, 2016, http://heterogeneities. net/publications/Law LinProvincialisingSTS20151223.pdf, 2–4, 8; and "Tidescapes: Notes on a Shi (勢)- Inflected STS," working paper, 2016, http://heterogeneities.net/publications/ LawLin2016TidescapesShiInSTS.pdf, 21.

48. Zach Dundas, "Wendy Red Star Totally Conquers the Wild Frontier," *Portland Monthly* (2015), http://pdxmonthly.com/articles/local-artist-wendy-red-star-totally -conquers-the-wild-frontier-march-2015.

49. Lou Catherine Cornum, "The Space NDN's Star Map," *New Inquiry* (January 26, 2015), http://thenewinquiry.com/essays/the-space-ndns-star-map.

50. Lou Catherine Cornum, "The Creation Story Is a Spaceship: Indigenous Futurism and Decolonial Deep Space," *Voz à Voz* (2015), http://vozavoz.ca/feature/lindsay-catherine-cornum.

51. Donna Haraway, "Staying with the Trouble: Anthropocene, Capitalocene, Chthulucene," in *Anthropocene or Capitalocene? Nature, History, and the Crisis of Capitalism*, ed. Jason Moore (Oakland: PM Press/Kairos, 2016), 39.

52. Sallie McFague, *Metaphorical Theology: Models of God in Religious Language* (Philadelphia: Fortress Press, 1983), 102, and *Models of God: Theology for an Ecological Nuclear Age* (Philadelphia: Fortress Press, 1987), 27–28; Haraway, "Situated Knowledges," and "The Promises of Monsters: A Regenerative Politics for Inappropriate/d Others," in *Cultural Studies*, ed. Lawrence Grossberg, Cary Nelson, and Paula Treichler (New York: Routledge, 1992), 299.

53. Sallie McFague, "Imaginary Gardens with Real Toads: Realism in Fiction and Theology," *Semeia* 13 (1978): 255–58.

54. Haraway, *Staying with the Trouble*, 12–15.

✎ Feeling Dead, Dead Feeling

AMY HOLLYWOOD

In all of my recent work, I am interested in asking what it means to make and read literature as a form of imaginative ascesis. What does it mean to read and write devoutly, religiously, mystically—and are these even the right words? Reading the writing I love raises these questions for me in particularly acute ways. I would venture to guess that for Henry James and Robert Frost, Djuna Barnes and William Carlos Williams, Susan Howe and David Foster Wallace, writing is itself a kind of reading and both writing and reading are inexhaustible attempts to hear God or, absent God, to hear that other, those others, that we glimpse, hear whispers of, just barely touch, in the acts of reading and writing themselves. Reading and writing are forms of divination. Howe and James and Frost (all of whom will play a role in what follows), may not hear God, but their writing is itself an inscription of the divine, however fragmentary and partial, for they are deeply committed to the movement of thought, to the articulation of affect, and to an engagement with that aspect of existence irreducible to the individual or to reified conceptions of the group. This work feels affectively, intellectually, spiritually, essential to me now more than ever. As our political horizons darken, we need literature and its affective play more than ever before.

> Starting from nothing with nothing when everything else has been said.
> —SUSAN HOWE, *That This*

This single, unpunctuated line is the second paragraph of Susan Howe's *That This*, a book-length poem in four parts dedicated to the memory of her third husband, the philosopher, Peter H. Hare. She has just described her discovery of his dead body: "I knew when I saw him with the CPAP mask over his mouth and nose and heard the whooshing sound of air blowing air that he wasn't asleep. No."[1] Howe juxtaposes her refusal—"No"—with Sarah Pierpont Edwards's letter of July 3, 1758, announcing the death of her husband, Jonathan Edwards, to one of their daughters:

> Oh that we may kiss the rod and lay our hands on our mouths! The Lord has done it. He has made me adore his goodness, that we had him so long. But my God lives; and he has my heart. . . . We are all given to God: and there I am, and love to be.[2]

"I admire," Howe writes, "the way thought contradicts feeling in Sarah's furiously calm letter."[3]

The furiously calm contradictions of Sarah Edwards's letter find their justifying source in the anguished psalm to which her words likely allude. Psalm 2 opens with a question: "Why do the heathen rage, and the people imagine a vain thing?" The answer, in the King James version, defies summation. Reading the psalm, I am not always sure who is speaking to whom, but there is no doubt as to what is being promised:

> Ask of me, and I shall give thee the heathen for thine inheritance, and the uttermost parts of the earth for thy possession.

> Thou shalt break them with a rod of iron; thou shalt dash them in pieces like a potter's vessel.

> Be wise now therefore, O ye kings: be instructed, ye judges of the earth. Serve the Lord with fear, and rejoice with trembling.

> Kiss the Son, lest he be angry, and ye perish from the way, when his wrath is kindled but a little. Blessed are all they that put their trust in him.

This is difficult writing: The rage and the violence seem directed—everywhere. Sarah Edwards feels this rage and this violence; she feels it directed against her husband and against herself and against her daughter, but she also, with ease, identifies the rod, which will "dash them to pieces like a potter's vessel," with the Son and so with the promise of blessedness.

For Sarah Edwards, the one who destroys is also the one who saves. Howe sees this clearly:

> For Sarah all works of God are a kind of language or voice to instruct us in things pertaining to calling and confusion. I love to read her husband's analogies, metaphors, and similes.

For Jonathan and Sarah all rivers run into the sea yet the sea is not full,
so in general there is always progress as in the revolution of a wheel and
each soul comes upon the call of God in his word.[4]

Scripture calls and gives a calling to Jonathan and Sarah Edwards. It calls them
to God, where, Sarah writes, "I love to be." Howe sees this in Jonathan and
Sarah Edwards, but she doesn't experience it: "I read words but don't hear God
in them."[5] Howe loves Jonathan Edwards's analogies, metaphors, and similes,
most of them biblically based, but she hears in these words "the unpresentable
violence of a double negative." The rod, perhaps, without the Son? Or more
troubling still, the rod with the Son but without any promised salvation? For
Howe, what is crucial is how unpresentable this is.

That This goes on to perform that unpresentable violence in often illegible
textual collages, strips of words and fragments of words cut from the writings
of the Edwards family and other, unspecified texts, placed seemingly at random
on the page. The psalms appear again, in a more hopeful light, although one
that remains tethered to Howe's framing question: "Where shall I find Real."[6]
"Maybe," Howe writes, "there is some not yet understood return to people we
have loved and lost. I need to imagine the possibility even if I don't believe it."[7]
These poems mark the impossible necessity of imagination; Howe returns to
her husband—she returns to the Edwards family—through these barely legible textual collages. Her reading and her writing—of her husband's autopsy
report, his emails, the detritus that catches her eye as she wrestles with the
reality of his death, the paintings of Poussin and the art historian T. J. Clarke's
reflections on those painting—and what she makes of them *are* the return:

This sixth sense of another reality even in simplest objects is what poets
set out to show but cannot once and for all.

If there is an afterlife, then we still might: if not, not.[8]

This is the background against which I want to talk about how we die now,
those of us who are no longer Christian. I am interested in how we approach
the difficulty of death, our own and that of others, and how difficult literature,
writing it and reading it, might be a training ground for approaching the difficulties of death—and of life. I will speak in terms of what Michael Warner
calls "ethical secularism," a version of secularism which asks how we live now,
those of us for whom religious practices are no longer formative. In Warner's
words, "It presents itself as a project for becoming the kind of person who can
rightly recognize the conditions of existence, and although it is an attempt
to overcome Christianity it does not secure its stance as a privileged default

against the particularities of religion." I'd like to say that I don't wish to over-come Christianity. I'd like to say that death demands particularity. But for me, as for many others, Christianity is simply—but there is nothing simple about it—gone.

When I think about religion and what we grandiosely call literature, I am less interested in the exploration of religious themes or images—although they are strewn through the work of those I'll discuss here—than in the anal-ogies and disanalogies between literary practices and religious practices of writing and reading.

The practices of religious elites—and increasingly not only elites—in West-ern Christianity circled endlessly around the psalms, with reading, recitation, song, and meditation leading to the production of new songs in and through engagement with the biblical text. In medieval monastic life, monks and nuns, either individually or in community, enact the continual praise of God that is heaven itself through their recitation or singing of the psalms. For John Cas-sian, a key figure in the development and theorization of Christian monasti-cism in the Latin West, the techniques of repetition central to the monastic life are not at odds with, but themselves produce, spontaneity.

Dying and dead monks and nuns are surrounded by their communities, who recite or sing the Psalter over them. By the high and late Middle Ages, these practices have moved out of the confines of the monastery. The be-guines, semireligious women living lives dedicated to God and Christian per-fection in the world, were often employed to care for the sick and the dying. This included reciting or singing the psalms over those they cared for, perhaps at times with them. (Did they sing in Latin? The French, Flemish, German, Italian, English vernaculars? Many of the dying may not have understood the words of the song.)

Those raised within Christian and Jewish traditions often forget how *dif-ficult* the psalms are—not just formally, but also in their vivid and incredibly complex imagery, in the harshness of the world and the God they depict, in the truths they purport to tell. For early theologians, theorists of the psalms and literary critics all, and often poets, the psalms are at the heart of the Chris-tian life because they contain the entire range of human emotion. Through uttering the words of the psalms and looking from the book of scripture to what Bernard of Clairvaux calls the book of experience, moving back and forth between the two so that the words of the psalmist become one's own and emerge, spontaneously, from one's lips, Christians come to understand who they are, who God is, how they stand, individually and communally, be-fore, with, and in that God.

The psalms are not my scripture. But since I was a small child I have *read* religiously, perhaps I have even begun to write that way. And that is what I see, vividly, complexly, with difficulty, in the work I love. An (a)typical juxtaposition, from Fanny Howe's (Susan Howe's sister—or is Susan Fanny's?) *'Tis of Thee* (2003), chosen (almost) at random. (X: African American Man; Y: European American Woman; Z: Their grown son.)

> X: and Z:
> Any discussion of race is really a discussion about the creation of the universe.
> (page break)
>
> Y:
> Now I believe that when the Messiah comes the world will have no images,
> since the image will be cut free
> from the object, released like beef from a cow,
> and competition will automatically founder
> as an instinct, having no visible object in sight.
> Then on that day I won't have to look for you in order to know you.[9]

I don't believe in the messiah, but I believe in Fanny and Susan Howe. What does that make me?

I have a fantasy, that when I am dying, someone will read to me the opening pages of *The Portrait of a Lady*:

> Under certain circumstances there are few hours in life more agreeable than the hour dedicated to the ceremony known as afternoon tea. There are circumstances in which, whether you partake of the tea or not—some people of course never do—the situation is itself delightful. Those that I have in mind in beginning to unfold this simple history offered an admirable setting to an innocent pastime. The implements of the little feast had been disposed upon the lawn of an old English country house in what I should call the perfect middle of a splendid summer afternoon. Part of the afternoon had waned, but much of it was left, and what was left was of the finest and rarest quality. Real dusk would not arrive for some hours; but the flood of summer light had begun to ebb, the air had grown mellow, the shadows were long upon the smooth, dense turf. They lengthened slowly, however, and the scene expressed that sense of leisure still to come which is perhaps the chief source of one's enjoyment of such a scene at such an hour. From five o'clock to eight is on certain occasions a little eternity; but on such an occasion as this the interval could be only an eternity of pleasure.[10]

There are three men on the lawn in Henry James's not so very innocent scene, an old man and two considerably younger—a father, a son, the son's friend. (And two dogs, a collie and a "bristling, bustling terrier" who only later, in passing, will we find to be named Bunchy. All of the names come later.)

Daniel Touchett and his son Ralph are both dying.

Their history, and that of the young woman who comes to join them, may seem simple, even banal. How can one speak of eternity with respect to an afternoon tea? (A little eternity and hence no eternity at all; and yet, beyond the irony and the boredom, on *this* occasion "an eternity of pleasure.")

I found myself thinking about this scene in James and my own imaginary deathbed scene, during which I am remembering James or listening to some unspecified person reading James to me, while reading, entirely by accident, David Orr's *Beautiful & Pointless: A Guide to Modern Poetry*. Orr wants to argue against the notion that poetry needs to be something grand, dealing with the sublime and the eternal, in order to be interesting and worth spending one's time on. Poetry, he writes "seems beautifully pointless, or pointlessly beautiful, depending on your level of optimism."[11] (An afternoon tea on a beautiful lawn dipping down to the Thames. James refuses to leave its beauty alone.)

Orr's line marks the end of a section; a new one begins, the penultimate one of the book:

> My father died of cancer in March of 2007, as I was beginning work on this book. He was sixty-one. It's difficult to type those sentences for many reasons, not least among them the fact that I've been a book critic for over a decade now, and almost always find myself cringing during the inevitable fetch-me-a-tissue moment in any personal essay or memoir. Still, throughout this book . . . I've tried to suggest what a relationship with poetry actually looks like, in both its limitations and strengths. I've described it as a private pleasure and an occasional irritation that can't easily be justified in public terms. Having said this, I'd be falling short if I didn't try to offer some sense of what—for me—poetry has proven it can and cannot give. Sad as it may be, we often discover the true contours of any relationship in the situations that matter most to us; and sadder still, those situations tend to be ones in which something we love is lost, or in danger of being lost. So pull out your tissues, and let's talk about it.[12]

(I've got a lot of these stories. My father, dead at sixty-five, when I was twenty-three. My oldest brother and mother dead nine years later, in Pedro's case almost to the day of my father's death. My mother four days later. My brother Michael died in 2013 on the same date as Pedro. Between them, a sister and another brother, my best brother, Daniel. And that's not all.)

(I could give a shit about tissues.)

"Cancer," Orr writes, "can kill you in many ways."[13] In the midst of and likely caused by chemotherapy, his father had a stroke that left him partially paralyzed and unable to shift the pace, intonation, or stress of his words. Suffering from what is sometimes called "flat affect" (surely a misnomer—the voice is flat, but is the affect? Perhaps it's just easier to think that what we can't hear isn't there), Orr's father couldn't "slow down and modulate his voice." A speech therapist gave him various exercises meant to help.

(Cancer can suffocate you; rot you from the inside out or from the outside in; make you hurt so badly you can't even scream. It can give you a heart attack or tangle your guts so that you heave your own shit. No one wants to know all the ways that cancer can kill you.)

As Orr self-deprecatingly explains, the not unself-interested thought occurred to him that poetry might also help his father. It deals, often, with—or perhaps better in—the stress of meter, the intonations engendered by rhythm and rhyme, the pacing needed to articulate assonances and alliterations. He searched his parents' house for leftover books from college, and "flush with inspiration" returned to his father "armed with the fruits of English poesy." He tells us he learned one lesson very quickly:

> Do not attempt to get a stroke victim to read Hopkins. "I caught this morning morning's minion, king-/dom of daylight's dauphin, dapple-dawn-drawn Falcon . . ." I can barely pronounce this myself, and I have full use of my tongue. We did a little better with Robert Frost.[14]

(I gave my father *The Complete Poems of Gerard Manley Hopkins* for Christmas a year or two before he died. He'd had an old, mottled edition, its wartime paper disintegrating under my hand as I tried to read it. Whose gift was this?)

Orr and his father read from Frost's "The Silken Tent"; Orr cites the opening four lines of the poem:

> She is as in a field a silken tent
> At midday when the sunny summer breeze
> Has dried the dew and all its ropes relent,
> So that in guys it gently sways at ease . . .

Orr reflects on what he loves in the poem; its technical virtuosity—the entire poem is one sentence—and what he calls "the delicate exactness of the first line." "'She *is as in* a field a silken tent,' rather than, for instance, 'She *is like* a silken tent in a field.'" For Orr, following the critic Robert Pack "'The metaphor of the tent does not merely describe the "she" of the poem, but rather the relationship between the speaker and the woman observed.'"¹⁵ (I am not at all sure that this is right.) What Orr likes about it is that Frost, in giving a relation—the metaphor itself—about a relation does something "more unusual and difficult" than poets normally attempt. (All the power in these relations, all the wealth in James's lawn, will have to remain unanalyzed. Not by James, who can't stop analyzing, but by Orr.)

Orr admits, though, that none of this meant anything to his father. Or perhaps better, he assumes, on the basis of what his father says to him about the poem, that its technical virtuosity meant nothing to him. For his father, the tent was interesting. It reminded him of tents pitched in open fields by traveling circuses, a sight he recalls from his own childhood. For Orr, though, the pleasure his father found in the poem wasn't adequate, for, he writes, "if reminiscence was all that was needed, we could just as easily have been reading a magazine article about P. T. Barnum." He worries that what is properly poetic about Frost's lines are not a part of his father's enjoyment, the sound of the poem, its syntax, "the expert maneuvering that Frost does in order to unload the poem's only four-syllable word in the poem's penultimate line: 'In the *capriciousness* of summer air.'" Orr wanted his father to hear that—and to have it "help somehow."¹⁶ But help with what? Orr doesn't tell us if the meter and rhythm of the poem made his father better able to bring intonation to his speech. That was, I thought, the point of the exercise. Given that Orr doesn't tell us whether reciting the poem helped his father's speech, I am going to assume that what served as the justification for the exercise was not its real agenda.

(Why can't a magazine article about P. T. Barnum be a poem?)

Instead of telling us about his father's voice, Orr tells us about his father's reminiscences. And the circus, clearly, isn't sufficiently profound, not least because it doesn't seem to require poetic form for its elicitation. But is the clever use of syntax and metaphor in itself valuable? Should his father be taking the pleasure in the poem that Orr takes, and without that specific technical pleasure, is the poem a waste of time? Does poetry require formal difficulty—in its execution and in our appreciation of that execution—in order to be worthwhile? And do we have to be able to recognize, analyze, and describe these technical achievements in order to take pleasure in them?

And then there is the question of meaning. Frost's poem isn't that hard to understand—arguably its technical virtuosity is hidden by the relative simplicity of its meaning. Some readers of poetry, those who love secrets, might scoff at its lucidity. But there are secrets and there are secrets.

Does Orr suppose his readers know the poem? That they will go look it up? (Or is he hoping that they won't?)

Anyway, I did, in my copy of *The Complete Poems of Robert Frost* (1930; second printing 1949). (On the fly-leaf, "For Jimmie/21 Dec'50/Joe." From my dad to my mom, on her twenty-ninth birthday. There is a Sunday "Peanuts featuring Good ol' Charlie Brown" folded into fourths and tucked neatly into the front cover of the book. "Sally! Your beach ball is floating away. It's going clear across the lake!" "Stay calm, big brother . . . stay calm!" She addresses the ball: "**Okay, you stupid beach ball, come back here right now, or I'll see to it that you regret it for the rest of your life!**" The ball returns. "You have to know how to talk to a beach ball!" says Sally. Who thought this was so funny they needed to save it? What did it mean to them? There is a golf joke in there somewhere. And my brother Daniel.)

Okay, sorry, the poem.

> She is as in a field a silken tent
> At midday when a sunny summer breeze
> Has dried the dew and all its ropes relent,
> So that in guys it gently sways at ease,
> And its supporting central cedar pole,
> That is its pinnacle to heavenward
> And signifies the sureness of the soul,
> Seems to owe naught to any single cord,
> But strictly held by none, is loosely bound
> By countless silken ties of love and thought
> To everything on earth the compass round,
> And only by one's going slightly taut,
> In the capriciousness of summer air
> Is of the slightest bondage made aware.[17]

The "central cedar pole" that is the "pinnacle" of the tent, "to heavenward" "signifies the sureness of the soul," of her soul. When no particular string pulls, the pole and its tent seem free (although Frost does not use the word) despite—in fact because—it is "loosely bound / By countless silken ties of love and thought / To everything on earth the compass round." The more plentiful our ties, the more sure—the more upright and capacious—the soul. But when one pulls—the speaker of the poem? a chance summer breeze?—only then is it (but of course, the tent isn't aware, only "she" is) only then is *she* made aware of its/her bondage, however slight.

(After my brother Daniel died, my sister had a dream. She was late for church, standing in the back looking to see if she could find a seat. Daniel was there, in a full pew, with his daughters and me and my other brothers and my other sister and my sister's kids. Far too many for one pew. (When we were kids we could squeeze six, but that still meant two pews for the whole family. And endless fights over who had to sit with my mother.) But Daniel gestured to my sister to come and sit in the pew. She did and we were all there and there was more than enough room for everybody. That was my brother's heart.)

There is more in Frost's poem than might immediately catch one's eye.

(As my father lay dying, I read Tertullian's *On the Resurrection of the Flesh*. My father's edemic leg hung outside the bedclothes—my always so composed, so elegant, so immaculate father's body cast into disarray by pain and disease. My father, who, dead drunk, passed out with a cigarette so carefully balanced between the fingers of his right hand as it lay, folded gently on his left, across his chest, that only a perfect column of ash was left, hours later, when I found him, afraid to move the stub lest the ash scatter over his unburnt hand or shirt or the white sheet on which he lay.

My father, who, his leg run over, twice, by a drunken friend, got up, walked to the driver's side, and took the wheel.

My father, who caught me when I fell, blood running down his bright white shirt.

His swollen leg and foot fell out of the bedclothes. I wanted to grab hold and pull him back into this oh-so-painful-flesh.)

"Poetry," Orr concludes, "needs a history with its readers." For Orr, poetry, to be useful, or helpful, or whatever it is he's seeking

needs to have been read, and thought about, and excessively praised, and excessively scorned, and quoted in melodramatic fashion, and misremembered at dinner parties. It needs, in a particular and occasionally ridiculous way, to have been loved. If poetry could do nothing for my father that a thousand other things couldn't do, that was because it hadn't been a part of his life—just as when I'm eventually laid low, I will take little comfort in cello concertos and origami.[18]

(So does a Christian need to have spent her lives reciting the psalms, being shaped by the poems' sound and their content, by the work monks and nuns do with and to them, in order for their recitation as she dies to be "helpful"? Why then sing psalms over the beds of the dying, even those of the laity who may not have been particularly devout—although the psalms were everywhere, and so everywhere heard, in the Middle Ages?)

(A friend lay with his eyes closed as the church choir sang around his bed. But what he seemed most to enjoy, or so I like to imagine, were the tidbits from a biography of Louis Zukofsky I was reading as we sat together in the late spring sun. He lay, with tubes attempting to stem the flow of waste that otherwise would come, periodically, from his mouth.)

Yet Orr knows that the story about technical expertise as a source of pleasure and distraction in the face of death is inadequate, because his father did respond, with intense pleasure, to at least one poem. But as Orr writes, "When he did so . . . it wasn't because of some rarity unearthed by the expertise of his clever son, or because of the uncanny genius of one of the definitive poems of our language."[19]

What Orr's father loved and enjoyed for a few of his dying days was Edward Lear's "The Owl and the Pussycat." (My friend loved this poem too, its divine foolishness.)

> The Owl and the Pussycat went to sea
>   In a beautiful pea green boat,
> They took some honey, and plenty of money,
>   wrapped up in a five pound note.

Lear's nonsense poem gave Orr's father intense delight for a number of difficult weeks before the most difficult ones that led to his death. Orr assumes that his father must have been familiar with the poem, or one like it; that the pleasure he took in it is tied to some dim memory of reading to his children many years before. "It was," Orr writes, "happy silliness, soon to end—and surely there were a hundred other things that might have given my father the same comfort—but this absurd poem was, in its own small way, *something*."[20] Orr cites the closing lines of the poem and his father's response to them:

> "Dear pig, are you willing to sell for one shilling
>   Your ring?" Said the Piggy, "I will."
> So they took it away, and were married next day
>   By the Turkey who lives on the hill.
> They dined on mince, and slices of quince,
> Which they ate with a runcible spoon;
> And hand in hand, on the edge of the sand,
>   They danced by the light of the moon,
>   The moon,
>   The moon,
> They danced by the light of the moon.

"I really like," said Dad, "the runcible spoon." Reader, there are worse things to like. Or to love.[21]

In *Infinite Jest*, a novel I've never read, David Foster Wallace has his character, Rémy Marathe, a Québécoise terrorist, say, "Choose with care. You are what you love. No?" Truth or truism, this is just the sort of literary pronouncement David Orr finds deeply embarrassing. So do I, a lot of the time; when writers proclaim that poetry and fiction can radicalize consciousness, transform the political sphere, re-create the everyday world, provide the sole and necessary grounds for ethics, usher us into an easeful death—I cringe. Poetry and fiction are marks on the page and sounds. And death, like literature, is difficult.

(When my father and mother, my brothers and sister and friends died, I wanted to read difficult books. Really really difficult. Only the incomprehensible was comforting in the face of how hard death is.)

Who knows why Orr's father liked Lear better than Frost, although I have a feeling it has less to do with prior knowledge of the poem than with its ability to help him articulate sound and with it, perhaps, feeling—feelings of whimsy and humor. (My sister was in a fever as she died. "Better get used to it," someone said. We laughed and laughed. My sister, I fear, was unconscious.) Sounds elicit whole worlds of feeling. They are among the strongest—and arguably the last—of the strings that hold us to earth and enable us to reach . . . heavenward? (My sister and I sang to Daniel, snatches of half-remembered songs, as he gasped out his last, morphine-slowed breaths.) A novel by Henry James or David Foster Wallace, a poem by Robert Frost or Edward Lear, a Beethoven violin concerto or a Dum Dum Girls song—it's the saying, the listening, the reading, the repetition, the way something we love pulls us back to earth even as it lets us fly—that's what I love. (In my (day)dreams, it's what I am.)

(In my (day)dreams, difficulty's reverberations sustain and shake and yet still somehow soothe.)

Someone close to me said that he doesn't care what goes on at his funeral, except that he wants loud music. Really really loud.

What's the aging hipster's version of the psalms?

Oh it's a game, hold tight
Can you shut your eyes?
Shut out the light
Death is so bright

From dreams you wake to shock
To find it's true
But, she's not you
No, she's not you

And you'd do anything to bring her back
Yes you'd do anything to bring her back

Oh I wish it wasn't true
But there's nothing I can do
Except hold your hand
Except hold your hand
'Til the very end[22]

The words are good, but it's the wall of sound, the layers of feedback, the echoing resonating chaos of it all, that bring the house down.

NOTES

1. Susan Howe, *That This* (New York: New Directions, 2010), 11.
2. Ibid., 12–13.
3. Ibid., 13.
4. Ibid., 12.
5. Ibid.
6. Ibid., 47.
7. Ibid., 17.
8. Ibid., 34.
9. Fanny Howe, *'Tis of Thee* (Berkeley, Calif.: Atelos, 2003), 60–61.
10. Henry James, *The Portrait of a Lady*, ed. Robert D. Bamberg (New York: Norton, 1975), 17.
11. David Orr, *Beautiful & Pointless: A Guide to Modern Poetry* (New York: Harper, 2012), 187.
12. Ibid., 187–88.
13. Ibid., 188.
14. Ibid., 190.
15. Ibid., 191.
16. Ibid., 192.
17. Robert Frost, *The Complete Poems of Robert Frost* (New York: Henry Holt, 1930), 443.
18. Orr, *Beautiful & Pointless*, 192–93.
19. Ibid., 193.
20. Ibid., 194.
21. Ibid.
22. Dum Dum Girls, "Hold Your Hand," in *Only in Dreams* (2011).

ACKNOWLEDGMENTS

This volume had its origins in the proceedings of the fifteenth Transdisciplinary Theological Colloquium, also titled "Affectivity and Divinity: Affect Theories and Theologies," which was held at Drew Theological School in Madison, New Jersey, March 18–20, 2016. That the TTC had managed to reach mid-adolescence had much to do with the unflagging energy of Catherine Keller, George T. Cobb Professor of Constructive Theology at Drew, who had originally birthed it and has continued to nurture it. "Affectivity and Divinity" also would not have been if Javier Viera, Dean of Drew Theological School, had not continued to believe in the TTC.

Foremost among the other people whom the editors wish to thank for "Affectivity and Divinity," and hence also for the volume you hold in your hands or peruse on your screen, are Eugenie Brinkema, Mel Chen, Patricia Ticineto Clough, Ann Cvetkovich, and Gregory Seigworth, affect theorists extraordinaires, who, against all reason (but affect theory is seldom about reason), consented to being locked up with a crowd of biblical scholars, theologians, church historians, and other scholars of religion for two full days, and in a chapel, of all places, Craig Chapel at Drew Theological School.

We are also deeply grateful to all the other faculty presenters and student presenters, both from Drew and elsewhere, and to the respondents, moderators, and discussants whose papers and other contributions also made the colloquium memorable. They included, in addition to the participants whose essays appear in this volume, An Yountae, Chris Boesel, Robert Davis, Carlos Ulises Decena, Lisa Gasson-Gardner, James Hoke, Dong Hyeon Jeong, Stephen Keating, Catherine Keller, Jennifer Knust, Jennifer Koosed, Gerald Liu, Joseph Marchal, Elías Ortega-Aponte, Lily Oster, Arthur Pressley, Erica Ramirez, Mary-Jane Rubenstein, Robert Paul Seesengood, Jenna Supp-Montgomerie, Thandeka, Eric Thomas, Kyle Warren, Karri Whipple, and Lydia York. The colloquium's logistics were handled by Lisa Gasson-Gardner and Kyle Warren, who maneuvered us all with indefatigable aplomb and ensured that coffee or wine were always flowing. A special shout-out goes to the Corona Group—Omar Montana, Elijah Kuan Wong, Elizabeth Garcia, Jansiel Polanco, Mac Morris, and Yeong Ran Kim, together with Patricia Ticineto Clough—whose performance of *Ecstatic Corona* immersed us in certain of the affects that the colloquium had been designed to debate.

Particular thanks, once again, go to Richard Morrison, Editorial Director of Fordham University Press, both for gracing the colloquium with his presence and, together with his outstanding editorial team—not the least Eric Newman and Teresa Jesionowski—for shepherding its proceedings into print. Our gratitude, finally, goes to Hilary Floyd for ably compiling the index.

CONTRIBUTORS

MATHEW ARTHUR is an information designer and community education activist in Vancouver, Canada. He is co-editor in chief of *Capacious: Journal for Emerging Affect Inquiry*, and he co-organized the 2018 conference, Capacious: Affect Inquiry/Making Space. He recently lectured on anticolonial approaches to affect studies at the Affective Societies' "Power of Immersion" Spring School, Freie Universität, Berlin.

KAREN BRAY is an assistant professor and the chair of the Religious Studies and Philosophy Department at Wesleyan College. Her research areas include continental philosophy of religion; feminist, critical disability, and black studies; and queer, political, and decolonial theories and theologies. Her work has appeared in such journals as *The American Journal of Theology and Philosophy*, *The Journal for Cultural and Religious Theory*, and *Palgrave Communications*, and several edited volumes. Her book on political theology, affect, and counter-redemption, titled *Grave Attending*, is forthcoming from Fordham University Press.

AMY HOLLYWOOD is Elizabeth H. Monrad Professor of Christian Studies at Harvard Divinity School. She is the author of *The Soul as Virgin Wife: Mechthild of Magdeburg, Marguerite Porete, and Meister Eckhart* (University of Notre Dame Press, 1995), which received the Otto Gründler Prize for the best book in medieval studies from the International Congress of Medieval Studies; *Sensible Ecstasy: Mysticism, Sexual Difference, and the Demands of History* (University of Chicago Press, 2002); and *Acute Melancholia and Other Essays* (Columbia University Press, 2016). She is the co-editor, with Patricia Beckman, of *The Cambridge Companion to Christian Mysticism* (2012). She is currently completing, with Constance Furey and Sarah Hammerschlag, *Don't Touch Me: Essays on Difficulty and Faith*.

WONHEE ANNE JOH is a professor of theology and culture at Garrett-Evangelical Theological Seminary. She is also the director of the Asian American Ministry Center as well as an associate faculty affiliate in the Departments of Religious Studies and Asian American Studies at Northwestern University. Her publications include *Heart of the Cross: A Postcolonial Christology* (Westminster John Knox Press, 2006); *Critical Theology against US Militarism in Asia: Decolonization and Deimperialization* (co-edited with Nami Kim; Palgrave Macmillan, 2016); *Trauma, Affect, and Race: A Postcolonial Theology of Hope* (Fordham University Press, forthcoming); and *In Proximity to the Other: Decolonial Theological Anthropology* (Westminster John Knox, forthcoming).

DONG SUNG KIM is a PhD candidate in Hebrew Bible at Drew University. His recent publications include "Queer Hermeneutics: Queering Asian American Identities and Biblical Interpretation," in *T&T Clark Handbook of Asian American Hermeneutics* (Bloomsbury / T&T Clark, 2019) and "Children of Diaspora: The Cultural Politics of Identity and Diasporic Childhood in the Book of Esther," in *T&T Clark Handbook of Children in the Bible and the Biblical World* (Bloomsbury / T&T Clark, 2019).

STEPHEN D. MOORE is Edmund S. Janes Professor of New Testament Studies at the Theological School, Drew University. He is author or editor, co-author or co-editor, of more than two dozen books. His most recent monograph is *Gospel Jesuses and Other Nonhumans: Biblical Criticism Post-poststructuralism* (SBL Press, 2017). With Jennifer L. Koosed he co-edited *Affect Theory and the Bible* (Brill, 2014), and with Kent L. Brintnall and Joseph A. Marchal he co-edited *Sexual Disorientations: Queer Temporalities, Affects, Theologies* (Fordham University Press, 2018).

A. PAIGE RAWSON is a visiting assistant professor of religion at Wingate University in Wingate, North Carolina. She spent eight years in the ministry before transitioning into academia in order to study the Bible through feminist, queer, and poststructuralist theories. Paige's research is animated by her commitment to social justice and antiracist epistemological activism and Africana and Afro-Caribbean philosophies; it eschews traditional Western European methodologies in favor of oraliturary interpretations of the Bible in a hermeneutic she refers to as bibliorality.

ERIN RUNIONS is a professor in the Department of Religious Studies at Pomona College. She explores how biblical teaching and citation shape political subjectivity, gender, sexuality, U.S. national sovereignty, and biopolitics. Her most recent book is *The Babylon Complex: Theopolitical Fantasies of War,*

Sex, and Sovereignty (Fordham University Press, 2014). Her next book is on the Bible and the prison-industrial complex.

DONOVAN O. SCHAEFER is an assistant professor of religious studies at the University of Pennsylvania, which he joined in 2017 after three years as a lecturer at the University of Oxford. His first book, *Religious Affects: Animality, Evolution, and Power* (Duke University Press, 2015), considered the relevance of affect theory for questions of religion, politics, and subjectivity.

GREGORY J. SEIGWORTH is a professor of communication studies at Millersville University. He has published widely, including in *Antithesis, Architectural Design, Cultural Studies, Culture Machine, Radical Philosophy,* and *Theory, Culture and Society.* He is co-editor, with Melissa Gregg, of *The Affect Theory Reader* (Duke University Press, 2010), and co-editor, with Mathew Arthur, of the on-line journal *Capacious: Journal for Emerging Affect Inquiry.*

MAX THORNTON is a PhD candidate in theological and philosophical studies in religion at Drew University. He is an alumnus of University College London and the Graduate Theological Union. His work focuses on disability, gender, technology, and theological anthropology. He is a recipient of UC Riverside's Holstein Dissertation Fellowship.

ALEXIS G. WALLER is a ThD candidate in religion, gender, and culture at Harvard Divinity School. She received an MDiv in New Testament and early Christianity from Union Theological Seminary. Her work focuses on the intersections of the study of the New Testament, queer historiography, and arts-based pedagogies.

INDEX

Abelard, Peter, 99

Abraham, Nicolas, 95, 107n44

Abu-Lughod, Lila, 89

Ackerman, Susan, 141n51

ACLU, 62

Acorn, Annalise E., 81n77

aesthetics, 9, 23–25, 44–46, 48, 51, 127–29

affect: and animality, 20, 22–23, 25–30, 33, 190, 195; and assemblage, 10, 177, 181; as bloom space, 10, 126, 128, 134–35, 141n47, 144n74; definitions of, 1, 19–20; and divinity, 1, 7, 11–12, 32, 43, 121, 126, 128, 130, 133–35, 206; and economics, 8, 30, 32–33, 46, 55–57, 60–61, 64–65, 68, 70, 80n75, 102, 104n4, 105n16, 113–15, 117, 175; and emotion, 1–4, 8–9, 12n5, 14nn14,16,17, 16n21, 19–21, 25–28, 55, 97–98, 112–13, 116, 118, 122n5, 123n14, 130, 133, 142n57, 143n70, 209; and feeling, 21, 26, 46, 48, 93–94, 111–14, 117–18, 121, 123n14, 130, 174–85, 191, 207, 217; and gender, 6, 10, 117, 148, 162n13, 164n21, 174–85, 197; and historiography, 10, 147–48, 150, 159, 167n35, 173n63; and language, 2, 4, 6, 14n14, 92, 96, 127, 134, 190–94, 197–99; and literature, 11, 127, 135, 157, 206, 208–9, 217; and politics, 7, 22–25, 28–31, 60–61, 85–92, 94, 99–100, 110, 112–18, 121, 123n24, 175–78, 181–81, 187–90, 192, 195–98,

217; and power, 4–6, 8, 20–25, 27–30, 33–34, 44, 57, 85–88, 90–92, 96, 100, 119, 175, 181, 183, 189–92, 194, 213; and religion, 5–8, 11–12, 14n15, 16n21, 19, 29–34, 40–41, 122n2, 142n62, 166n25, 190, 209; and rhythm, 10, 25, 29, 120, 126–34, 137nn14–15, 139n33, 140n41, 143n71, 212–13; and theology, 6–9, 11, 64–66, 68, 80n72, 87, 98, 100, 122n2, 187–99, 202n18; theories of, 2–6, 20–21, 27–28, 33–34; and transgender experience, 174–75, 178–82, 184

The Affect Theory Reader, 1, 4, 12n1

affective remainder, 85–86, 89, 92, 95

affective resonance, 111, 115, 126–29, 131–32, 134, 137nn17,19, 138n21, 139nn28,32, 143nn65,71, 144n74, 182, 191

Agamben, Giorgio, 4

agential realism, 178–81

Ahmed, Sara, 5, 8, 13nn7–8, 14nn16–17, 15n20, 20–21, 26–28, 30, 34n4, 36nn37–38,49, 74n2, 109n71, 112–14, 122n6, 123nn11,14,18,22, 139n28, 194–95, 201n7, 203nn30–31

Akenson, Donald Harman, 160n2, 166n27

Alexander, Jeffrey C., 107n41

Alexander, Michelle, 62, 78n47

Amich, Candice, 15n20

Anaximander, 43–44

TC

TRANSDISCIPLINARY THEOLOGICAL COLLOQUIA

Kent L. Brintnall, Joseph A. Marchal, and Stephen D. Moore, eds., *Sexual Disorientations: Queer Temporalities, Affects, Theologies.*

Karen Bray and Stephen D. Moore, eds., *Religion, Emotion, Sensation: Affect Theories and Theologies.*

Lightning Source UK Ltd.
Milton Keynes UK
UKHW011320261019
352348UK00013B/280/P